# Singin' Your Subway Blues

# Singin' Your Subway Blues

## A Busker's Memoir

**NICK TURNER**

First published in 2024
Copyright © Nick Turner
Perth, Australia

ISBN 978-0-6453097-3-7

This book is memoir. It reflects the author's present recollections of experiences over time. Some names and characteristics have been changed, some events have been compressed, and some dialogue has been recreated.

All images Copyright © Nick Turner except on pages: vi, vii, 68, 78, 128, 146, 190, 264, 280, 306, 328, 334, Copyright © Briony; x, Copyright © Lucy Forrester; 42, Copyright © Rob Hatley; 52, Copyright © Shutterstock; 336, Copyright © Lindy Nield.

Edited by Ingrid Waltham, thewritingeditor.com.au
Designed by Anna Maley-Fadgyas, bookdesigns.com.au
Drawing by Robyn Varpins, robynvarpins-artist.com
Printed in Australia by IngramSpark

Cover image: The road atlas we used to hitch across America.

*This book is dedicated to my wonderful dad*

*Howard John Turner*

*and to the remarkable*

*Briony*

*These crazy adventures would not have happened without them*

*Thanks to both of you for trusting and believing in me*

*And it would not exist without my son*

*Callum Larsen Turner*

*I wrote it for him, to help him believe you can do ANYTHING you set your mind to*

*It worked*

Simon and I pretending to be Jack Kerouac and Neal Cassidy in Paris.

# CONTENTS

1. Blowin' in the Wind — 1
2. Down in the Tube Station at Midnight — 43
3. Like a Rolling Stone — 53
4. A Simple Twist of Fate — 69
5. Sous le Ciel de Paris — 79
6. A Simple Twist of Fate (2) — 121
7. Strike Another Match (Go Start Anew) — 129
8. Tangled Up in Blue — 147
9. The City That Never Sleeps — 191
10. Hejira — 225
11. Prisoner of the White Lines — 265
12. A House in New Orleans — 281
13. Nothing Left to Lose — 307
    Epilogue — 329
    Acknowledgements — 335

Room 17.

*I'm down in your subway*
*Singin' your subway blues*
*I'm down in your subway*
*Singin' your subway blues*
*Oh lord*
*I ain't got much more to lose*

Dave Green
Nottingham busker
1983

Peroxide blonde posing; the summer before I dropped out of uni.

# 1 BLOWIN' IN THE WIND

*How many roads must a man walk down*
*Before you call him a man?*
Bob Dylan, 1963

### Nottingham, January 1984

Paris. That was the plan. To go to Paris with Simon and Garry. To try our luck busking. But here it was, the day of departure, and I couldn't find them. I spent the morning roaming the streets checking in with the other buskers. Everyone, of course, knew the plan, anything new travelled fast around here, but no-one had seen them.

I felt a bleak and growing realisation that I might get left behind, or maybe have to go to Paris alone. Where were they?

### Nottingham, September 1983

Until now, I had done pretty much what I was meant to. Kept out of trouble just enough at school to get the grades I needed to get into university. Chose a good career-focused degree in Chemical Engineering – largely because it had the longest list of jobs waiting if I got the bit of paper! This, I reasoned, would allow me to put off the daunting decision of what to do with my life for as long as possible. I barely scraped through my first two years at uni, spending most of my time and money in the pub, hating the tedious boring sterility of endless lectures. I scraped over the line at the end of my second year with the lowest possible pass mark. The next year was the toughest year on the course and I knew I would fail if I didn't do something drastic, so that summer I really tried to generate some enthusiasm for being there. I went back at the start of the third year and lasted three weeks. I was drunk just about every night of them, and lots of days as well, and I found myself sitting morosely in corners, depressed and even crying, often on some poor undeserving ex-girlfriend's shoulder. Finally, during a particularly extreme performance at a party, the poor girl whose evening I was ruining looked me in the eye and said if it was really that bad, I should face facts and get out. *Baba O'Riley* by The Who was cranking out on the stereo at the time: "I don't need to fight to prove I'm right, I just need to be forgiven".

In my drunken state this seemed like a bolt of white lightning, a solution to my unbearable situation. The next day, wincing through another inevitable hangover, it didn't seem so simple, but the more I thought it through the more attractive the idea seemed. The only problems would be convincing my parents it was a good idea, convincing the university it was a good idea, and working out what I would do with myself. The last part was the easiest. Fuelled by a diet of Jack Kerouac's *On the Road* and Laurie Lee's gentle masterpiece *As I Walked Out One Midsummer Morning* – which traced him walking and busking across Spain in the 1930s – I thought I would take up my trusty guitar and make my way through the world by singing on street corners. I'd never busked before, but it sounded simple enough.

# 1 BLOWIN' IN THE WIND

Persuading my parents proved remarkably simple as well. My dad happened to be coming up that weekend from our family home in Bedford, and he picked up very quickly that I had something on my mind. Somehow I got talking about it, and, remarkably, once he'd worked out I was serious and had something approaching a plan, said he'd back me in whatever I decided to do. Dad was made to leave school at fifteen to 'bring in a wage' and for as long as I could remember he'd been passionate about giving me and my brother the chances he'd never had. So for him to support my decision to leave uni was amazing – heroic, even. I remember he looked me steady in the eye and said, "You'd better do it well then, eh son?"

Uni proved the hardest to convince, not because they had any great desire to retain me as a student, but because, incredibly, no-one else had ever taken a year off in the middle of the course. I would be doing the awful thing of setting a precedent! I applied to suspend my course for a year and they responded by withdrawing me entirely, with no guarantee of readmission. I would have to reapply, and they would assess my application if and when that happened. My tutor made it clear that given my chosen vocation and my past performance on the course, he didn't expect me to reapply, and certainly didn't think they'd want me back even if I did!

The door I'd opened – or was it a hole I'd jumped down – went round and round in my mind that night, and I resolved the next day I just had to make it work.

It was that simple.

My first attempt at busking in Nottingham was scary and exhausting. I walked around for something like two hours in a cold sweat of fear trying to find a good spot, watching an endless procession of people playing all the good places with never a gap between them. It was a cold and overcast October day in Nottingham, and everyone seemed to have that grey, big-coated, 'winter is coming' look about them. No-one cared about me and my guitar in its cheap brown plasti-fabric case. Finally, when I did find a free spot, down in the subway underneath the Broadmarsh Shopping Centre, I broke a string ten minutes after I started. I hadn't made a penny. I didn't have a spare string, and had little choice but to give up and make my way home. That night I had to think long and hard about where I was. Very much out in the cold from my own doing was a pretty good description.

The second day began better. I had developed a theory that year that I had some kind of guardian angel hovering around me, one with a perverse sense of humour who would guide me in the right direction only to chuck me in the deep end to keep me on my toes and remind me who was boss. I reckon this day in Nottingham he was at his perverse best.

It was a perfect tangy early autumn Nottingham day, and the sun was out. The first playing spot I came across was empty. This was a prime spot on the pedestrian arcade from Slab Square down to the Broadmarsh Shopping Centre, with lots of people passing, not too much background noise, and generally occupied full-time by someone singing or playing something.

I hauled the guitar out of its forlorn brown bag, avoiding eye contact with anyone while I spread the case on the ground. Clumsily shrugging the guitar strap over my head, I pretended to tune up while I caught my breath. The world carried on around me, totally oblivious to the feeling of cold, tight terror in the pit of my stomach. I started playing, and, fixing my eyes firmly on the far side of the street, began to sing. I really can't remember what I played first, but I remember life got better rather than worse as I strummed and crooned away. My voice started small and hesitant, and I carefully avoided any eye contact with the people passing. The first coin on the case was joy beyond belief, and I almost lost the thread of what I was singing. The coins were small and silver, five and ten pence pieces, but they kept coming in a slow but consistent trickle. I was bubbling with excitement and wanted to go chasing after people to thank them, or even ask them "what is it I'm doing right – how can I do it MORE!" but a much larger part of me just wanted to put the guitar back in the bag and go home. The bottom line was I was actually a reasonably good singer/guitarist, but I was a very long way from being a good busker.

After about half an hour I spotted a long, lanky form loping towards me with a saxophone case slung over his shoulder. This was the rightful owner of the playing spot. He wandered up and squared off in front of me, legs apart, with his hands resting on the top of his case. A rollup dangled out of the side of his mouth, his head was tilted back slightly to let the smoke get away. A tad provocative, but also leaving me enough space so that the punters could still get to the case. I kept playing to the end of my song, wondering what was going to happen.

I finished up and nodded at him. He drew a long haul on his rollup and said in a broad Birmingham accent.

"Like er, can I 'ave me pitch back – mate?"

I didn't know what to say and hesitated for a long second or two, mouth opening and closing like a stranded fish. This turned out to be a very good ploy, as the faintest of smiles twitched up around the seemingly immovable rollup.

"Tell ya what, I 'ad a bloody big night last night and I feel like shit – 'ow about I go and get meself some brekky and you see what you can do."

I think I would have kissed him if not for getting burns from his rollup – not to mention being punched out. I muttered something inane and nodded.

"Now then, oi'll be back at twelve. No slopin' off early or givin' the pitch away to some other booger or oi'll be very upset, orlright?" Eyebrows and end of rollup raised together, questioning.

I nodded furiously, and, with another ghost of a smile that signalled to me very loud and clear how very green I was at all this, he loped away. After this trauma, the playing and singing was an absolute doddle and I started to loosen up a bit. It felt good that I'd just learned some of the secret language – I was playing on a 'pitch'.

I already knew a reasonable amount of the staple busking material – Bob Dylan, Neil Young and the inevitable Simon and Garfunkel. I was very far from sure, but in the first half hour before Mr Rollup showed, the money coming in seemed to be totally independent of the song. Maybe I got the faintest inkling of the first big secret of busking after that. Because I was more relaxed, I looked happier and played better, and it was noticeable that the money went up. I tentatively found myself starting to actually look at the people I was playing to rather than looking at my boots in embarrassment or staring across the arcade at a shoe shop. Old people seemed to be much more friendly and generous than anyone else. But other than that, I couldn't work out any patterns.

# 1 BLOWIN' IN THE WIND

The sun stayed out and the money kept dripping in. Mr Rollup, who turned out to be 'Mogs', came back at the appointed time and was surprisingly communicative. Once I got more experienced myself, I realised I had 'passed' with Mogs in those first few minutes of playing, and by standing my ground just long enough. I was there for real. I didn't stop playing and scramble for cover the moment he showed up, and I was good enough that people would part with hard money for my efforts. I was worthy of notice. If, on that first day, I'd stopped as soon as Mogs arrived, muttered some apology or other and scuttled away, I would have beamed out 'fookin' student, fookin' time waster', and would have got no slack from Mogs whatsoever. The general philosophy was, if you haven't got the guts for it, go get a job in a pub pulling pints. On the other hand, if someone passed that first test, they were generally in the club, and became part of a very loosely knit and ever-changing mutually supportive network of local buskers.

As I packed up my gear and Mogs set himself up, he gave me a rundown on the good pitches, most of which I already knew, and, vitally, the protocol. When you want a go on a pitch, you ask the current owner when it's free. If someone else is already booked in, you rock up at changeover time and negotiate your turn. Leaving a pitch early when you had an agreement was pretty much unforgivable unless it was pissing down with rain or the police moved you on, and it paid to be aware of regulars' timeslots even if they hadn't showed that day to book in.

Lesson ended, Mogs sent me packing, and I sat down on a bench across the other side of the mall to count my take and watch him in action. It was remarkable how his body language changed. He was a funny looking guy, with slightly buck teeth, mousy blond hair that was thinning on top, and highly improbable National Health wire-rimmed glasses. While we'd been talking it was obvious he was hungover to hell, with that bent-up aching head and body look that I knew so well. However, once he was 'on' it was like he'd expanded in size. Head flung back, legs apart, the saxophone dancing in front of him, and every inch of him saying 'I BELONG HERE and fuck I'm good'. What he was playing was not as important as *how* he was playing it – every ten seconds was a show on its own, with the sax chortling away seductively to the old ladies as they waddled past him, genuinely brightening up their day, and occasionally receiving a reward for doing so. It was another good lesson on what it was all about, and I watched him closely while I counted out the money. I'd made about six quid in two hours, which wasn't going to make me rich but, importantly, was enough to keep me alive – providing I kept at it.

Flushed with success I decided I could head back home, feeling somewhat assured that my new vocation could succeed in Nottingham at least, if nowhere else.

Even after such a short time out of the student loop, it already felt different going back to the house I shared with five other guys, all students. I caught the bus from Slab Square up the hill, through Canning Circus, then down the Derby Road to Lenton, a hotchpotch inner-city suburb of students, old-time locals, Pakistanis and West Indians.

One of the few people I really connected with at university was Rob. He got me. In the share house, we were soulmates. We had found the house in a desperate quest at the end of our first year at university, to escape the regimented life of living in the halls of residence. We just

# 1 BLOWIN' IN THE WIND

loved the vast decaying bulk of the house rising out of the crazy overgrown garden, like the Norman Bates hotel in *Psycho*. It was an enormous crumbling Victorian mansion on the corner of the road that led down to the Raleigh bike factory, and just across the railway bridge from one of the most popular student pubs in the city. This had been an important factor in the year or so I'd lived there. At one point I worked out with Rob that we'd been to the pub for at least thirty nights in a row. Not surprisingly, we got to know the landlord, Mick, pretty well. It was quite a special feeling to shoehorn your way into a very large and teeming pub on a Saturday night, catch the eye of the landlord, and have your usual sitting on the bar by the time you got there. The usual was a lethal concoction of Shipstones Bitter and White Shield (an anagram of Shipstones being 'honest piss'). Our main excuse for needing to go to the pub so often was that the house was so bloody cold, and the pub was the only way to keep warm. (This wasn't completely fanciful. In Rob's west-facing attic room, some of the glass was missing and there were holes in the brickwork; one night during a howling westerly blowing we watched in disbelief as the entire carpet lifted off the floor and hovered about two inches above it).

The boys were fairly impressed with my earnings for about two hours' work. We lived on about thirty quid a week, so six pounds was a decent amount of money in such a short time. We'd decided that when I started my career as a travelling busker I would hang onto my room in the house. Nottingham was right in the middle of the country, and was a hell of a lot more inviting than relying on my parents' place. The downside of this was that I needed to keep on paying the rent, and therefore, for now, needed to sign on the dole to give me some kind of insurance to make ends meet. (Having a source of income while signing was, of course, illegal, but that was the least of my worries).

I stayed in Nottingham for a couple more weeks, testing the water at other pitches, learning how to deal with the other buskers, and sorting out the seemingly endless paper trail to drop out of university. I would go into the city every day and do two or three hours, making reasonable money, and getting the feel of what I was trying to do.

There were maybe six established pitches in Nottingham and about ten regular buskers playing them. All the serious players were older than me, with a few in their mid-twenties but most in their late thirties and a couple over forty. Some stuck to the same pitches and some, like me, wandered round a bit more. Banjo Allen just about owned the pitch outside C&A on the way down to the Broadmarsh. He would play four or five hours a day every day on a little banjo-ukulele, playing real dyed-in-the-wool old timey stuff. He'd sing a couple of lines then talk to a punter as they passed, trying to reel them in.

"My old man said follow the van, love the smile!" And "don't dilly dally! Don't worry – be happy! On the way, hi gorgeous!" and on and on. This was a hell of a lot harder than it looked and needed a very fine touch to make your take better, not worse. I tried it a couple of times but couldn't make it sound relaxed – and if you sounded like you were forcing it, it didn't work.

Mogs rarely strayed from his favourite pitch, but stuck to two to three hours a day. This was about the optimum amount of time to play each day for me as well. It may not sound like long, but imagine standing up in a carpark and giving a three-hour speech every day to a constantly changing audience with no microphone, and you might have an idea of the effort involved. Playing longer also generally meant you gave it less and the money ended up about the same. You had to remember you were doing it all again the next day, and the next day after that. Burning out wasn't an option.

After a couple of weeks it was time to stretch my wings and try my luck in some other parts of the country.

First place on the list was Sheffield. I would stay with my brother Matt, who'd just failed his degree. I had fully intended to hitch but the weather was classic Midlands – autumn fog and pissing rain – so I played a couple of hours beforehand in Nottingham to make the fare and bought a ticket for the late afternoon bus. I thought my luck was really in, as a guy with a very cool haircut stopped and listened to a couple of songs, then asked me if I wrote any of my own stuff. I gave him a hopeful 'yes' on the basis that I had lots of bits and pieces lying around, although little that could be called a finished song. He said he was involved in the recording industry, and would be really interested in hearing some of my stuff. Could I give him my contact details? Neither of us had a pen but I said he could find me on the streets 'when I was in town', feeling very cool saying so. In the back of my mind as he walked away was the niggling doubt that I didn't actually have a damn thing to give him, but I reasoned all this travelling and new experiences would probably yield an album's worth of songs within the month!

Nottingham bus station is among the most godforsaken locations on this planet; a giant, draughty, badly lit concrete box perched on top of the Victoria Shopping Centre that smells of diesel, fag ends and piss. There doesn't seem to be anywhere for sound to get out and every bus that goes past is an assault on the eardrums, with the insanely irritating beeping alarm of reversing buses being a particular refinement. Getting on a warm, dry, quiet bus was a blessed relief.

I fell asleep on the bus for a while and woke to a heavy fog on the motorway. The bus was making slow progress. Large floodlit signs ghosted out of the grey amorphous fog as I travelled alone, away from security and regularity. I was sure there was a bloody great song somewhere in this and jotted down a couple of lines, but mainly I just watched the fog go by and let my mind drift back on how I'd ended up where I was.

Playing the guitar had always been a part of me that I found hard to explain. I'd asked for a guitar for two or three years before my parents finally got me a real one instead of some plastic toy when I was ten years old. I still remember the first time I sat it on my knee, because it felt vividly like I was welcoming back an old friend. I never had to fight to learn how to play, it was more like coaxing some distant memory back to the front of my mind. Weird.

I didn't do much the conventional way, either on the path I took to learn the instrument or how I played it. Most significantly, I was left-handed but played right-handed, it just felt right. I went to a couple of lessons run by a teacher at my primary school and found the group approach irritating and limiting, so up until I was twelve I taught myself, without knowing there was such a thing as chords. I learned lots of melodies and how to work my way round the fretboard in a tuneful way. When we moved house, my new school was very alternative and had a laidback guitar class that I went to for a while and picked up the chord thing. With what I already knew about melodies, I found I could play both the chords and the tune without too much trouble, which freaked out the teacher (she was only about three lessons ahead of her pupils). She left the next year, and the new music teacher couldn't play guitar at all, but once she saw me play, asked me and one of the other kids to take the class! I was twelve, and I did OK – though I doubt any of my proteges went on to fame or glory.

I wasn't really learning much new so Mum booked me some lessons with a classical guitar teacher. This was a nightmare. I was told I was doing everything wrong and had to change everything about my finger and hand positions, which slowed me down no end and didn't seem to have any point. I endured six lessons then decided I would stick to my own path from then on – I was a lefthander who played righthanded and had a strong sense of melody with the chords sitting behind, all of which was completely upside down from the 'conventional' approach to playing. This made me very difficult to teach – and generally confused the hell out of the person I was learning from.

While I was still at the alternative school I performed regularly at school assemblies and during drama productions. Things came to an abrupt halt when I got a free place at the posh public school, where it was all Shakespeare and classical music, and I went back to playing in the bedroom for a few years until I hit the teenage rockstar phase that most guitarists go through. I had the advantage over most sixteen-year-old wannabes in that I could really play, so it was fairly easy to crank up a punk band that sounded halfway decent. There was also an occasional folk club that one of the teachers ran at the school, where I did my first hesitant singing. It didn't feel half as comfortable as the playing. The punk band helped my singing a good deal – confidence and loudness were far more important than holding the tune, and it gave me the chance to find out where my voice worked, without the scarily quiet and attentive folk audiences. The band was a huge amount of fun but, weirdly, the sense of belonging I had with acoustic guitars just didn't carry over to the electric instrument. The solid body, thinner neck, much lighter strings and the need for a whole different touch just didn't feel right. It took me another thirty years to learn how to make an electric guitar sing. But my forty quid no-name electric was great for slamming out Stiff Little Fingers and The Jam when I was seventeen.

When I left school and went to uni, I toyed briefly with starting up a band with a couple of guys, but the three of us had completely different ideas about what music we should be playing. We lasted about three rehearsals and that was it; I was back in the bedroom on an acoustic, nylon string guitar, playing anything from folk tunes to thrashy punk to the endless riffing up and down the fretboard that was, I suppose, my own stuff, since it certainly wasn't any song I'd ever heard. I played guitar when I was happy, when I was sad, when I felt like being loud and when I felt like being contemplative. It was never, ever something I had to do, always something I wanted to.

The big, heavy brown steel-string guitar I travelled to Sheffield with found me in a music shop up in Canning Circus. In the midst of my college depression, I'd gone up there to test-drive all the expensive guitars I couldn't afford, just to make me feel better. She was sitting on the wall, amidst all these instruments at three or four hundred pounds each, at a mere sixty quid. I almost didn't touch her, but when I did I was immediately struck by the weight in the sound box

# 1 BLOWIN' IN THE WIND

and the big solid sound she made. I played my way around the entire wall of instruments and came to the conclusion she sounded as good or better than things five times her price. I went home that night thinking it was all in my head, but showed up the next day and she still sounded that good. I handed over the money, with another fiver for the case. As with all my most special instruments, it felt more like us finding each other rather than a simple purchase.

Sheffield is a tough, down-to-earth city. It felt good coming into town, seeing the giant bulk of council flats rising starkly against the skyline on the hillsides, with the lifting fog snaking around them. The bus to my brother Matt's place was packed with commuters in the late autumn dusk. Matt lived in a poky little bedsit on the ground floor of another crumbling Victorian monstrosity, which seemed to be the principal abode of students all around the country. I arrived at 5.30pm and Matt got out of bed to let me in. It was a while since I'd been there, and the place had got more crazy since my last visit. Matt had an obsession with collecting news cuttings from *The Guardian*. There were mouldering piles of damp newspapers, smelling like rotting mushrooms, all over the flat. A leaky pipe from the flat above had destroyed the wallpaper above his bookshelves, and was starting to do a pretty good job on the plaster. The books on the top shelf were exploding at their spines and made a bizarre piece of wall sculpture. The curtains hung tiredly from the curtain rail by a couple of hooks. They didn't look like they'd moved in a long time. This didn't matter too much because the window looked out on an overgrown postage stamp that had once been a garden surrounded by a high brick wall. No-one wanted to look in or out.

Matt and I weren't close. He was way more intelligent than me, but had always seemed to go out of his way to isolate himself from the rest of the world – compromise and sociability didn't appear on his map. He was slowly turning into a recluse. He'd been there for over five years and just about everyone he knew had moved on. I found it all very depressing, but he seemed comfortable with it. He didn't have a plan and seemed unfazed by not getting the degree after all that time. He'd failed for not handing in enough of the course work, and had used up three deadlines. Crazy to my mind, but then again lots of things about my brother were crazy as far as I was concerned, and I think he felt the same about me. To Matt, the concept of making a public exhibition of yourself on the street corner and setting yourself up as a target for ridicule was as insane as my view of his ever-growing piles of newspapers.

My first day of busking in Sheffield was tough, but not disastrous. I didn't see any other buskers so I set up in a subway just near the bus station. This turned out to be too busy and too noisy. The passage was narrow and people were having to back up to get round me. It's amazing how much noise can come from people just walking and talking. The money was much lower than Nottingham. This was Thatcher's Britain, and Sheffield was one of many cities that was slowly having the heart torn out of it while the politicians dreamed of a new industrial age, free of all those unprofitable and smelly steel factories and shipyards and coal mines. None of these 'new' industries were starting north of Leicester but no-one voted Tory there anyway so it didn't matter. I worked four hours in Sheffield that first day and made about seven pounds. I never saw another busker. This was tolerable but there was no way I could

# 1 BLOWIN' IN THE WIND

do four hours every day. I could only hope that the other places on my 'trial tour' – Manchester and York – would be better. It was also noticeably colder in Sheffield than it had been in Nottingham, and I had to spend good money on some fingerless mittens. These made me look like Fagin and were a pretty good sympathy prop, but they were necessary – my finger ends were nicely callused but the cold steel of the string, coupled with my tingling half-frozen hands, was exquisite agony.

I spent a couple of days in Sheffield, playing for about three hours a day. The police never bothered me and I pretty much had the run of the city. I liked the raw, tough steeliness of the city, but the money just wasn't good enough. After long hours in the cold I was looking at the city through a veil of fatigue and tiredness. I knew I couldn't keep this up for too long.

Each day after playing I would go back up the hill to my brother's place and try to find some common ground with him. We toured his favourite pubs, me spending the money I'd worked so hard to earn and him delving dangerously into the next two weeks of dole money, but we didn't really connect.

We got on better on the day we took a bus out to the west of the city to walk on the hills round some reservoirs. It was good to get away from the grime and bustle, and it made me realise how very urban my existence was becoming.

With the low take in Sheffield and my brother making the most of my generosity, I went backwards on the money while I was there, and actually had to get some out of the bank for the first time. This was very bad news, as the plan was obviously to slowly save money for bigger things, like air flights. Things had to improve, or my dreams of roving the country and then the world with guitar in hand would be just that – dreams.

Next stop, Manchester. I did the rounds of the city centre, trying to track down the other street musicians and get some info on the lie of the land, unknowingly setting up a habit that would soon become second nature. My plan was to make some money before heading out to my mate Mike's. The city centre was absolutely pumping with people, particularly on the wide pedestrian precinct next to the Arndale centre, but buskers were noticeably absent from the landscape. I eventually found a guy playing at the top of a wide set of stairs of a restored historic-looking building overlooking a square. He had an amplifier for his guitar, a mike on a stand for his voice, a fold-out seat, a hi-hat cymbal that he operated very deftly with his jigging left foot, a bass drum coming out sure and solid from his right foot, and above it all a mean blues harp clamped into a carrier hung round his neck. He gave it everything he had, singing every song with a big bluesy voice, the tortured harp coming in every couple of lines to back him up. He leaned into the mike as he sang, gyrating away as he pumped the guitar and the hi-hat. He was very good, and he seemed to have found the perfect pitch. There was a café at the top of the stairs, and the stairs gave him stage height for the people passing by in the square. His presence was such that he could draw people up the stairs to drop money in his case, as well as catch those coming in and out of the café. The case was positively groaning with money.

The thought of me even asking to have a go on this guy's pitch was laughable, and life seemed suddenly very bleak. However, as I watched him, pondering what to do,

# 1 BLOWIN' IN THE WIND

I spotted a guy walking across the square with a guitar case and a smart looking bluesy hat perched on his head, with the hatband full of plectrums. This was surely another busker, and one a bit more in my league. He spotted my guitar case and came over for a chat, offering the ritual cigarette as an opener. I hadn't smoked for a fair while when I started busking, but it was almost a requirement of the job. The way to talk to any busker was to wander up at the end of the song, throw a small coin into the case, and offer a cigarette. When someone returned the favour it was a whole lot easier to accept than turn it down, and smoking became an integral part of my life playing music on the streets. I soon found out from my man with the picks in his hat the lowdown on Manchester. The Arndale and Kings Street were the two main pitches and although there were a fair number of other players around, it usually wasn't hard to find a slot. Mr Blues was the undisputed king of town and, as I suspected, no-one ever went near his pitch and he never played anywhere else. We shared our view that it was bad for business having guys like Mr Blues around as it reflected very badly on us less well-equipped mortals. I headed for King Street on the advice of my new-found friend, who, as it happened, I never set eyes on again.

King Street was a lot quieter than the Arndale, and a good spot to start. I played for about an hour and made a couple of pounds, and then came upon something new. A couple with a violin and a flute set up about twenty yards away from me and started playing classical music. They looked very unlike buskers, wearing big owl glasses and black evening attire, and I decided they must be from some local music college or other. As most passers-by were coming from their direction, my take nosedived. This was piss-poor etiquette and I wandered up and made it plain they were breaking the rules. They blinked back at me through those big round glasses and made it clear that as far as they were concerned there weren't any rules. I went back and strummed my way through a couple more songs but it was clear I was wasting my time and I decided to pack up. I was counting my meagre take when another singer-guitarist came striding purposefully up the street. He wasn't quite as well equipped as Mr Blues, but he had a portable Vox amp slung round his shoulder and his guitar was in an enormous flight case. I nodded as he came up the street and he stopped over for a chat. I asked him what he did about Little Lord Fauntleroys who travelled in pairs and didn't obey the rules and he laughed, nodded at the Vox and said it wasn't generally a problem for him. He was also most adamant that I would do a lot better outside the Arndale as the crowds were too good to miss. I had nothing to lose so I tagged along with him. As I did, he kept up a constant stream of advice and anecdotes of how he made a couple of thousand quid in fifteen minutes down in London one time and was thinking of going back to Cannes after Christmas because it was too bloody cold in Manchester. Everyone on the streets tended to err on the side of optimism in telling their stories, but this guy certainly pushed the limit more than most. However, he was friendly enough and showed me a reasonable pitch at one side of the enormous pedestrianised precinct outside the Arndale. As I set up I could see what he meant about the crowds. The place was absolutely heaving with waves of people going up and down like packhorses, with bulging bags from all the big department stores hanging off them. There was obviously a lot more money around

## 1 BLOWIN' IN THE WIND

in Manchester than Sheffield. I hoped this would reflect in how much money ended up in my case.

I doubted I'd have enough belt to make much of an impression at the Arndale and I was right. People didn't ignore me as much as not notice me with so much going on. I was overwhelmed. Again I packed up the guitar, hefted my pack on my back and looked for a better spot. The best I could do was to get some big ornamental lamppost to my back, slap bang in the middle of the huge river of people. Playing here was a new experience because everyone came at you face on, which was quite confrontational. I was just getting used to it when two stern-looking policemen strode up purposefully saying they'd had complaints that I was causing an obstruction and it was time to move – now. I decided that today was not my day.

I was quite proud of myself for finding the right bus out to Mike's place in West Didsbury, then getting off at the right stop and finding the block of flats he lived in. I asked a few directions and found his room somewhere up on the fifth floor. I staggered down the corridor with my pack and guitar, thinking I'd had enough for the day and looking forward to winding down over a beer or three.

My enthusiasm was short-lived because he wasn't there. Given it was three o'clock on a Saturday afternoon this wasn't exactly unexpected, but I could really have done with him being home. I set myself up in the common room and waited. I was pretty knackered after all the wandering up and down the streets of Manchester lugging all my worldly possessions with me, and I had to fight not to fall asleep. Three hours of Saturday afternoon TV later I was still there. I was starting to get a bad feeling about things and wandered back to his room again. A neighbour told me he was away for the weekend – he wanted to get away from things because he was feeling down that a good mate of his had just pulled the plug on his university career (me). I was flattered that he would care so much but this was more than overshadowed by a feeling of dull panic that I had nowhere to stay and no plan in a big city that I didn't know at all.

I realised my only real options were either to try and get back to Nottingham or to travel on again to York, my next stop, in the hope that Sarah, an old Bedford mate, would be there. Determined not to beat a retreat just yet, I opted for York, and wearily shouldered my pack and trusty guitar once again. Mike's gaggle of corridor associates wished me a cheery farewell as I headed back out into the cold and dark. I am pretty sure this was the day I first evolved my theory about the guardian angel who occasionally had a day off. I had a strange vision of this angel sitting on some sun lounge next to a swimming pool in tropical sunshine sipping on an enormous cocktail, looking down on me and pissing himself laughing at how clever he was.

I caught the bus back into the now deserted city, to discover that the train station was about a two-mile walk from the bus station. The walk took me down the same mall outside the Arndale where I'd been playing seemingly an age ago. It was a very different scene now, with all the shoppers gone home and just the street lights and glowing shop window displays for company. There was a fish restaurant at the end of the mall, and I was suddenly acutely aware that the last time I'd eaten was a hastily gobbled bowl of cereal back in Sheffield, a lifetime ago. It was about to close but I think I looked so pathetic they took mercy on me. I was so hungry I pretty much shovelled down the tired-looking

## 1 BLOWIN' IN THE WIND

fish and limp chips without stopping for breath. I only had fifteen minutes to get to Victoria Station. My back, arms and stomach were all aching from carrying around my gear all day long and I just wanted to curl up and go to sleep. I got the train with a couple of minutes to spare, virtually the only passenger.

At that time a certain dusty, tired smell permeated backwoods-line British Rail diesel trains that automatically put me in an immediate state of dull 'life is taking me nowhere' depression. This train absolutely reeked of that smell, and I waited for the dull ache to descend on me. Surprisingly it didn't, and I realised that, beyond being bone-tired from the day's exertions, I was actually quite enjoying all this self-induced torture.

The train pondered slowly on, stopping at every station, with few getting on or off. For the first half hour or so I went back almost exactly the way I'd come that morning from Sheffield, which seemed about a thousand years ago now. I did a huge amount of travelling that year on just about every kind of transport you can name, but this journey really sticks in my mind. I remember the hiss of the airbrakes and the jolting clunk of the train as it pulled out of each station, the mournful whistle in the inky winter dark, the shadow figures of people on the other side of the grime-encrusted windows, the steely-bronze taste of guitar strings on my sore fingers as I tried to suck some heat into them, a ghost clock seemingly hanging in the sky, someone paying it enough attention to keep the backlight working but not fix the clock itself, as it permanently read a quarter-to-midnight. Most of all I remember all the millions of lights I saw from the train window as we juddered slowly across the country, and wondering over and over just how many people were out there and what on earth they all did with their lives.

By the time we finally rolled into York station I was feeling very detached from reality, and I had to really push to get the gears clunking inside my head again. York had by far the most cheerful station of any I'd stopped at on the journey, well-lit and high-roofed and built in big chunky stone, in contrast to the endless parade of crumbling Victorian red-brick stations I'd come through. I was now east of the Pennines and further north, and there was a gentle north-east wind stirring through the station that came straight from Siberia. For the thousandth time that day I hefted up my pack and my guitar and waddled out of the station to find a bus up to the university. All I really knew was that Sarah lived somewhere called Alcuin College. I'd found a city map somewhere on a wall in the station and worked out a bus waiting at the terminus was heading vaguely that way, and jumped on. I asked an old-timer on the bus if we would be going anywhere near Alcuin College. "Are we bloody buggery mate," was the amused response. He went forward to the bus driver to discuss my plight, collecting the only other passenger on the way for assistance. They all pitched in heartily to work out where the hell I needed to go. They were a very friendly lot, and once they had an answer approved by a unanimous majority, it was decided that the bus would take a fairly significant diversion to get me a bit closer to where I needed to be. I found this a refreshing approach to public transport. It may have upset anyone shivering at a bus stop further down the line, but I wasn't going to argue.

We stopped at a very quiet junction and the driver and passengers pointed me confidently up the gentle hill of an

# 1 BLOWIN' IN THE WIND

affluent-looking suburban avenue. If it hadn't been for the confidence of the committee and the deliberate diversion of the bus I would never have believed I was going in the right direction, as, after a couple of hundred metres, the houses petered out and from what I could see in the dim streetlights, I was pretty much walking through a field. However, there were lots of lights ahead and so I headed towards these. Turned out the bus crew were right, and the field was actually the edge of the university campus.

Tracking down Alcuin College and Sarah's room was straightforward enough, and I burst in to her block kitchen with quite a flurry, not quite believing I'd finally made it. Two guys in the kitchen were quite taken aback at my entrance. I explained who I was and what I was doing only to be told that Sarah had gone home to Bedford for the weekend, depressed because her friend Nick had dropped out of university.

My angel was at this point no doubt laughing so hard he was spilling his banana daiquiri all over the pool, but, luckily for me, he decided at this point that holiday time was over. It was time to deliver me from disaster.

When the guys in the kitchen worked out who I was, we all started guffawing at the ludicrousness of the situation – me a little maniacally by then. I truly didn't care what happened to me anymore at that point, which of course meant that things suddenly started to work out fine. The two were chemistry students, and in a very chemistry student way methodically set about making life more bearable. Chem 1 put on some cheese toasties while Chem 2 took on the daunting task of persuading the hall porter to provide me with the spare key for Sarah's room. He returned successful in his mission, then moved onto the next stage of the plan, which was to provide me with a glass of red wine or two to help the cheese toasties go down. After such a mongrel of a day this was pure heaven, and I gave a wry wink up to my angel.

I asked a few probing questions about the possibilities for busking in York, and got some mixed news. The city was built for it, with lots of quiet pedestrianised streets and medieval squares, but there was a tendency for street performers to be big on the performance front – fire eaters and jugglers and Henry the Eighth-era recorder players in period dress. I wasn't sure how a raggedy young guitarist would do against competition like this, but felt that my luck had changed and I was due for a break.

I rang Sarah's house in Bedford and, remarkably, she answered it. After getting over her incredulity that I was actually there, she said she'd be back the next day. Sarah, the ever-supportive friend. I turned into her warm and comfortable bed with a full belly and a pleasant glow from the red wine, revelling in the gorgeous smell of being among things female, looking forward to catching up with her.

Sarah was a couple of years younger than me and just in her first year at university. She was one of the few people who knew how many misgivings I'd had about going away to uni in the first place. I'd been about the only person from the home crowd who'd actually got the grades I needed to get in, despite my final year at school. That year was a great time to be seventeen, with the Sex Pistols' crazy moment of genius under the manipulative hand of Malcolm McLaren changing the turgid, stale music scene forever, along with The Clash, Stiff Little Fingers and Elvis Costello. The Jam were at their furious best, and Paul Weller was everything to us. We went down to see The Jam at the Rainbow shortly after

# 1 BLOWIN' IN THE WIND

*Going Underground* had released straight to number one, and watching the raw fury, power and anger of Weller onstage we knew we could smash Margaret Thatcher to pieces and take on the world with just a Rickenbacker guitar, a sharp suit and a howling giant voice that tore your head and guts to pieces. Eighteen years later I discovered a CD of collected live Jam recordings. I bought it purely on the basis of a quote on the sleeve notes "The Jam at the Rainbow in 1981 was the most heart pounding, root squashing, body surging experience a fifteen-year-old boy ever felt". He must have been in the crowd next to us. I've seen countless bands over the years since then, but nothing will ever match The Jam. They ruled our lives, and we would have died for Weller and for each other. I'd seriously toyed with the idea of not going to university just so as not to betray my punky mates. Thank God I did go. Two years later The Jam had split up, and the old crowd were all still drinking in the same pub at home. Put simply, I left home, and they didn't.

First day in York. Time to try my luck. It was a bright, clear morning as I took the bus down to town. I tapped out rhythms on the fretboard of the guitar underneath its plastic cover, looking forward to getting back on the streets.

York was a different universe to Manchester, a serene maze of winding streets of Tudor and Elizabethan houses. There were few cars, lots of pedestrian arcades, and the cathedral towering above everything, glorious and magnificent. I couldn't find any other buskers at first, but it was Monday morning. I set up at the end of a pedestrianised street and eased into it, playing a couple of soulful numbers, revelling in the quiet background noise that actually let me sing instead of yell. I even contemplated doing a bit of finger-picking, which wasn't generally worth the effort because no-one could hear you. I thought the world had ended after ten minutes or so when two policemen appeared in front of me, with slight grins on their faces. But this was York, and they merely told me that they would escort me to a much better spot just around the corner. This was the first and last time this ever happened, and it was quite wonderful.

The spot they showed me was a cracker, on another pedestrianised street opposite a windowed café where the punters could watch and listen to me while they ate, rewarding me handsomely more often than not when they left. The passing foot traffic was generous too, and best of all, I noticed a couple of shops prop open their doors so they could hear me better, and a dark and dreamy looking girl opened the window of her first-floor office and smiled and waved at me. The idea of an audience that listened longer than the ten seconds as they walked by made me try harder and think more about what I was playing, and I did very well indeed. After half an hour or so the dark and dreamy girl wandered across from the office with a cup of hot steaming tea, telling me in an adorable eastern European accent that she "luffed Bop Dylan and had moofed to the office nearest de window to 'ear me bedder". I played *Hollis Brown* as a thanks, which is miserable even by Dylan's standards, but she leaned out the window at the end of it and gave me a little clap and a big smile. The café owner popped his head out after a couple more songs asking when I was coming in for a meal, but I wanted to make the most of this – Sheffield and Manchester had been very average, and I really wanted to get some decent money back in my pocket.

That first day in York persuaded me that not only did I have the guts to be doing this, but I also had enough talent to validly claim my place on the streets with any of them. I didn't have any illusions of being catapulted to immediate stardom but I was brightening up the day for a lot of people and earning a reasonable amount of money doing something I loved. What more did I really need?

I also reckon my appearance would have helped me through those difficult early days. I was just twenty years old and had a very young face, plus I'd dyed my hair almost white-blond that summer. The hair was good for two reasons: firstly it made me look even younger, and secondly it gave me an unusual look, vaguely punky, vaguely arty – just the right look for a street musician.

I made sixteen pounds in two and a half hours, which more than made up for the Manchester disaster. If nothing else, I knew I could wander between Nottingham and York for the year, slowly building up my war chest for my big move – whatever that would be.

That evening I met Sarah off the train from Bedford and we went out to one of the campus bars with her gaggle of first-year friends. Later in her block kitchen I pretended to be Paul Weller for a while, belting out *That's Entertainment* and *Down in the Tube Station at Midnight* to a very appreciative audience. Sarah loved me playing, but I still got the floor and the spare duvet.

I stayed in York for a couple more days, and really enjoyed myself. It was a very low stress place to play, with the best money I'd come across. The entire centre of the city had an air of timeless majesty, where it was seemingly automatic for people to slow their pace, take their time, and above all make the effort to listen rather than hurry by. All this was perfect for busking. The warning bells that had rung when I first talked to the chemistry boys hearing about fire eaters and jugglers turned out to be false alarms. I don't recall seeing another busker anywhere that first time in York. This may have been something to do with the weather, which was bloody freezing, but at least dry. Maybe no-one else was crazy enough to play when it was this cold, but I was just passing through and I didn't have time to wait. Wearing fingerless mittens was the only way I could keep playing, but with practice I found I could still do a remarkable amount of my repertoire with the gloves on.

I tried various pitches, including outside the cathedral and a picture postcard Kings Square. Outside the cathedral didn't feel right for either me or the punters; a raggedy busker singing Bob Dylan songs just didn't fit the serene timeless mood of the place. If I'd had a lute, some silly trousers and a falsetto voice I'd have been perfect, and I think if I'd lived in York I may well have given this a go – well, maybe not the trousers. Kings Square was the most perfect collection of medieval houses in the whole city, and an absolute magnet for the tourists. However, takings were surprisingly average in comparison to my favourite spot outside the restaurant. The Square had a way of funnelling the wind through it, so you'd get dust in your face and dead leaves on the pitch and everyone would be freezing cold and not particularly in the mood for music. So I kept going back to the pitch outside the restaurant, and in so doing reinforced another important lesson. By the third day, the restaurant owner had stopped smiling and the shops weren't propping open their doors, though my adorable East European office girl still gave me cups of tea. It was very easy to outstay your welcome on a pitch. Also my take, though still good, was tailing off noticeably. I played four days straight in York and the last day it felt like I'd been there too long, which was fine, as I'd managed to get hold of Mike and arrange to go back and give Manchester another go.

Mike was very well set up in his tower block. He was just about my best mate from home these days, after the demise of The Jam idealists. We'd grown up together skateboarding. He was a couple of years younger than me, but was advanced for his age, particularly on the womanising front. Mike had this combination of boyish enthusiasm, humour and dark good looks that just seemed to hypnotise women. I can't count the number of times I'd seen Mike disappear off into the night with some woman he'd just met. He would always have this look of vague surprise that this could possibly be happening to him, which was one of the things that made the bastard so lovable.

An unexpected bonus of Manchester was that another Bedford friend, Richard, was at the polytechnic there. Richard had a very relaxed approach to studying and preferred to invest his energy in learning about the wilder side of big city life. He was in good company. Manchester was, and remains, a great city for music. We wandered through all the wild basement clubs along the Oxford Road, absorbing the energy and pump, including a couple of the Rasta places, which were pretty scary – several times we were the only white guys in the place but somehow Mike seemed to be accepted there. I pumped out *Love Will Tear Us Apart* when I was busking and thought about crazy Ian Curtis wandering up and down these streets wondering what to buy his mum for Christmas before disappearing into those same Oxford Road clubs to front Joy Division. The Smiths were just starting to happen, and *Oh Manchester, So Much to Answer For* rang in my head every time I played on the street. Manchester was musically light years ahead of Nottingham, whose biggest claim to fame was Paper Lace winning the Eurovision Song Contest ten years ago with that great rock anthem *Billy Don't be a Hero*.

Manchester was big, tough and proud, and made no pretence at hiding its grime. There was such a contrast between busking on the Kings Street pitch, where lean-faced women waited for buses, and the massive Arndale shopping strip up the road, where women from the wealthier outer suburbs paraded with armfuls of boxes and bags. As usual, it was the people with the least money who seemed to be the ones who gave most generously to struggling musicians like me.

Manchester was also the first place I busked where the police were an occupational hazard. They could really mess up your day. When I got moved on from the Kings Street pitch I just wandered up to the Arndale and started playing again, and in so doing came very close to getting myself arrested. Ten minutes after starting up I spotted the same two women coppers who had nailed me on King Street walking up towards me on the Arndale, looking very unimpressed. The guitar was in the case by the time they reached me and I held my breath and grovelled. They asked for ID and radioed in and asked straight if I was signing on the dole as well as playing. They kept me there for ten minutes or so while they checked I wasn't wanted for drug running or any armed robberies and then made it clear if they saw more of me on the streets again that day I was in big trouble. Officialdom over, they also said I might like to bear in mind the foot patrol shifts changed at 2pm each day. It made me realise again just how easy it all was in Nottingham.

The shift change time was vital information but still made life difficult. If you got moved on after 2pm your day was over; if you went down to get the early shoppers and got moved on, you could have a four-hour wait on your hands. It mystified me why the division one buskers with their amps and drum kits didn't get hassled and I did, and I never really got an answer. It may have been some kind of quality control thing – a big amp and an expensive guitar doing Simon and Garfunkel was the sort of image they wanted rather than an emaciated punky-looking kid singing Clash songs. I could play plenty of Simon and Garfunkel songs as well, but I just couldn't make myself heard in Manchester doing the nice stuff. Plus playing the tougher stuff seemed to me to fit the mood of the city much better.

My division one busker friend did me a big favour one day when the bespectacled classical duo again did their trick of setting up ten feet down the road. Wandering past, he quickly sussed out what was happening, and, giving me a grin, calmly set up just the other side of them and gave them a blast with his amp. They tutted and flustered like a couple of old owls and packed up their music and stands in a jolly big huff, but still hung around to see if he would move. He nodded at me, stopped playing and – leaving everything set up – settled down on a wall to smoke a fag or two, applauding at the end of each song and giving the owls a contemptuous look. They buggered off after ten minutes or so, and I nodded my thanks to him. It brought home another couple of lessons – not following the rules could make for serious trouble from the local pack, and having to resort to these tactics didn't do a damn thing for the general busking vibe. A lot of shoppers and store owners witnessed this showdown, and those who didn't know the lowdown were giving the two of us daggers, obviously thinking we were bullying the poor owl duo. The store owners also took a dim view of three kinds of music duelling for airspace on a quiet mall. This was all very bad for business and increased the likelihood of someone calling the police to get us all out of the way.

After four or five days, it was time to head back to Nottingham and sign on at the dole office. This was 1983, and Margaret Thatcher was busily dismantling the battered but proud industrial heart of just about every town and city north of Leicester. There were over three million unemployed, and for many people in that dreary, lightless hole of a dole office, there was little to hope for.

In Alan Sillitoe's angry young man classic 1960 film *Saturday Night and Sunday Morning*, Albert Finney rode his bike past our Nottingham house on his way home from work in the Raleigh bike factory. Every kid in England had a Raleigh bike at some time in their life, and I was proud that I rode one to uni every day. When we first moved in you would be woken in the early morning by the sound of hundreds of pairs of feet as the guys coming off the night shift walked home past our house. During the course of the two years I lived in the house the sound of passing feet pretty much dried up, and a couple of years after that the factory closed altogether. Add to that most of the textile factories going broke, and John Players Cigarettes and Boots Chemists factory moving out of town, and it's no exaggeration to say that Thatcherism tore the heart and guts out of a community that had been a happy, thriving place to be. I don't ever remember any banner waving, and you never heard anything directly, you'd just notice another mill suddenly had broken windows and a giant, desperate 'Space for Rent' sign out the front. Every dole office in the north of the country was filled with millions of men for whom the country now had no need. It was desperate, hopeless and tragic, and I will despise

# 1 BLOWIN' IN THE WIND

Margaret Thatcher till the day I die for what she did to all those men and their families.

In the back of my mind was the fact that way back I'd promised some guy on the streets a demo tape of songs next time I saw him. I had a scribbled half-verse of one song that I thought was crap, together with a couple of lead riffs, but had left them at home. As it turned out, it was just as well. The little prick worked in the dole office. I was daydreaming my way to the front of the queue when I saw him – the same sharp haircut and trendy red-and-black shirt looking busy on the far side of the glass counter. I remembered how keen he'd been to get my name and address. If I'd had a pen on me that day I might be now looking at a charge of failing to declare earnings. I found something very interesting to look at anywhere that let me keep my back to him, trying to maintain the look of bored nonchalance that everyone else in the building had, but not doing too well. When I got to the front of the queue they asked the usual questions about whether I'd done any work or been actively looking for employment and I had to try very hard to keep the right tone of resigned hopelessness. I resolved to be very careful about who I would give my name out to on the streets in future.

Walking out of the dole office after my narrow escape, reflecting on how I actually had a choice, it came to me how lucky I was to be able to do what I could do. It made me even more determined to make a go of it, and I set about organising my first swing through the southern half of the country.

I decided to make my first trip relatively simple. I'd visit my parents in Bedford, and then straight on to London, hitching all the way. This would be simple. The Derby Road we lived on ran straight to the M1, and I'd already done the hitch to Bedford a number of times – I regarded myself as having failed if the trips took as long as it would take on the bus. I would start walking up the hill from our house towards the uni and the hospital, a cardboard sign with M1 hanging nonchalantly off my arm and the guitar showing prominently, as I'd always felt that the more interesting you looked while hitching (within reason) the more likely you were to get a lift. I examined how I felt as I left the house again to hit the road, and it felt good. I was more than ready to be on the move again.

I had bought a hard case for the guitar, partly to protect my beloved companion from all the shocks and knocks of travelling, and partly because it moved me off the bottom rung of the busking league. If you were serious, you really needed a solid case, and it had become obvious that the fabric case was a message to other buskers that I was still new and green. I knew I would need to look very confident before I tackled London, so regarded the case as a wise investment. Wise it may have been, but it was also bloody big and heavy, and I was glad I didn't have to walk too far up the road before I got a lift.

I made Bedford in less than two hours, and with several hours of daylight left, decided to try my luck before going home. This was a strange feeling, as I was looking at a place I knew like the back of my hand from a completely different perspective. I couldn't recall ever seeing a busker in Bedford and couldn't immediately think of a place to play. Amazingly I found another busker within ten minutes, playing on Pigeon Square near the bus station. It was a great pitch. You had the entire glass wall of a supermarket at your back, with no inconvenient doors or shop displays to cramp your style, and some thoughtful town planner had provided several park benches and landscaped areas for people to sit and listen. The thought they might have just wanted to sit down without getting the benefit of a song of course never crossed my mind!

The guy playing was even younger than me, maybe eighteen, which was very unusual. He was also playing some fairly obscure Pink Floyd track from *The Wall*, rather than the standard busker fare of *Wish You Were Here* and *Another Brick in the Wall*. This was interesting stuff and I settled down to watch. He of course spotted the shiny new guitar case and my pack and nodded me over when he'd finished the song. His name was Martin, and as the only busker in town, he was as surprised to see me as I was him. He made the most unusual offer of knocking off immediately to let me have a go on the pitch, which I was sure was so he could size up his competition. I threw a couple of less common Pink Floyd numbers out to acknowledge I'd known what he was playing, which raised a smile and, to my surprise, a reasonable amount of money as well. Pigeon Square was just about the perfect pitch; over and above the conveniently provided seating you could wander up and down outside the supermarket, keeping step with shoppers to get a laugh if you felt like it, and, best of all, due to a quirk of architecture there wasn't one shop within earshot of where you played to get upset about the disturbance. Very easy.

The general protocol with other buskers when you changed over was to listen to a couple of songs then chuck a coin and get on your way, but Martin settled himself down to watch the whole gig, so to speak. This unnerved me slightly, but he seemed quite content to just sit in the sun and watch, so I kept testing for common ground. Neil Young was enthusiastically accepted, and I showed off by playing *Needle and the Damage Done,* with its fairly tricky intro riff. Martin got that glazed look musos get when they're trying to work out and memorise something as they watch it. Not much else I played got a reaction, and he positively turned his nose up at The Jam and Joy Division. This was a strange phenomenon indeed. Being a hippy at eighteen was very uncool in 1983.

I walked home along the Goldington Road, feeling good that I would be able to tell Mum and Dad that everything was going well.

I stayed in Bedford for my customary four or five days, spreading my time between busking, getting to know Martin, doing my duty by Mum and Dad and tip-toeing my way through the minefield of the mates who had never got away from home. I'd had an idea that once they found out I'd chucked in uni, things might go back to the way they once had been. I wandered up to the local to catch up a few times, but found anything I had to say about what I was doing generally stopped the conversation dead. It's not for me to say why this was, but I imagine it was because I had freedom, and all these guys could see ahead of them was more of the same. I guess you had to learn to like it or go crazy. I realised that I had left for good and there was no going back.

One person who was genuinely pleased to see me was my oldest friend and former childhood sweetheart, Helen. Helen and I had long had a pact of complete honesty with each other. We might have ended up together, except for the fact she hated uncertainty and taking chances in life. It was good to be able to share things with her. She was very supportive, while making it clear she still thought I was bonkers! It was nice to know I had someone else from home on my side and who would always be there for me, whatever happened.

With Martin as the only other regular busker, busking in Pigeon Square was very straightforward, but I learned a lot. I learned to work the throng rather than just standing there playing a song. To make money from busking, you need to try and get inside a person's head while their mind is on a thousand other things, and persuade them that you are worth them stopping, going through their pockets, and parting with some hard-earned cash. This needs exactly the right kind of eye contact and body language. I needed to look young and a bit vulnerable for old ladies, maybe a bit world-worn for businessmen – particularly after work when they've had a drink or two – cool and punky for people my own age and maybe school kids, happy larrikin with a bit of flirtation for girls and particularly mums with kids, and hypnotising for the kids themselves. To make money you had to scan constantly for the faintest hint that anyone was interested in you then do everything possible to hook them in, but not be so pushy that you put them off. I'd also realised that lots of people hated stopping and digging around for change in front of you, and would often come back ten minutes or an hour after they'd first seen you with whatever they thought you were worth sorted and ready to throw onto the case. This meant that even if someone was obviously going to walk past without giving, you had to work them in case they were the 'pay later' kind. This was really quite hard work, but watching someone slow down and put their hand in their pocket always gave me a warm glow inside.

The seats in Pigeon Square gave the pitch an interesting but quite difficult to handle dimension. You might get a businessman, an old lady and a feral hippy-looking type sitting next to each other. The businessman would probably have got *House of the Rising Sun*, the old lady *Piano Man* or *Streets of London* and the hippy anything by Pink Floyd or Neil Young. Having them all sitting next to each other made it a bit difficult and at times frustrating. You could see the body language warm up and cool down as you played to their taste, and innumerable times I would watch while I got the positive reaction with the right song only to lose it again when I played to the person next to them. The trick was to try and play a song that got in their headspace soon after they sat down, which was easy enough, and another one just as they were about to leave, which was a whole lot harder. The best money was almost always unpredictable, as it would generally occur from playing someone's special song. I got a five-pound note one day from a guy in tears because I played the whole of Dylan's *Tambourine Man* (generally people only know the wimpy version by The Byrds, which misses out all the best words). Probably the most important thing to realise was when you'd had enough. Singing full-on and working the passing throng, I could achieve a maximum of three hours a day. I found standing there for the sake of it playing half-heartedly was a waste of time and the money would fall away drastically.

Martin proved a sociable type but very into his dope and acid. He lived in a large, damp one-room flat just out of town, another decaying Victorian monolith. I went back there a couple of times and we smoked and listened to music and chatted. I remember being introduced to Roger Waters' *Pros and Cons of Hitch Hiking* while floating in a cannabis-induced haze, the psycho-paranoia of it all and the constant revisiting of melodies really got inside my head. It was wild. Martin was unusual in that he was a dope fiend who didn't have to talk about the stuff all the time, so you could have a reasonable conversation with him. He didn't have any acid around at the time but asked if I'd be interested in some if he could get his hands on it. I'd never tried it – it was a drug that scared me in that it was about the only one that really interested me. Pushing the mind limit thing intrigued me a little too much. I said I was interested.

Staying home was the usual mixed blessing of having people around that love you. I could honestly tell Mum and Dad that I was enjoying my crazy journey, and within the context of what I was trying to do, being successful. Dad would occasionally drop by from work when I was playing in Pigeon Square and I'd give him a special song or two, with all eighteen stone of him sitting there grinning like a cross between Buddha and Father Christmas.

Bedford was a resounding success and a relaxing break before taking on London. As I packed to leave, with Mum wittering away in the background about whether I was SURE I wanted to go while trying to pair up socks and iron everything she could get her hands on, I was humming my way through *London Calling* and *Down in the Tube Station at Midnight*.

This would really test me I thought, and I was spot on.

## 2 DOWN IN THE TUBE STATION AT MIDNIGHT

*The distant echo of faraway voices boarding faraway trains*
*To take them home to the ones that they love and love them forever*
*The glazed dirty steps repeat my own and reflect my thoughts*
*Cold and uninviting, partially naked except for toffee wrappers*
*And this morning's paper*
Paul Weller, 1978

The weather was kind to me as I hitched down to London and I made it in less than two hours. I decided to go straight to work.

I'd thought a fair bit about how I would attack the mighty metropolis. I knew that what I had already learned would not plug in to busking in London. Manchester was the only thing that came close, and it was still very different. Manchester had a defined centre with lots of pedestrianised places where people went to shop. London was a vast sprawl with a middle that was given over to the mighty car. The only place I could think of that fitted the bill was somewhere called Covent Garden, which I'd heard of but never been to. This would be my first stab. I'd also check out the Underground. I'd at least seen buskers play there, but I knew it would be a different planet to anything I had done before.

I got the tube at Brent Cross, where the M1 got into London, and headed for Covent Garden on the tube. Working my way back to the surface from the Underground, I felt overwhelmed by the maelstrom of people, noise, smells, relentless, hurrying movement and hot stinking dirty air. There was no fun to be had underground. I decided that playing there would be my last resort; pure desperation to make a buck. Covent Garden was great. A nice pedestrianised square with the Opera House in the middle, a decent sized market and lots of tourists wandering around looking to be entertained. This would be marvellous. I set up in an archway that faced out onto the square and fired up, hugely relieved that it could be this easy. The money came in comfortably, the sun shone and life was perfect. It couldn't last. Fifteen minutes after I started up a guy dressed as a court jester with a wild set of juggling paraphernalia made a beeline for me from the far side of the square. I imagined this would be the normal negotiation for next spot and decided to avoid commenting on his frankly edge-of-sanity dress sense. It would have to be bloody worthwhile for a conservative Englishman to dress like that in November. His accent said Yorkshire, and he wasn't a happy lad. "'ave you got a permit?"

I smiled and made it clear this meant nothing to me. I just tried the usual, "When do you want to start?" routine.

"Bollocks to when do I want to start. To play 'ere you need to audition, PASS the audition, and then wait for yer permit". There I was thinking jesters were meant to make people laugh.

I held out for a couple of minutes, but Blackadder was in no mood to compromise. Grave threats and warnings of calling the market management and even the police tumbled out, with production of the said permit as a final flourish. It would have been sacrilege anywhere else I'd been for a busker to talk like this. I realised that Covent Garden was very much off limits. Once I packed up, Yorkshire became at least vaguely civil and expressed a view that it would be highly unlikely that I would pass the audition to play there with my current 'act'. Given his dress and other kit I was inclined to agree with him. I didn't think a few Beatles songs would really stack up. Plus it took about a month to go through the process. He knew little and cared less about other possible places to play. I sat on a bench and watched him do his stuff to a couple of hundred people and wondered what to do next.

It was all too hard, so I beat a retreat. Sarah had arranged for me to crash at her friend Kate's hall of residence at University College London, a short walk from Euston station. The hall was a huge maze of a place on four floors stretching between several different houses, with corridors snaking up and down to join them all up into something viable for communal living. There was a security lock on the front door and it took me about an hour of hanging around outside to find someone who would find someone who would find Kate. She was very gushy and excited at my arrival and dragged me up to her room where a group were sitting around doing the first-year student coffee thing. I found them uninspiring trendy London types, gobbing on about Stringfellows and the Hard Rock Café. Hanging out at such places was ridiculous to contemplate on a student grant, but most of these people were obviously not existing on just a grant. From what I knew of Kate, her budget wouldn't stretch to hanging around with these people too long. She was a hyperactive, short-kilt-wearing, dope-smoking student who was way ahead of me on the latest music scene.

That night we went to the UCL bar and saw a band composed of the bits of Wham that were let go when they signed up George Michael and Andy Ridgeley. I would have thought being separated from those two would have been a cause for celebration, but the band were awfully bitter about it all. One or two tirades against the terrible industry were bearable, but it was all they had to say and I got bored. Then I got pissed, and spent the night yelling down Kate's ear about what I'd been up to, and trying to quiz her and her friends over likely places I could play. No-one was much help; the only suggestions were Camden Markets on the weekend, and the dreaded Underground. It seemed like the most obvious first option.

Kate had already left for a lecture when I woke up next morning, but her roommate was still in bed, reading and trying to pretend I didn't exist. I tried to be invisible, but Room Mate clearly wished I was anywhere but there. So with a throbbing head, guts suffering from a diet of beer and crisps and that blank post-dope empty brain feel, I headed for Euston tube station. I didn't really have a clue where to go looking for a pitch so I picked names I'd heard of that were right in the middle, like Oxford and Piccadilly Circus. The only people who would have any real idea how vast the labyrinth of tunnels under London are would be the people that work the trains, the tramps who sleep in the tunnels, and the buskers. I spent about an hour wandering round Oxford Circus getting my bearings – it was a vast maze and very difficult to know where to play. The buskers here were also a different species to friendly, hippy Martin back in Bedford. I came across a few and waited till the customary end of the song but didn't get the nod and hello, just a blank stare and into the next number. This wasn't good, but if they didn't want to be sociable, then fuck 'em. At least they weren't dressed in a hat with bells and asking me for a licence. The choicest spots were at the bottom of the escalators where people could see you all the way down, or at the end of long

## 2 DOWN IN THE TUBE STATION AT MIDNIGHT

passages, because the tunnels would just bounce your sound down to the other end and people could hear you for miles. All the pitches I came across of this kind were either manned up already or had a big sign saying No Playing Allowed, with dire warnings of death and destruction if you tried. I would say that Oxford Circus when busy would have about ten people playing at any one time somewhere in the maze of tunnels. My aching head wasn't standing up too well to all the bustling energy and white light and I knew I had to get going soon or I would lose my nerve.

I set up on the exit tunnel from one of the main lines, in a convenient little corner where the tunnel threw a right-hand bend. I waited for the whoosh and swish of a stopping train and opening doors, then started playing. A wall of people came at me and just about swept me away in the rush. I was actually hanging onto the case to avoid it getting washed away in the tide, with many a curse and jibe as I quite literally caused an obstruction. A minute after it started the platform emptied and the tunnel was deserted again. This was obviously hopeless, even though I'd seen plenty of other buskers playing corridors that seemed perfectly identical. There was either some trick to picking the right tunnel at the right time of day that I hadn't yet worked out, or else the nutters who regularly played these spots put up with some serious stress and abuse.

I desperately wanted something easier to nurse me through my hangover. I just about press-ganged another busker into talking, albeit briefly, and he made it clear there wasn't any room on his pitch – at all – all day. When I asked about the signs warning of penalties he just shrugged his shoulders. The chances of getting nailed were the same wherever you played and sometimes it was just not your day. Some days they would even have a general round-up of the musical fraternity for a fining session. The sign was basically irrelevant. While the idea of the fines was a bummer, the sign in fact was the best indicator of a good spot – it meant the spot was used regularly enough to warrant being banned from it.

I found a reasonable pitch at the end of a main tunnel between two lines where the tidal wave effect had a chance to stretch out a bit, with people going in both directions. This made for a reasonably regular throng who had time to hear you and get the money out, which was much more bearable than playing at people straight off the train. I could revel in my voice and guitar rolling down those acoustically perfect tubes, sounding magnificent, though I say it myself. My head still felt it was going to explode though, so after playing for about an hour and getting a very reasonable take, I fed some change into a machine on the platform – I couldn't bear to waste my tube ticket by heading back to the street. The Coke and chocolate restored my energy levels. An old guy with a guitar hanging off his back wandered off a train and, in a rare phenomenon for London, smiled and stopped to say hello when he saw the case. He gave me a few more hints on where I should play. Incredibly, he busked on the moving train. Saying it was the best money, he urged me to do it too – but that I should carefully coil the loose ends of my guitar strings into a circle on the machine head "so I wouldn't take some poor little kid's eye out while I was goin' round the coach". Playing on the trains was too daunting for me, but he gave me a couple of good stations to try. Apparently Bank and Monument had the longest corridor of any tube station with a bend in the middle that was just designed to hold a busker.

I think at that point my hangover got the better of me and I headed back to Kate's to crash. Over the next few days

## 2 DOWN IN THE TUBE STATION AT MIDNIGHT

I immersed myself in the crazy world of the tube stations. One day I just fronted a player on one of the best pitches in Oxford Circus and demanded a spot. He told me to come back in an hour when he changed and when I did it was a different guy. I staked out the pitch after this and when the swap came I waded in, making it clear I meant business. It turned out they really didn't know how long the pitch was occupied for; everyone had their slot for the day and didn't know more than a couple of players on in the chain. It seemed in London you just had to keep pushing to get in the door, and that night, I finally got on for an hour, having spent all day travelling the lines looking for places I could call my own.

I did two hours at that good pitch and knew that the slot was mine. Word of mouth had got round about this nutter who just wouldn't go away and I was finally accepted. God knows how I had the energy but that same night I decided to try and get on at the Bank and Monument slot. I'd wandered past there a couple of times already and it was truly an awesome spot to play – you could hear the player for miles. I got there about 10.30pm and it was unoccupied. There weren't many people coming through, but I was pretty manic by this time and I set up anyway. Most people passing seemed to be half or very pissed businessmen with guilt in their eyes about families waiting for them back home. I gave *House of the Rising Sun* hell and made a fortune. Pound coins and even a fiver, and me playing the same song non-stop for about two hours. I gave it everything I had, which in that spot produced an awesome effect. Though I say it myself I was fucking good that night – even though a two-hour gig playing one song was more than even Pink Floyd could get away with.

I seemed to be drawing on energy from the electric hum of the tube and felt I could play all night, but finally gave it away when it occurred to me that the trains were likely to stop sometime and I was miles away from Euston. I made the last train back to Kate's, staggering along with a huge amount of change in the case. This was my best day other than York so far. Mind you, it ought to have been, as I think I spent twelve hours straight down in the tunnels.

The dope crew were sat around in the usual circle when I got back and I gave them the money to count while I had a beer and wound down. I made around forty quid, which impressed even the London set. I tried to be sociable but was just too exhausted. I woke up still sitting upright against the bed with everyone gone, the lights out and a blanket thrown round my shoulders.

The next day I knew I'd overdone it. My voice and my fingers were raw, and I didn't have it in me to go back down into the tunnels. The money I'd made would last a couple of days. I felt I had a grubbiness in and on me from playing underground all day long that nothing would wash away. Like so many other things that year though, this had a good and bad feel to it. It seemed proof to me that I was now really on the journey to becoming what I had set out to be just a couple of months ago.

I went to Regents Park to give myself a reward and Kate some space to get some work done. Winter was really coming in now and I realised one of the good things about the tubes was the warmth. I found myself near the zoo and watched the big animals from afar. A polar bear paced up and down his concrete enclosure, obviously longing to be anywhere but there.

It was in London that I realised just how through-the-floor my self-esteem had gone in Nottingham. In stark contrast to the nervous, unconfident introvert drunk I had become in my final months at university, I liked the person I had become. I was confident, happy and relaxed.

The fretboard on my guitar was starting to develop grooves and dips in the fretboard that only my fingers could match – the guitarist's fingerprint that you can only get from hours and hours and hours of grinding away on the frets. My finger ends were as hardened as the soles of my feet, and I could put matches out on them without feeling a thing. I soon knew exactly what kind of strings I needed to reach the compromise between making the guitar get the big sound, give my fingers at least a chance of not getting too pulverised, and last as long as possible before having to put on a new set. I knew how to retie the strings when they snapped to save on new ones, and could get three uses out of a thinner string. This involved tying knots into the little circular end stops using your teeth as a third hand, and I have grooves in my front incisor teeth now from the grinding they got from those wound phosphor bronze strings. I could stand on any street corner and set up, change strings, eat a pie, do pretty much anything without a shred of nerves about being on show. I knew how to case a place for somewhere to play, and how to tune into the passing crowd to extract every coin possible from being there. I could fend off about anyone that came my way – drunks, tramps, nutters, shopkeepers having a bad day or the police. Most of all, I knew that if I could cope with the aggro of getting a pitch in London I could do it anywhere in the world. In short, my apprenticeship was over. I would spend a few more months pulling money together in the cities and towns where I could get a bed or floor to sleep on, and focus on more distant horizons.

Europe and America were more than just some crazy dream now. I might actually get there.

## 3 LIKE A ROLLING STONE

*How does it feel*
*Yeah how does it feel*
*To be on your own*
*With no direction home*
*Like a complete unknown*
*Like a rolling stone?*
Bob Dylan, 1965

Life became a blur of journeys and city streets.

The combination of money on the streets and a friendly place to sleep was best in Nottingham and Bedford. York was good for three or four days, and I could survive in Manchester for a couple of days, limited by the average takings. London was limited by the time I could crash on Kate's floor without tension, and the energy-sapping madness of playing the Underground. I never went back to Sheffield.

A pattern emerged where I would hitch south and catch the train back north. Every two weeks I would end up back in Nottingham to sign on. I was a regular on the streets by now. Getting to know the other regulars was a fragmented process, as virtually all conversations happened as you were swapping your pitch, and people were either in a hurry to get started or go home. In addition to Mogs and the relentless Banjo Allen, there were a few other regulars I got to know well.

Ron, an older singer/guitarist with a very big voice, was the undisputed king of the Broadmarsh subway and played the early shift religiously every day, having a family to support on his precarious income. I really got onside with him one day when he was late for his usual 10am start and I started on the pitch, thinking he'd missed the day. When he showed up fifteen minutes later I stood down immediately, saying I'd just been holding it for him. This wasn't true, I needed the money, but at the time I knew I needed to learn off guys like Ron more. From that point on I was very much in favour with him, and if I saw him on the street we'd swap cigarettes and he'd tell me if pitches were free on the other side of town.

Terry and Simon were of a different breed. Both were only a few years older than me and had obvious aspirations to stardom. Terry specialised in Motown stuff and did a belting *Tracks of my Tears*. He dressed very cool and sharp and moved around a lot, with a long coat that flew out behind him as he gyrated. He was unusually attractive for a busker, and didn't really fit the mould of the rest of us ragged-arse troubadours.

Simon bore a passing resemblance to Stan Laurel. He wore a big floppy cap – a look that was a cross between a dustbowl refugee from Steinbeck's *Grapes of Wrath*, and an extra from Sillitoe's *Saturday Night and Sunday Morning*. He was about the only other ex-student on the circuit but was a Nottingham boy, born and bred. Both he and Terry were only busking until their true talents were discovered and they made their rightful millions, when they could start driving round in their Ferrari (Terry) or Cadillac (Simon). I tuned into Simon's sense of humour very easily over a beer or two when we were waiting for a pitch, and we enjoyed jousting over our various tastes in music. Simon claimed 'purity' in his repertoire, sticking to his punky roots and not resorting to crowd pleasers like Simon and Garfunkel and Ralph McTell, as I did. I could leave him for dead on The Jam though, which vexed him a little. I felt the time would come when I would get to know Simon a lot better.

But Ron was king, and between the four of us we just about owned the pitch in the subway down under the Broadmarsh Centre on the way to the bus station. The clear advantages were that it was undercover and had great acoustics. It was also at the bottom of a long, wide, gently sloping tunnel, so people could see and hear you from a long way off. There were also no shopfronts close by, so you didn't drive a shopkeeper completely nuts playing the same stuff day after day. More subtly, it was on the way to the bus station and car parks that marked the edge of the city's main shopping area, so you were the first and last thing people saw when they came into the city to do their shopping. "Thank God that's over for another bloody week, 'ere y 'are lad, sounds very nice." Also, if someone came back after two hours in a nice warm department store to see you still outside in the cold, it was good sympathy material. "You still 'ere young un? You must be bloody freezin'."

The regular busking company was completed by two notable 'floaters' by the names of Scottish Jimmy and Dave Green.

Scottish Jimmy was a crazy Glaswegian who was almost always pissed and often meant trouble. He would have been handsome once upon a time, tall with black twinkling eyes and wild unkempt jet-black hair, but the grog had turned his face the colour of uncooked dough, and often the light in his eyes would go out, or worse, would take on a glint of craziness when his gander was up, which was often. It was generally pointless trying to arrange a time to take over from Jimmy because more often than not he'd pack up early to go to the pub. Worse, he'd often rock up and decide it was a great idea for the two of you to play together. This could be fun if you'd already made your pile for the day but a pain in the arse if you hadn't. Several times I saw the money I'd made before Jimmy showed up disappear into his half. But you didn't mess with Jimmy. He had a defeated, sad, tired-looking woman who looked a lot older than him but who I think was just worse for the wear from too many years on the grog. She was always wandering the streets "Lookin' for Jimmy, 'ave you seen 'im love?" and often had a black eye or other bruises. The two of them were pretty hard work but were part of the landscape.

Dave Green sported a chequered cap that sat squarely on his balding head, and if what he told me was true – and I think it mostly was – he had done a lot of things in his time. He reckoned he was mates with Ralph McTell of *Streets of London* fame, and also of Denny Laine, who was the third part of the Wings triangle along with Paul and Linda McCartney. I heard a lot of stories from a lot of buskers that year about who they were mates with, most of which I dismissed, but Dave wasn't a bullshitter. I think it was true. Dave regarded himself as the godfather-cum-protector of Nottingham's busking fraternity, and with some justification. The police had a crackdown on busking a few months earlier, and Dave had gone through the laws of the city and found some bylaw a couple of hundred years old that said a man could not be prevented from making his living in an honest fashion on the streets of Nottingham. (There were probably lots of 'ye's' in there, but that was the general idea!) This meant that the worst that could happen to you was to be asked to move on if someone complained.

# 3 LIKE A ROLLING STONE

Dave and Scottish Jimmy had a long history together – and not a good one. One day I was playing with Dave when Jimmy rolled by and joined in. As usual, Jimmy was pissed and wouldn't be put off, so we moved from the subway out to the winter darkness to play on Slab Square. Jimmy followed us and, too drunk to play, made huge theatrical runs in front of the punters and passers-by, yelling our praises in raucous Glaswegian. To avoid getting arrested, Dave suggested a gig in a pub just off the square. The landlord there was keen, but not with Jimmy tagging along. So we headed across the road to Yates Wine Lodge, a vast three-floored drinking hole with sawdust on the floor – just the place for ragged-arsed buskers.

It turned out Jimmy was banned from Yates, and Dave knew this. We sculled a quick half, watching as Jimmy peered intently through the fag smoke and lights trying to keep an eye on us. Then we bolted out the back to the other pub for our gig. Jimmy found us just as we were finishing our sound check and waded up towards the stage with eyes blazing and guitar swinging round his head like a battle-axe. We did some damage control with the landlord, and Dave somehow managed to convince Jimmy that we hadn't tried to abandon him in Yates, and that we would all get together on stage later for a jam. During our gig, Jimmy kept erupting out of his chair with blazing eyes and clenched fists and then, remembering himself, tried to calm down, muttering, staring wild-eyed at the floor and shaking his head. Not surprisingly the landlord by now was looking for any excuse to get rid of all of us. He got what he needed when Dave hopped off the front of the high stage, caught his heel in the drink shelf, and was sent sprawling in front of the punters in a mess of broken glass and frothing beer. All three of us were thrown out into the night. I was scared Jimmy was going to completely lose it, but once we were all in the sin bin he turned sorrowful, "Forgive me lads, it's all my fault". We bought some beers and kept playing on Slab Square for hours, not caring whether we made money or got arrested.

Busking in Nottingham was generally uneventful – except when Banjo Allen was interviewed by the papers and he said he made up to a hundred quid a day, and that while he wasn't signing on, most of the other buskers were. A massive influx of no-hopers promptly hit the streets, keen to get their hundred quid a day. It caused me major paranoia every time I queued up at the dole office. It took about a month for the no-hopers to realise that it wasn't that easy. From memory not one of them survived to become a regular, but in the meantime getting a pitch became nigh on impossible, the number of people on the streets went up five-fold and the money was dreadful. We regulars banded together London-style to freeze out those who were so awful they were bad for business. You couldn't stop people playing, but there was no point in making life easy for someone who just hadn't got it.

One of the braver things I did in Nottingham was play on the streets when the Glasgow Rangers came to town to play Nottingham Forest in what was obviously a big deal to everyone but me. The city was crawling with pissed Scotsmen all hell bent on having the best possible time and showing the Sassenachs that the Scottish were the best in the world at drunken bonhomie. I sat watching the scene, wondering if I would get the crap beaten out of me if I started playing. A girl from uni called Ali passed by and stopped for a chat. I decided to give it a go and gave Ali

## 3 LIKE A ROLLING STONE

fifty pence to prime the guitar case just after I started up. I used the very pitch I'd played on when Mogs had given me my first chance – it felt lucky.

Less than a minute into the first song I was surrounded by pissed, scarf-waving Scotsmen, all singing along out of tune. There was a rustle in the crowd as Ali appeared, blushing bright red, to daintily put the fifty pence in my case. The Scottish guys thought this was magic and immediately started digging in their pockets, proclaiming at a million decibels what a generous and open-hearted race they were. Then the requests started. The most memorable was "Play *Flower o' Scotland* or we'll attack yas". I'd never heard of it, so I suggested they sing it and I'd play along. Twenty drunks yelling at the tops of their voices wasn't the easiest thing to play along to, but it really didn't matter what I played. As more and more fans turned up, I was in danger of getting overwhelmed. Each mob would cluster round me, request a song with varying degrees of enthusiasm and politeness, generally take no notice whatever of what I played and sing whatever they felt like. The money was great and it was brilliant fun too. Fun and a bit scary – this was the Catholic Glasgow team, with strong ties to Belfast and Northern Ireland, and the requests included IRA rebel songs – the *Soldiers Song* being the most popular. I wasn't sure of the law around singing songs on the street supporting political groups that blew people up, particularly if they weren't on the side of the government. But saying no to playing what these guys wanted would have been a very foolish and dangerous game, so I stood in the middle of mob after mob, singing along with the rebel anarchists.

One guy asked for a go on my guitar and promptly went jogging off down the road. Fortunately for me his mates brought him back. Another bizarre moment occurred when an extremely drunk young guy kept insisting he played guitar too. "I'm fuckin' famous me, I'm in a band called … called … what the fuck is it – ay, Aztec Camera. No, really I am." I nodded and grinned and said fine and promptly forgot it. About two weeks later I saw Aztec Camera playing on *Top of the Pops*. It was him. I reckon he would just about have got over his hangover by then.

As the weather grew colder I needed to upgrade my street clothes to survive. My one pair of shoes had a split right down the side, and after the first fall of winter snow had turned to dirty slush and ice on the Nottingham streets and I nearly froze my foot off, I invested in a massive pair of steel-capped boots that were on sale. The soles were about two inches thick. I figured this would give me as much insulation from the cold as I would ever need. I dug out a hat that I'd stolen from some party a year or so back that had a Tom Waits look – a grey trilby with a narrow brim and slightly too small. It made me hold my neck and head straight and was also a good prop for doing Mick Jagger struts, when I would tip the hat forward over my nose. It was great for business. On a more practical note, I found that wearing a hat was the best way to stay warm on the cold days – all that singing seemed to push the heat out of the top of your head like a chimney. I had a donkey jacket for the days when it was reasonable and a vast green overcoat from the Oxfam shop for the really cold days. When I was wearing the hat, the big overcoat, my chunky brown boots and the fingerless mitts I looked every inch the authentic thing, and a lot of the other Nottingham regulars took the piss out of me for dressing up for the part.

When I wasn't busking I spent a lot of time hanging out with Chris, an ex-student who'd become the DJ of choice for the most popular student club in the city and for every hall party on the university campus. I felt much more at home behind the decks with Chris, pumping out music and watching him work the crowd, than sitting at home while my housemates slogged through their degrees.

I got to know Dave Green better the night we both got booked to play a gig at the university, of all places. I had been playing in the subway underneath the Broadmarsh and two Indian guys stopped to talk. They explained they wanted some entertainment for their Christmas party. The money was fifty quid and it sounded too good to be true. It was. It was a nightmare. The party's guest of honour was an old lecturer of mine who recognised me. It was pure torture as I bombed in front of an audience who spoke almost no English and had never heard of any of the songs I knew how to play. I thought the set would never end as I tried to be soulful, funny, light-hearted – *anything* – to get more than a too-polite smatter of applause. I didn't know what I was doing.

Dave was the other busker they'd picked from the streets, and I watched as he gave a superb demonstration of why he'd been at the top of this game so long. He had all the kids up the front dancing to some train song or other and then persuaded a couple of adults to join them. The audience loved every second of it, and it was a big lesson that entertaining a crowd on stage was a whole different country to blasting out punk songs on the street.

I stumbled through a minute of mutual agony with my old lecturer, then retreated to a corner with Dave for our free feed. I soaked up his anecdotes and advice like a sponge, all the more so because he gave it without a hint of smugness or crowing. He was kind enough to say that I had it in me to do what he did, I just had to learn how to play the audience, not just the song.

It was soon obvious that he and I were the only people drinking, so we left the party and headed back to the city, stopping at a few pubs. When they shut, we took some beers and sat talking on the steps of a factory entrance. It turned out to be near the Irish Social Centre, the main student drinking hole, and by coincidence the lads from my house wandered past. When I saw the look on their faces I knew I'd broken away completely from the student life. They passed by with as little talk as possible. This was part of the price I paid for doing what I did.

A final irony of that night was that to save money I had ridden my bike up to the university for the gig and left it there when Dave and I went on our pub crawl. By the time I returned the next day all that was left was a snipped bike lock. The bike cost about fifty quid and I spent another ten on booze, so I was down on the night and minus a bike.

The upside was that Dave – around thirty years my senior – became a valued mentor, adviser and guiding light. We got on so well that we would often get together on the streets. I really don't know why he bothered with me, but he did. Maybe he saw something of himself thirty years ago. One great day we did a wild blues medley which started out with Dave singing some song which had the line "I'm down in your subway, singin' your subway blues". I've never found the song and he may have made it up on the spot, but it hit the mark exactly of what we were doing. A blues harp player appeared from somewhere and, fuelled by a bottle of ginger wine to keep out the cold, we went off. At that moment, it was about much more than the money.

## 3 LIKE A ROLLING STONE

I was spiralling up and down the subway weaving in and out of the faceless crowd, pumping out these blues riffs with the harp howling above and Dave's rock-solid train rhythm and bucket-of-gravel voice wailing out the truths of our crazy street life. For a few brief minutes we touched some deep nerve of what this playing on the streets was all about. It was wild.

There are so many moments of those times that will stay with me forever. Like when the two homeless drunks wanted to share their bottle of cheap sherry with me, whether I liked it or not. They watched intently, making sure that I took a swig from the same bottle that their blistered lips and rotting teeth had just sucked from. And the time I got bailed up by a tramp who had almost no voice left. Somehow he managed to communicate that he wanted me to play Bob Dylan's *Hard Rain* and when I got to the line "I heard the song of a poet who died in the gutter" he nodded, pointed at himself, and walked away in tears. Another day a guy rolled through who I had never seen before and never saw again but who knew the chords to *Amsterdam*, a brilliant, dark song by Jacques Brel covered by David Bowie as the B-side to an obscure single called *Sorrow*. He scribbled down the chords on a small piece of blue cardboard for me and disappeared forever. This song has stayed with me longer than any other I play and I still love its maniac theatre. It's a great song for the streets.

I got to know my fellow busker Martin a lot better when I was in Bedford. We occasionally busked together on Pigeon Square, and did well. It was so easy it was more like a busman's holiday. Martin and I shared out the time so we each got a fair go at the people having lunch in the square. In addition to the normal punters, there was the usual gaggle of derelict-looking types that seem to gravitate to public places. Occasionally one would give me a bit of a run-around, but they were harmless enough, and generally very friendly. One particularly intense one would regularly sidle over and tell me all the past glories he'd had as a musical legend of one kind or other. Some of his stories got a bit far-fetched, but his best was the day he told me in deadly earnest that it was he who had written the theme to *Neighbours*. Another occasional highlight was friends or old schoolteachers wandering past and recognising me. I'd gone to the local public school and so the teachers were a fairly rugger and rowing lot, which meant they were either totally horrified at an 'Old Boy' sinking so low, or, in a couple of the more eccentric cases, highly enthusiastic at me doing something so individual and character-forming. One teacher, who had always regarded his classes as a stage performance and encouraged my disruptive contributions to class, boomed out words of encouragement from fifty metres away, to the great amusement of the lunch throng. He thought it was all a wonderful thing I was doing and far more character-building than boring old university.

I hit a major setback in Bedford when I became the victim of a policeman having a bad day. He threatened me with arrest for disturbing the peace and causing an obstruction and radioed around various places trying to nail me for claiming the dole while earning – but of course he knew nothing about Nottingham. I'm pretty sure he would have taken me in but for the crowd of supporters who gathered to watch and who made it clear they were happy for me to be there. One very well spoken old lady in particular gave him a very refined earful about how people like me brightened the place up. He let me off but made it clear if he saw me again before Christmas I would be off on a visit to the cells.

Coming back to London after my regular trips north was always hard. Each time I left, I fell off the food chain for all the good pitches and had to fight my way back. Slowly I established my own spots, which was a lot easier. I even got the hang of playing the crazy pitches straight off the platform that were either swamped with people or totally deserted. I hated it but sometimes it was the only choice, and, amazingly, the money was bearable. If you put the case beside you and not in front of you, and made sure the fretboard of the guitar didn't stick out in the traffic, you could just about get away with it for most of the time. You also had to time this right – peak rush hour was a waste of time, partly because you could get overwhelmed by the crush and partly because the commuters were like robots and totally uninterested in giving money to buskers who got in their way. At other times it just about worked, though I was stunned that anyone could find the time in the fifteen seconds they had rushing past to give an offering, but somehow, they did.

Playing in the Underground was one long blur of grimy tunnels, whooshing, grinding trains and an endless, seething, exhausting mass of humanity, and I have almost no vivid memories of playing there. An exception was a day when I realised a guy I'd been to school with was walking up the tunnel, wearing a three-piece suit, looking every inch the city banker, but with a look of total desolation on his face. I remembered he'd failed in just about everything a year before the end of school and his old man had pulled him out and fixed him up with some kind of job in the City. He was still only twenty but looked ten years older. He was staring down the tunnel with empty eyes and it seemed like the weight of the whole world was on him. I was singing away and so much part of the scenery that I was invisible to him. I wondered whether to say hello, but never did, and he continued his weary way down the tunnel. A quite surreal reminder of a direction my life was not going in.

I tried to learn at least one new song every week, and spread them between things I liked, things that were 'stayers', like Beatles songs and top twenty stuff. I've forgotten a lot of the more pop stuff but *Love of the Common People* was one I remember because of the line about the hole in your shoe that lets the snow come through.

*That's Entertainment* by The Jam became my hallmark in Nottingham, while London was *Down in the Tube Station at Midnight.* Playing it on guitar was no mean feat and was good ammo for impressing the miserable London mob. I used to play them both to get my energy back up on bad days, and most times they worked.

As Christmas grew nearer and the Christmas shoppers and decorations got more intense, I headed to Nottingham. There was a whole crop of buskers who only appeared for the Christmas period and it messed up the regulars something rotten. It got a bit surreal; in my favourite subway a man appeared playing dreadful clichéd Christmas carols on a piano accordion with a Jack Russell dog huddled up in his accordion case and a piece of tinsel wrapped round his straw boater. He looked all sweetness and light but was an absolute prick, refusing to give any time when he would move, and regularly hijacking a pitch by playing just up

## 3 LIKE A ROLLING STONE

or down from where you were. Another had a monkey and a barrel organ that he cranked all day long (the organ that is, not the monkey) making a bloody awful row for pretty much zero effort, collecting bugger-all money and wrecking the whole street for everybody else to play.

Things went ballistic just before Christmas and I knew I had to play every moment I could to make the most of the ridiculous money. I was bringing in fifty pounds a day – twice the weekly dole money. My fingers were raw, and I had to keep drinking milk to put some kind of layer on my tortured throat. It was freezing and if I couldn't get a spot in a subway the air stung the back of my throat every time I breathed in. On the last day before going home to Bedford for Christmas, I nearly killed a couple of people coming down the stairs of a double decker bus because my guitar case was so full of money it just pulled me off my feet and sent me down the stairs on top of them. I felt on top of the world. For the first time in my life I was doing exactly what I wanted, and no-one – *no-one* – could stand in my way.

## 4 A SIMPLE TWIST OF FATE

*They sat together in the park
As the evening sky grew dark
She looked at him and he felt a spark
Tingle to his bones
'Twas then he felt alone
And wished that he'd gone straight
And watched out for a simple twist of fate*
Bob Dylan, 1974

Christmas finally arrived and I scored a lift home with Rob. The tradition in Bedford on the day before Christmas was wandering round every pub in town, bumping into everyone who'd come home for the holidays. I met up with Sarah and Kate and Mike and Richard and various other people whose floors I'd been sleeping on during the year.

When the pubs closed after lunch I found myself wandering around with Kate's boyfriend. Tom was a farmer's son and a good bloke, but he was in a foul mood because he seemed completely obsessed with the idea of finishing it with Kate and highly resentful that he was going to have to buy her a present. Tom had even less time than I did for Kate's trendy London set, and this seemed to be the main theme of why he wanted to finish things. I thought of Kate's wonderful vibrating energy and decided he was a bit daft. He disappeared soon after, but I happened to meet up with Kate in one of the high street pubs. At this point something I've never really been able to work out clicked, and in the space of an hour Kate and I crossed every barrier of personal body space and started getting very close. I had dim feelings of guilt about Tom but figured this was just a harmless Christmas piss-up – and Tom wanted to finish it all anyway.

The final part of the Christmas Eve ritual was a curry, followed by an attendance at midnight mass. Bearing in mind we'd been drinking for nearly twelve hours at this stage we were very far indeed from the state of mind of most other people in the church. I sat very close to Kate in the church, feeling her heat and energy. Richard was as loopy as ever and wandered up to the front in the middle of the service and asked if he could have his free biscuit and glass of wine early because he was busting for a piss. If they'd had bouncers we would have been thrown out, but as it was we got lots of black looks on the way out. Kate's mum was waiting outside and offered to drop the rest of us off, so the final thrill for the night was Kate perching on my lap for twenty minutes breathing in my ear. I got out the car in a swirl of emotion, waving the car goodbye with Kate smiling and waving over the back seat, and wandered into the house confused and hormonally fired up.

The next day there were various family obligations to be got through and I had my usual crashing Christmas Day hangover. The general family rule was that you were allowed to escape from the proceedings after the third enormous plate of food for the day, which we called 'Christmas tea' to differentiate it from Christmas breakfast and Christmas dinner. The phone rang sometime in the afternoon and it was my old friend Helen. She didn't mince words.

"What's happening with you and Kate?"

I stuck to our pact of complete honesty. "I don't know. It was very weird, but nothing happened. How did you find out?"

"Because she rang me about ten minutes ago asking for your number to ring you to see if you were going to Jim's party." Jim was one of the old crew and had established something of a tradition of having a party at his place on Christmas Day. He and I didn't talk very much anymore and I knew I wouldn't really be welcome.

"So – what are you going to do?" Her tone of helpful friendliness had significant undertones of potential for scandalous gossip.

"Hmm, dunno – but if she does ring I really should go along to be sociable, shouldn't I?"

Helen made some dry comment about the different interpretations you could put on 'sociable' then got off the phone fast to leave the way open for Kate.

Fifteen minutes later the phone rang. I tried to sound relaxed. I could tell Kate was curling up and dying from embarrassment at the other end, but it still felt like there was some kind of serious chemistry happening. There were lots of breathless pauses at both ends and I agreed to meet her at the party. I felt highly confused. Yesterday we were both pissed and it was a Christmas celebration. Today we were both sober (or heavily hungover, in my case).

I endured the family glutton thing for as long as I could, then bolted for the party.

The whole Bedford crew who'd never made it away from home were there, diluted with the people who were back for Christmas. For the hundredth time I wondered why it was that other people could leave and be forgiven but I appeared to be walled out forever. I really knew the answer. I'd been the closest to them and the first to go, and once the bond we'd had was gone it was impossible to have anything in the middle.

Kate was there, and Tom wasn't. Making eye contact with her across the smoky room was like some naff sequence in an American teen movie, with lots of confused energy going back and forth, and more than a little straight-out lust. We circled each other warily for the first part of the evening, but later got together and ended up curled up in a corner half asleep – a combination of the excesses of the last two days and a couple of spliffs. Everyone steered clear but I could see a number of black looks coming our way; not surprising since Kate and Tom were 'official'. I suppose I took my lead from Kate on that one and also had my recent experience with Tom to go on, but no-one else knew about that.

About midnight I walked her home and we ended up sitting on the garden wall talking and getting steamy. At about two in the morning we did an extended Romeo and Juliet goodbye scene outside her parents' semi-detached house in Brickhill and I staggered home in a haze of love, lust, alcohol, exhaustion and dope.

The next few days were ridiculous. As soon as Tom found out what was happening he suddenly decided he was still madly in love with Kate and several highly theatrical scenes were played through as the love triangle pushed back and forth.

There was no particular reason for either of us to hang around in Bedford after New Year so we made a romantic escape to my place in Nottingham by bus (well it seemed romantic at the time). We had the whole house to ourselves and it was so cold we had little choice but to spend most of our time in bed to keep each other warm. Three days of this and I was firmly convinced that I was hopelessly in love, and life was wonderful.

Being in love was great but I knew I still had to make some money, and figured the crowds for the January sales would be very lucrative.

How wrong can you be.

I played for two hours in Nottingham on a good pitch when the place was seething with people and made about two pounds. Whereas a week before everyone was suffused with that pre-Christmas glow that England does so well, now it was a cold and hopeless January, and everyone was getting bargains at the sales – not a time to be generous. The difference was amazing, and after trying and getting the same result in Bedford, I decided to take a month off and put my energy into being in love, rather than howling on street corners for no money.

This of course involved going back down to London to stay at Kate's halls of residence, with the trendy set and Room Mate. Of course things were very different now, and coordinating room activities with Room Mate became a major part of life.

Being with Kate was wonderful. Her energy was amazing and I loved the feel of her small powerful body next to mine. We went for long romantic walks by the Thames and talked for hours and hours and hours about nothing interspersed with some highly enthusiastic and energetic lovemaking. Being Jack Kerouac and seeing the world suddenly seemed far less of a priority.

Everything was wonderful for about two months before it started to wane. I found Kate's set of trendy friends hard work and was having problems hiding this. It also became apparent that socialising with them started to take precedence over our time together. I would hitch down for a weekend to find that she'd spent the previous three days doing wild and crazy things with the trendies and was now focused on getting up to speed with her lectures. I was exiled to the tube stations to try and earn some cash while she worked. There was one really awkward scene where I was off to catch a bus to Bedford and she obviously couldn't wait to see the back of me. I was in a huge depression for the entire journey, then was back on cloud nine the next day when I got a letter she'd written as soon as I'd got on the bus saying how sorry she was, and how wonderful what we had together had been.

I pondered the ecstasies and trials of being love while I went back to Nottingham to sign on and catch up with the boys on the streets. Revolting January had drizzled into just as revolting February and March, and the busking was still very average.

In those tough couple of months I spent a fair bit of time sitting in cafes with other buskers. That's when I really got to know Simon – the John Steinbeck wannabe – and Garry, a new man on the beat. Both of them were at least five years older than me.

First impressions were deceptive. Garry looked like an innocent who'd breezed in from some middle-class upbringing to play at being a busker for a while before going back to stockbroking. He had neatly cropped blond hair, a trimmed moustache and soft, deer-like eyes. He was also on the bottom end of the busker food chain as far as guitar and singing ability was concerned. He had a good voice but didn't belt it out, and he was a bit of a four chord wonder on the guitar. He was also just about unique in that he regularly played his own songs on the street. I quite liked his stuff, but it wasn't catchy enough to make up for the fact that no-one knew it. We got into the habit of meeting for a coffee or a beer after we'd both finished playing for the day, and I slowly started to pick up a very different story. He was from Hyson Green, which was about the toughest part of the city, all falling apart 60s-built council housing, where only the roughest and the toughest got housed. There were dark hints of violence from an abusive father a long way back, and a descent into heroin addiction to get away from it. A lengthening list of buskers I knew around the country would tell me in hushed tones of their fights with the devil heroin and I generally placed these alongside the stories of narrowly missed fame in the past and big breaks just around the corner as part of the busker smokescreen, but Garry was different. He didn't talk about it like it was a badge of honour, in fact he hardly referred to it at all. The mild eyes and nice-boy haircut also camouflaged some serious muscles – his shoulders and forearms were huge, and I noticed some major tattoo work peeking out from the ends of his sleeves and at the back of his neck. He had me pretty convinced his background was for real until he said he joined the French Foreign Legion to clean himself up from the smack and get away from his father. When he added that he'd deserted from the Foreign Legion in Corsica and got a bar job a few miles away from his regiment, I thought he was stretching the envelope of truth. But the truth, or otherwise, was his business. Garry was a nice guy who was decent company and pathetically grateful for any advice or help I gave out about his beloved self-penned songs.

It was easier to see through Simon's carefully crafted impression of the hard-bitten street muso. He was an honest showman, and a good one at that. The big floppy Steinbeck hat and the broad Nottingham Alan Sillitoe accent were both pretty much film props. It turned out he was a Nottingham University graduate and a local boy, and his dad was a dealer in books. Ironically, he and I were really like what Garry looked like, and we were both playing at what Garry was trying to get away from. Simon's saving grace was that amidst the theatre act he could look back at himself and laugh at his antics, and accept it if you did the same. I remember one time we got to talking about musicals and he said he had played Fagin in the school production of Oliver, and when I called him out on this, he sang *Reviewing the Situation* right through in the middle of the bus station café, complete with spidery Fagin fingers and wringing hands. He was magnificent and got a standing ovation from the grandmas waiting for their buses. He milked this for every clap he could get, doing an enormous Elizabethan bow and then exiting stage left with chin held high and arm extended in theatrical pose. Simon also did a great Stan Laurel, but he *really* wanted to be Tom Joad from *The Grapes of Wrath*. He was the first person I'd come across who I thought might understand my ideas about doing America.

Simon and I had started talking about going somewhere different to freshen up life, but while I was in love this seemed like something I could put off and we'd never really got anywhere with it. However, while talking with some of the old-timers round town we came up with the idea of Paris and, given the fragile state of things with Kate, I raised it as a serious idea. It was spontaneous and easy enough to commit to over a beer in the pub, but Simon agreed and proclaimed that we would leave in two weeks. He was at the end of the lease in his flat and just had to organise somewhere to store his few belongings. With my head in a spin, I got phone numbers and addresses off him and agreed that two weeks from now we would start our great new adventure. Kate was a significant complication in this but I knew in the back of my mind that this was the next step I needed to take to have any chance of making it to America. I told the dole office I was going to Paris to look for work, and was able to stay away a whole month. If Paris worked out, I figured Kate would somehow fit in with the travelling back and forth from Paris to Nottingham every two weeks to keep the rent paid on my room and pick up my twenty-five quid a week from the dole.

The next visit to London was disastrous. After our letters – hers just words and mine a little too blunt – together with the news that I was thinking of going to Paris, it was a tense and angst-ridden couple of days. We ended up pissed and stoned and sobbing all over each other in a borrowed room, and when I woke next morning I could feel something had changed. Still, this was love, and love couldn't fall apart so quickly, surely. What do you reckon?

Simon, me and Garry jamming in Room 17.

## 5 SOUS LE CIEL DE PARIS

*Sous le ciel de Paris / Beneath the Parisian sky*
*Marchent des amoureux / lovers walk*
*Leur bonheur se construit / Their happiness built*
*Sur un air fait pour eux / upon a tune made just for them*
Giraud/Dréjac, 1951. Performed by Edith Piaf.

If ever there was a day when my guardian angel worked overtime, it was the day we were due to leave Nottingham for Paris. Simon was missing in action. I rang him – his phone number had been disconnected. I cycled miles to the address he'd given me – it turned out to be deserted. I went down to the Broadmarsh subway and met up with Ron, who'd been the first person to suggest Paris to us. He'd seen Simon and yes, he was off to Paris that day, and what's more, Garry was going with him too. They were on their way to the bus station. In case I missed them, I asked Ron where I should head to in Paris to find the right 'turf'. The Mazet bar on Rue Saint-André des Arts in the Latin Quarter, from Saint-Michel Metro station, was the highly specific answer. This was the acknowledged buskers' hangout. The only complication was that Garry and Simon hadn't asked for any such guidance and as far as Ron knew, they didn't know the place. I might end up having to go it alone.

I worked my way across town towards the Victoria Bus Station where all the long-distance coaches left from, asking the regulars on the way if they'd seen the intrepid duo. Banjo Allen and Mogs both told me the same thing Ron had. With little hope I wandered into the enormous cavern of Victoria and there in the travel centre, literally at the front of the queue and about to buy a ticket, was Simon, with Garry right behind him. I resisted the urge to get down on my knees in thanks to my guardian angel.

They were both reassuringly happy to see me, but there was little time for chatting as I had to go home, pack and get back to the bus station in the space of about three hours.

Heading back out along the Derby Road on the bus I felt a pounding in my heart that had been missing since Christmas. Spending time with Kate and enjoying the heat of a new love affair over the bitter English winter months had been wonderful, but there was now a new adventure ahead, and I was feeling the excitement. Perhaps I had only been in love with being in love, after all. I put these thoughts aside to deal with another day.

I got back to the house in Derby Road, threw everything I thought I would need into my well-worn backpack – which wasn't much more than what I had been lugging around the country all year, with the addition of my passport. I was out the door again in less than an hour.

I'd arranged to meet Garry and Simon in a seedy old pub next to the bus station. We made quite a windswept and interesting trio; our packs and guitars artfully arranged in haphazard chaos around the tiny, glass-ring-stained table with its overflowing ashtray.

It turned out that the reason behind the unlikely alliance of Simon and Garry was because of a shared relationship experience. Garry had just found out he was a father, due to a one-off reunion with an old girlfriend just before he'd run off and joined the Foreign Legion. (I still couldn't believe this). Meanwhile, Simon had just found out that his ex-girlfriend, of about three months back, was pregnant. Both Garry and Simon had offered to do the noble thing by their respective women but had been sent packing. From what I could gather both women thought they'd be better off without a busker to put up with, as well as a baby. Both men were in a sensitive state, and it occurred to me that my dramas with Kate were distinctly minor in comparison.

It was good to be able to change the subject and I raised Ron's suggestion of heading for Saint-Michel. Neither really had any other plan, but as we discussed the option it became apparent that there was a bit of strutting going on for who would rule the roost for the trip. Both wanted to be the big chief decision-maker, even though it had been my suggestion in the first place. I was happy to sit back and let them deal with it. I had no interest in pretending to be the leader. My relative youth was a real advantage sometimes. Eventually we agreed that we would head for Saint-Michel.

We had a final beer to toast our impending adventure, then waddled back to the bus station, guitar cases bouncing off each other and bags and packs hanging off at all angles. This was exciting stuff.

Excitement levels dropped during the long bus journey to London, though the company and the prospect of where we were going made it much more bearable. We staked out the rear end of the coach; Simon sat in the middle of the back seat, his enormous boots splayed down the central aisle, his hands behind his head, the Tom Joad cap raked at a jaunty angle. This was really one big acting chance for Simon, and he was making the most of every scene. Garry was quieter and more reserved, taking the double seat in front and staring out the window lost in thought – not surprising really in the circumstances. As for me, I had been very unsure last time I'd seen Kate whether I was really going to do this trip, and as we travelled through the March fog and rain, I reflected that I really ought to try and see her in London as I passed through. I left messages at her hall of residence, but she either didn't get them, didn't make it to the bus station in time, or just didn't come. I tried to get worked up about leaving her behind, but the prospect of the big adventure ahead was all too exciting. So much for love.

I'd naively expected that when we transferred from the crappy old Nottingham to London bus to the London to Paris one, we would be on something a bit more comfortable and exotic, but if anything, the bus was crappier. Back then you were still allowed to smoke on buses, and the dusty stale bus smell – smoke with the hint of vomit – seemed to follow me around that year. The bus driver, who seemed as dodgy as the bus, made a huge fuss over having to carry our guitars in addition to our rucksacks, telling us they were excess baggage and it would be another pound each. We watched the pound notes disappear into his pocket with no hint of a receipt; the bus company probably wouldn't be seeing the benefit of those excess baggage payments. Both Simon and Garry made noises in protest, but the bus driver weighed about as much as the two of them put together and said if we didn't like it, he'd leave us and 'our fucking hat boxes' on the pavement. We gave up and boarded for another journey through the rain and gathering dark, battling our way out of the London rush hour and on to Dover, only stopping for the inevitable rest call at a tired service station where a washed-out, disinterested woman stood behind a counter full of washed-out, disinterested food, not even pretending to look like she gave a damn.

I've lost count of the number of times I've been through Dover now and I still don't think I've ever seen it in daylight, or even seen much of it at all for that matter. Just a blur of vast car parks, endless ranks of trucks under blazing neon-lit signs, a vague impression of huge cliffs that may or may not have been white, and not a hint of any bluebirds flying anywhere. We locked into the queue of trucks and buses shunting onto the ferry. Ten-ton bus driver wouldn't let anyone off to stretch their legs, even though we didn't move forward in the queue for about an hour. Garry and Simon were getting stir-crazy from all the sitting around and were starting to take it out on each other. The battle for who was in charge seemed to be intensifying, and both were trying to tell the other exactly what we should do when we got to Saint-Michel. I began to wonder if I might not have been better off having missed them and gone it alone and, surprising myself, said so. This diffused things a bit, but I could see there would be trouble in Paris if we didn't have a decent run of luck and find something they could both be happy they'd organised.

Customs and passport control finally came aboard and did their thing and we juddered slowly into the depths of the ferry. Once parked we filed out and threaded our way through the labyrinth of other buses and trucks to find the stairway up to the warmth and light of the upper decks. As Simon remarked a little too loudly, while still within earshot of ten-ton bus driver, you could see how you could become an absolute first division wanker if you had to do this every day to make your living.

As we stood on the stern of the ship motoring out into the freezing darkness, we ceremoniously said goodbye to England with more than a hint of 'good riddance'. All three of us gazed at the disappearing shore for a moment longer than the gesture required. My mind was on Kate, and I'm sure the others were thinking about women and babies born or to be born. An unexpectedly intense moment.

Back inside we decided to skip a crappy meal, a couple of beers and the duty-free. None of us had enough money to last more than a couple of days in Paris. We were going to have to make this venture work quickly or we would be straight back home. We'd all bought return tickets so at least we had some kind of safety net, but the thought of having to give up and go back to Nottingham was too awful to contemplate for all of us, for very different reasons.

During the trip I got the chance to observe Garry more closely. There was something deep and dark going on behind those eyes. Simon and I were on a jaunt, and had at least something and somewhere to go back to. From what Garry said there was nothing back in Nottingham for him, or anywhere else for that matter. He was the biggest of us by a long way, but several times that night I remember thinking he looked small, vulnerable and scared. Simon continued to role play; this time he was playing a part that was a cross between the Joads from *Grapes of Wrath* and the troops sailing away to war. He was very transparent about this, and I loved it for the fun of it, but it really grated on Garry, who had enough real-life dramas on his plate. The two of them prowled separately during the ferry trip, using me as the common link, both expressing doubts as to whether the other would last the course in Paris. Maybe they said the same about me while I was doing my own prowling, but I doubt I rated a mention.

Our arrival in France was an eye-opener. We had all trooped dutifully back down to the coach to join the queue through customs, and I was staring, bored, through the window when the French passport control officers appeared.

## 5 SOUS LE CIEL DE PARIS

I became aware of an electric tension next to me and out of the corner of my eye saw Garry tense and sit up rigid. He'd told me earlier that when he deserted the Foreign Legion he had left all his papers behind, including his passport. He'd got out of the country on false ID and, like all Legion deserters, he was a wanted man in France. I'd put this on the shelf with all the other wild busker tales I'd heard, but on seeing his reaction I had no doubt at all that he was for real. With a huge effort I tore my eyes away from him and pretended to be dozing as the officers made their way down the coach, flicking through passports and muttering *s'il vous plaît* and *merci* as they checked everyone's papers. I handed over my shiny new passport, receiving barely a glance, then pretended to try and go back to sleep, waiting for something to happen with Garry. Fortunately, nothing did, and the officers moved out of the bus as bored and slowly as they came in. I caught Garry's eye and he tried a tight-lipped smile, but I could see real fear in his eyes. I had no doubt now at all that everything he'd told me was real.

My memory of travelling through France towards Paris is dim. I must have slept for some of it, the remainder I was staring out the window trying to get a glimpse of the countryside. The whole bus seemed asleep except the three of us, lost in our own thoughts. It felt like we were going to war, my two companions older and scarred, with nothing behind them to leave, and me a mere twenty-years-old, young, carefree and naive, just signing up for the sheer adventure.

Dawn was just starting to liven up the murky, low-cloud sky as the bus reached the outer suburbs of Paris. It was disappointingly predictable in most ways – steel warehouses and low-rise flats, but with occasional flashes that let you know we were somewhere different – bakery windows piled high with baguettes, a fish shop with a hundred kinds of seafood and fish in the window.

We finally ground into Place Stalingrad, the windswept and featureless bus terminus for northern routes into Paris. We should all have been completely exhausted, having hardly slept at all, but adrenaline was keeping us pumped. We had one last slanging match with ten-ton bus driver over some other surcharge he wanted for our luggage, and then headed in for the Metro.

The joust for top dog position started up again with Simon and Garry both talking to the ticket office girl at the same time. Simon got a win because he knew to buy a wad of tickets at the same time (a *carnet*). However, Garry's French seemed considerably better than Simon's, with an accent that was further evidence of the Legion thing being for real. The vibes between Simon and Garry were now getting openly hostile and it felt like there would have been a showdown if we didn't have so much to think about for the day. We'd agreed that we would hit Saint-Michel, have breakfast, try and get a shared room in the cheapest hotel we could find, then hit the Metro to see what the money was like. We were near flat broke – a situation that wouldn't have been a problem on home turf because we knew that with a couple of hours' work, we would be able to survive for the day. I was thankful for my return ticket safety net.

We clanked down the line to a big station called Châtelet, and changed trains to get to Saint-Michel, excited and tense at the same time. The Paris Metro is a different creature to the London Underground. Metro carriages are almost art deco works, lots of chrome and big square windows. The trains run in a common tunnel in both directions on two wide tracks, so you can observe passengers on the opposite platform and fall hopelessly in love with some girl you know for absolute certain will disappear before your eyes in less than a minute, never to be seen again. The Metro has a completely different smell to the Underground for reasons I've never worked out. Parisian cigarette smoke smells three times as bad as English, and the Metro stations back then were just as filthy and grubby as tube stations are today, but the Metro has a smell that is quite invigorating, in stark contrast to the desperately depressing dead dusty smell that the Underground always seems to have.

The train ground to a halt at Saint-Michel and we found our way up to the daylight. I didn't know it then, but we'd surfaced at the *Rive Gauche* – the Left Bank – a place of legend. The Parisians lead the world in effortless street café chic, and wherever I looked there were perfect snapshots of the uniquely Parisian approach to seeing and being seen. Sharply dressed businessmen sipping tiny cups of espresso while studying newspapers efficiently balanced on tiny tables. Perfect girls with perfect hair in perfect clothes jiggling expensive shoes on crossed legs while talking animatedly together, Gitane cigarettes arcing through the air at the more expansive gestures, chins always pointing up with impish fleeting grins that break your heart. Waiters weaving through an impossible maze of tables, chairs and patrons with loaded trays, supremely confident, the absolute antithesis of the grovelling servant – never *ever* click your fingers at a Parisian waiter if you want to be served before you die. Understudy waiters bringing in the next lot of fresh baguettes, wrapped in brown paper but with the top open to tempt you with their heady warm smell. Even the tramps – the *clochards* – are not merely tramps, but existentialists drawn to Saint-Michel by the ghost of Jean-Paul Sartre, living out the sartorial nihilist lifestyle, sneering and thumbing their nose at the world while sitting on the exhaust grate from the Metro to take advantage of the warm air coming up from below.

All this hit me square in the face as we looked for the fairy-tale street name Rue Saint-André des Arts. It was an impossibly gorgeous, narrow little street that could barely take a car and would take a brave driver to try. We passed bookshops, art shops, boulangerie, tiny restaurants – all unique but all meshing to produce a feel like nowhere else I'd ever seen.

The Mazet, about a five-minute walk down Rue Saint-André des Arts, was obviously not a morning place. There were a couple of worse-for-wear looking guys nursing hangovers outside over a coffee, but the lights were out and it smelled of late nights rather than early mornings. Possibly not the right spot for our first breakfast in Paris. We walked on, thinking we would return later, and came to a crossroads where five tiny roads met. Here was a handful of cafes to choose from, all perfect, and we picked one beneath Le Petit Hôtel to have our ceremonial breakfast. Simon knew the score and ordered an espresso and baguette. Like a good Englishman, I ordered coffee with milk and paid four times the price. Garry asked hopefully for a cup of tea, which the waiter finally produced with evident disdain. It became clear as we paid for breakfast that we would have to tune into making money very quickly – I would last about two days on a starvation diet with what I had in my wallet, and the others were about the same. It would have been very tempting to stay at the café and watch life go by but we needed to get a place to stash our gear so we could get to work. Le Petit Hôtel didn't have anything we could use, and Petit Trianon just across from the Mazet was the same. Garry and Simon both suggested we try Hôtel de Nesle, off Rue Dauphine. I wasn't that keen as it was just out of the zone of cafes and energy, down a tiny little side street (called, amazingly enough, Rue de Nesle). We battled our way through the tiny entrance door and crowded into a tiny front parlour.

The room was comfortably full of residents enjoying their breakfast of baguettes and bowls of Turkish coffee. The smell was delicious. The room was walled with several enormous ornate gold-framed mirrors, interspersed with Turkish or Moroccan rugs and tapestries. Some of the guests were sitting on a couple of old rug-covered sofas pushed against the mirrors, while others squatted on low stools and cushions. The largest woman I've ever seen in my life was squatting on her own stool in the corner. Renée was dark-skinned, with huge almond-shaped eyes and jet-black hair tied back with red and gold braid. With an air of supreme matriarchy over her brood of residents, she was obviously the person to speak to about a room. She was very excited by all our guitars and prattled at a hundred miles an hour to a Moroccan guy about half her height and a quarter her weight. They seemed to be consulting over whether they had room for us. They reached some kind of agreement and the Moroccan guy beckoned us through a narrow hall to a tiny circular staircase at the back of the building. Negotiating this with a rucksack and guitar case was tricky work and between the three of us it was very slow going indeed. We climbed five flights of stairs, with, incredibly, the staircase getting narrower and narrower as we got higher. Soon it was wide enough for only one pair of feet, and we had to climb with pack and guitar fore and aft to avoid getting jammed. On the very top landing the guy, who we now knew as Gillel, rattled a key in a lock and opened the door onto a reasonably sized room overlooking a heavily overgrown rear courtyard. One entire wall of the room was covered in scrawled graffiti and pictures – a maelstrom of different languages and levels of artistic skill that had obviously grown with different tenants over the years. Three very tired but adequate looking beds ran along the walls, and there was a small table, a bookshelf and a lethal-looking light hanging from a frayed, burned light cord. It even had a tiny room with a wash basin off to the side. It was perfect. For the three of us to find a room together in a place that welcomed musicians within ten minutes of starting to look in a place we only went to because of a two-minute conversation I had in Nottingham, said to me that once again my angel appeared to be at work.

Gillel was very happy that we were so enthusiastic about the room, and, after extracting a promise that we would come down and play in the reception room very soon, disappeared back down the winding staircase to give the big momma the good news.

The rent at the hotel was reasonable but would wipe us out in a couple of days, so getting back on the streets was a priority. The best spot I'd seen so far was on Châtelet station – a nice long tunnel with a decent amount of people but not overwhelming and reasonably light and cheerful. I announced that I was going back there to give it a go and the others, with little else presenting itself, tagged along. It was the first time any of us had set out to busk in a team, and it felt more than a little strange. There is a very independent streak running through any busker, and neither Simon nor Garry was particularly happy about tagging along with the youngster to get them to their first pitch in a new city. I breathed a silent thanks for all that angst and trauma I'd put myself through in the London Underground. That time had taught me so much.

We dived back down the Metro at Saint-Michel and got the train back to Châtelet. I staked out my spot and bid the others adieu (this being about the limit of my French at the time). Once in place I felt quite comfortable and ran through a few standard numbers. I didn't think that singing in English would be a huge drawback, and indeed, the money tinkled in comfortably, but at considerably less than the rate I would need to be comfortable without working myself to death. While I was playing, I saw Garry cross the tunnel a couple of times in the distance. He clearly wasn't happy with any spot he'd found. A band of South Americans came past carrying a variety of guitars and drums and small ukulele-like instruments. They were very enthusiastic to see me playing there, tossed a couple of coins, and disappeared. I was highly confused when they appeared from the same direction fifteen minutes later, tossed a couple more coins, and disappeared up the stairway they'd climbed before. This made no sense at all, and when the same thing happened again fifteen minutes later my mystified expression had them guffawing in glee. By a mixture of pantomime and long-neglected schoolboy French I managed to work out that they were playing on the trains, shuttling back and forth between the two stations. I had never dared try this in London, and in fact the guy I met on my first day in the Underground was the only person I'd come across who'd ever talked of it. The idea of it didn't appeal at all, unless you had safety in numbers like the South Americans.

I carried on playing for about another half an hour. I saw Garry another couple of times, and Simon once. Eventually they appeared together, and I stopped to check on how they were going. I had done the best by a long margin as I had managed to pick the best spot (I tried to be humble) but I was still a fair way short of the rent. Simon had a bit of cash, but Garry appeared to have spent most of his time wandering around looking for the perfect spot, which he never found.

The rate at which I was making money meant I would need to work four to five hours a day to stay alive, and this just wasn't viable for more than a few days. I wanted to raise the subject of playing on the trains, but if Garry was nervous about playing the tunnels, he'd never make it playing in a carriage. I very much doubted I'd have the nerve to go for this either, though I reckoned Simon might just about have the ego for it. I had some vague notion that maybe we could all play together to give ourselves the balls to do it. This evaporated quickly when I saw how the South Americans worked. When the train came in, they climbed aboard like it was a stage, all Spanish exultations and waves to the crowd. As the door closing siren sounded, they started to play – very tight and with amazing rhythm, and as the carriage started moving I heard this wonderful four-part singing begin. This was seriously good stuff and the three of us would never get close to such polish without a huge amount of work. I'd just about written the idea off when a strange little guy appeared at my side and, again with a mixture of sign language, a bit of French and a bit of English, struck up a conversation. I was cautious, as he had the sleepy-eyed look and dry hesitant cough that I'd come to associate with junkies who'd occasionally hit me for some spare change in London. He reckoned he was a busker but had had a terrible run of bad luck ending when he 'fell asleep' on the platform and woke to find his guitar had been stolen. He didn't waste much time in asking if he could borrow my guitar to play a song or two. This obviously wasn't going to happen, and he giggled nervously at how sure I was about this.

The next suggestion he came up with was that he would introduce me on a carriage. I would play a minute or so of a song, he would do a bit more patter, then I would finish with a full song while he went round with the hat and we would split the takings. I was far from keen on playing on the train but, bearing in mind how long I'd have to play each day to stay alive on the corridors, it had to be worth a go. I also had this feeling that my angel had placed this guy here and I had to go along with the deal. Simon and Garry had only been half tuned in to our conversation, spread out as we were on the bright orange plastic bucket seats that lined the noisy platform, and looked as nervous as I felt when I announced I was going to give the carriages a go.

I stood with my new-found friend and waited nervously for the next train. It came far too soon for my liking. My instructions were to set myself up opposite the open doors, with my back to the wall, and look happy. I accomplished the first and had a brave go at the second but was probably the most nervous I'd ever been performing – this was so in-your-face and beyond anything I'd ever tried before. I was introduced with a flurry of French, most of which I only half understood – something about a once-only opportunity to catch this talented young English singer before he carried on his tour of Europe. Meanwhile commuters were getting on and off, banging the folding seats up and down, the warning siren for the door went off and then the rumble and clank as the train started to move. I dived straight into a song; I have no idea what it was, but I kept to the one minute, trying to look happy and relaxed for my audience, some of whom were only within inches of my face. It was a horrendous experience, and at the end of the minute I just wanted to turn round, smash a window and jump off the train. My MC clapped gleefully when I finished my first offering then went into some spiel – which I assume plugged the fact that we were here to make money – before gesturing for me to start again. I worked my way through a second song as the train pulled into stations, doors opened and closed, people got on and off and either stared into space, regarded me in a half-bored way, looked at me in obvious disdain, or completely ignored me. The little Frenchman threaded his way through the crowd, shaking the change in his hand in front of downcast eyes and imploring my audience to contribute. I kept one eye on him and was reasonably surprised to notice that he was getting at least a couple of 'hits'. He finished at the far end of the carriage and nodded back at me to finish up. The train was slowing for the next station, so I timed the song to end just before the train came to a halt and gave my audience a lacklustre bow and a smile. No-one smiled back. I half expected the guy to bolt with the money, but he met up with me on the platform. I'd made nearly thirty francs, as much in four minutes as in half an hour on the platform. I was happy to split this with the diminutive junkie, knowing that he'd given me the key to survival here, if I just had the guts.

I met up with Simon and Garry and we headed back to Saint-Michel to debrief. Could we do this? I could tell that Garry was out of the running for playing on the carriages – he was too nervy and his style just wasn't 'big' enough. He stared into his coffee, withdrawing from the conversation. Simon, after a bit of discussion, warmed to my suggestion of teaming up and giving it a go with the one guitar, sharing the playing and maybe singing together for one song, then one of us roving to get the money. This was a plan that had every chance of working and within a couple of minutes we were trying to work out which songs we both knew – that was easy, none – and which might appeal to the French, which was much harder to predict.

Through all this Garry remained aloof, sucking nervously on a cigarette and gazing down the terrace. As I finished my coffee my body reminded me that I'd slept for about three hours in the last forty-eight. We weaved our way through the never-ending crowds of Saint-Michel and the Latin Quarter to the hotel. Thankfully, reception was deserted. We climbed up the narrowing staircase until we reached our fifth-floor haven. I put my guitar back in its case, threw off my boots, and fell asleep face down on my sagging bed with its rough grey army blanket.

I awoke with my face warm and sore from lying face down in a damp soup of my own saliva and snot. Simon and Garry were arguing again. I listened with my eyes closed for a minute or so before realising things were about to come to a head. Garry was basically calling Simon down into the street to 'settle things once and for all'. I risked a peek. They were standing chin to chin, Garry with no shirt on. His back was a maze of colour; tattoos spiralling across his shoulders and down his arms. It was also quite evident that he was very well muscled, and the thought of getting into a scrap with him would be one way of committing suicide.

Yet again I played referee for them. I pointed out that starting a fight in the street outside our hotel on our first day would result in us having nowhere to stay. None of us had any kind of insurance, so any injuries would end up costing money that none of us had. I also raised the possibility of the French gendarmes taking a dim view of two mad English bastards using the street as a boxing ring, and that it was quite possible they could get themselves arrested. The two of them blinked at me in mild disbelief at this eruption from the junior member of the party. Garry grabbed a shirt and his guitar case and disappeared out the door to cool off and, I hoped, make some money to cheer himself up. I tried to prise out from Simon what it was that was causing so much shit between them, but he wasn't really interested in talking about it. I did, however, make a point of noting Garry's very impressive set of muscles, which, along with the fact that he'd been raised in Hyson Green and had been, I was now sure, in the Foreign Legion, meant that anyone going up against him would need to be prepared to sustain serious damage. My dazzling logic finally seemed to break through. Whatever went through his mind, that was the last time I saw the two of them confront each other directly, thank God.

Simon and I took the opportunity to go in search of food; we hadn't eaten anything substantial since Dover. There was a street market just down the road from the Nesle, which was magnificent to look at but totally impractical for our situation, selling mostly seafood and exotic cuts of beef and lamb. Tucked away behind it, however, was a small *supermarché* selling more practical consumables. We stocked up on what became our principal diet in Paris – French bread, pâté, tomatoes, cheese and a rough red wine called Villageoise. It came in one-and-a-half-litre square plastic bottles with a flip-top plastic lid and only cost seven francs a bottle. It was brutal stuff but fitted perfectly with the crazy rundown hotel room and our state of mind. We deemed it to be our drink of choice while in Paris. Other than that, the food prices were high but not astronomical, in fact probably less than London. Being able to stay alive in this place got another notch easier.

Once we'd decided to play the Metro, it was a straightforward toss of the coin as to whose guitar we would use and who would do the actual playing. We'd decided that the big intro thing was a waste of time as neither of us really had our heads around the language enough. As I'd endured the agony last time, it seemed only fair that Simon go first this time round. As the Metro came rumbling into the station, all chrome and big windows, it was obvious the trains were much emptier than during my morning session. It turned out this was an advantage, as we had a bit of room to move and weren't singing straight into some poor commuter's face. Simon cranked up and I realised that the only thing harder than singing with the guitar was not having it. I felt naked singing without something round my neck to strum, and I didn't know the words anyway; Simon was singing *I Want You Back* by Michael Jackson. It was a great boppy song and Simon gave it heaps but there wasn't even an identifiable chorus I could join in with, so I was reduced to putting in some imaginative 'oohs' and 'aahs' and dancing to the music. I used the chrome pole in the carriage as a dance prop, swinging and gyrating and feeling a complete idiot, but somehow managing to smile encouragingly up and down the carriage at the audience, who were reading their papers, staring out the window, or watching us in disbelief. The Metro started and stopped, the doors opened and closed, the door siren went, and Simon ground his way through the song – for once looking a bit overwhelmed by an audience. He flashed me a look that I correctly interpreted to start hoofing the carriage for money, and I set off. I was wearing my Tom Waits hat, which I reckoned would look good for collecting the money, and started weaving my way through the passengers, saying *s'il vous plaît* and *merci* in my best French accent. There was a reasonable amount of silver dropping into the hat, but I hadn't yet got the feel of what these coins were worth – in England I could pick the value just about by the sound it made as it hit the bottom of the case. Getting all the way round the carriage took a surprisingly long time, and Simon finished the song while I was still doing the rounds. I flicked him a 'more' stare and he came up with a BB King number. I finally reached the furthest corner of the carriage, then made my way back to Simon, feeling a reasonably satisfying weight of change in my hand. At the next station we took a quick bow as the doors opened and bolted. The whole thing would have only lasted about five minutes, but I felt like I'd just run a marathon and Simon looked like he had.

We had a smoke break on the station, Simon stretching his legs out and throwing his head back, quietly incanting obscenities at the madness of life while I counted the money. It was good. We worked out that doing what we just did on ten carriages would get us about a hundred francs each, just enough to pay the rent and stay alive. It would be possible to do ten carriages in about two hours, but the nervous energy it took out of you – I've never done anything quite like it, before or since, and it sucked the life out of you through the floor.

We carried on up and down the line for a couple of hours with mixed success, but each time it got just that little bit easier. At the end of it we'd made our hundred francs each but we were completely buggered. It's hard to say which was harder, taking the money or singing the song. Probably the toughest thing was staying standing while playing a guitar on a moving carriage – and trying to look happy doing it. The erratic acceleration and braking constantly caught me off my guard and I would stumble, poking some poor sod on an innocent journey who really didn't need a guitar in his kidneys. But we survived, and we made enough.

It was getting dark as we emerged back on the Saint-Michel streets, and I realised we'd still only been there for less than a day. It already seemed like forever.

Back at the Nesle, the lobby was crowded. It was a diverse lot – a middle-aged Afro-American with a booming voice, a couple of beautiful young girls, a wild punky-looking girl with pure white back-brushed hair, dressed all in black and with more earrings in her ear than I'd ever seen before. Gillel was holding court, and his eyes lit up when we walked in. I think he'd been warming up the crowd with the promise of great things from the new tenants, because there was a ragged cheer from the gathering at our arrival that signified a request to play.

We were both exhausted, but Simon slipped into actor mode again and went into an elaborate and theatrical introduction of ourselves in his colourful hybrid Anglo-French. Even with my limited schoolboy French, I could understand Simon's butchered attempts far more than the Parisians present, partly due to his less-than-lightning pace, and partly because of the liberal use of English substitutes when he didn't know the right French word! The general gist was that we were on a European tour of the great capital cities, that we were very happy to be in Paris, and that we had just returned from our first gig, playing to a crowd of thousands on the Metro carriages of the Saint-Michel line. The lobby audience clapped and cheered and shuffled up to make space for us in the wonderful and colourful chaos of beat-up old sofas and stools. Simon got wedged in between a jaw-dropping six-foot blonde who just had to be German, and an equally amazing looking dark-skinned black-haired girl, both of whom welcomed him with huge grinning fluttering eyes. Simon was in heaven and launched into a big-voiced blues song to an ecstatic reception. I could see it was going to be a long night.

I tried to pick up on all the accents and languages around me. We appeared to be the only English people, there were a couple of American accents, including the punk girl, along with German, Italian, Dutch, French, Arabic from Gillel and another dark-skinned guy with a big Jimmy Hendrix afro who introduced himself as Barraq. Most spoke some kind of English, and I discovered that my first assumption that they were all backpacking tourists was way off the mark. A tall, histrionic Italian with a wonderfully mischievous grin and a glint in his eye was Andrea, a starving Italian artist. The German blonde and her friend were, not surprisingly, actress/models. A guy who turned out to be the blonde's boyfriend, Hugo, was the male version of the perfect German – all angular face, deep-set blue eyes and a shock of white hair. He was an aspiring session drummer who kept himself by modelling when he couldn't get work as a drummer, which seemed to be most of the time. A dainty, shy Swiss-German girl sitting across from me turned out to be a ballerina. Nathalie and Rosene were two French girls who appeared to be even younger than me and were in Paris to get a break in "films, theatre, all things like this."

Bottles of wine appeared from somewhere and the guitar got passed to me, no mean feat in the cramped conditions, and at Gillel's request I launched into Neil Young. This got an ecstatic reception, which would have no doubt vexed Simon as he thought Neil Young was rock dinosaur garbage, but he was engrossed in a conversation with the dark-haired model and not in the mood for proclaiming musical purity. Andrea was effusive in his praise when I finished the song. "Is greeaaat 'ave you 'ere in 'otel. You will love us. 'ere is like home, many happenings – MANY happenings – quelle histoire – these girls and boys you know, dey too much party, too much wine drink – is WONDERFUL, eh?"

The evening passed in a haze of cheap red wine that sucked the saliva out of your mouth, and the bitter aroma of Gitane and Moroccan cigarettes. Andrea continued to communicate by sheer force of presence; both his English and French were technically atrocious, but he had no trouble communicating because his message was always embedded in happiness and positive energy. "Jus' remember is wonderful 'ere, so much 'appiness, so much good people, *quel monde, quelle histoire!*" He was gloriously and wonderfully overpowering.

More and more people seemed to cram into the tiny lobby until it was impossible to hear the music. It didn't really matter, it was a party not a gig, and I liked playing as it kept the energy going and was probably my most effective way of communicating at that stage. I realised I was going to have to brush up on my French very quickly to avoid spending all my time struggling to get any conversation beyond the simplest level.

The party finally broke up and we all trooped up the tiny little spiral staircase, numbers dwindling as we climbed higher and higher. Simon and I reached the fifth floor and discovered Richard, the Afro-American with the booming voice, occupied a tiny room across the hall, while the two French aspiring actresses, Nathalie and Rosene, were in the room right next to ours. Simon rolled his eyes in ecstasy as we watched the two nineteen-year-olds wave and giggle their way into their room. I dimly recalled that in a different universe called London I had a girlfriend.

We entered the room to find Garry lying in the dark staring at the ceiling. He stared at us for a second with big empty eyes then turned to the wall without saying anything.

Next morning – still only twenty-fours since arriving in Paris – I woke early. Looking up at the peeling paint barely clinging to the ceiling, I was certain that we'd stumbled on the best place in the whole city to stay; more than just a bed for the night, it was a wonderful group of like-minded people who were trying to do something different with their lives. Already I felt the most at home I'd felt for months. All those months moving around and sleeping on floors hadn't bothered me, but being the outsider everywhere I stayed had started to get me down. Here I was one of an extraordinarily exotic pack. It felt superb.

Simon and I slipped into an almost euphoric routine. We would wake with the noise of the streets, take a guitar down to the lobby and, under the watchful eye of the clucking Renée, feast on big bowls of Turkish coffee and baguette with rich butter and jam before hitting the streets. We both knew there would come a day when we would decide that playing alone was a better option, as the money would almost certainly be better, but this could wait for now. This was new territory and we both wanted to get comfortable with it.

We quickly learned the ropes. The regular runs – Saint-Michel to Les Halles and Odéon to Montparnasse on the Porte de Clignancourt line, and Charles de Gaulle to Tour Eiffel on the Trocadéro line – tied in with major tourist icons and ran between major change points. By far the best line for visual spectacle was Trocadéro, because you emerged from underground into daylight and crossed the Seine on a high bridge, with the Eiffel Tower as a backdrop. However, this was a twenty-minute ride from the Latin Quarter and made the day longer. It was also solid with other buskers, and you sometimes had to wait to get a space on a carriage. We eventually settled on the Odéon to Montparnasse run on the Porte de Clignancourt line. This was perfect in length, not too busy, not too quiet, and had just enough competition to make it known and accepted but not overloaded with other buskers, so you didn't have to wait too long to get a carriage. It was also about a two-minute walk from the Nesle to the Odéon station.

The level of tolerance from the Metro ticket inspectors was amazing. The only real crime was travelling without a ticket, and we soon got into the habit of weaving a valid ticket into the strings of the guitar machine head, so the inspector could check without us having to stop playing. Our audiences were often amused at such audacity, but the inspectors took it in very good spirit. Some days it was obvious that an order had come from somewhere to clear us off, and it was best to just pack up and wait for the next day. My worst experience happened when Simon was off buying cigarettes at a kiosk while I was being frog-marched off the platform out of the station. I had no idea where I was, and I knew Simon would be wondering where the fuck I was. I waited five minutes then used another valuable ticket to get back in. I was travelling down the escalator when I realised the inspector was at the bottom checking tickets. He was already glaring at me, and I knew I had to get away to avoid a hefty fine. I waded back up the escalator, fighting my way past people avalanching down like some Polanski nightmare film scenario. When I finally got back to the top, I had to jump the barriers the wrong way to get out, to the puzzlement of the punters coming the other way. Generally, people tried to get *into* the Metro without paying, not out of it. I wandered the streets for half an hour to find another station, then made my way back to Saint-Michel. Simon showed up hours later fuming, until I explained what had happened. Days like this were very rare though, and we generally had little hassle from the inspectors or the police.

Then there were the clochards, the junkies and the Metro beggars. The clochards were really part of the Paris scene. They lived on the stations, many crawling into the tunnels to sleep at night, timing their entry to avoid getting mowed down. They would generally hit you for a couple of francs once they had seen you pass a couple of times and knew you had some money in the bag. Once when we were having a particularly lean time, one of our regulars shuffled up, a giant barrel of a man with a wayward greasy beard, a decaying trilby, and a tweed coat held together with baling twine. Simon shook the bag forlornly and shrugged. Our friend shrugged a smile back at us and offered us a cigarette he'd bummed off someone else, and we were firm allies from then on. Some days they all seemed to go mad and would do crazy things like shitting on the station or lying down across the corridor to stop people passing. One day we came into Saint-Michel to find sand on the platform. A clochard had crawled onto the line to get to the opposite platform, mistimed it and got hit by the train. Over the course of the day the blood-soaked sand was kicked across the platform and onto the line by the passage of feet, a macabre symbol of the inevitability of death. Another day the train screeched to a halt just as we were entering the station, and from the sounds ahead we knew another person had been hit. We were stranded on the carriage and played for a couple of minutes, but to be bopping away happily when we knew some poor bastard was getting scraped off the line just down the way was wrong, and we gave it up. Sure enough, when we got to the station, the sand was down on the platform again.

The junkies were everywhere in Paris. They didn't often give you grief, but when they did it was bad. One day I put the hat under the nose of a guy who appeared to be hunched over picking something up off the floor. He was a junky missing a hit, and this intrusion broke into his withdrawal misery. He erupted from his seat, sending my hat and the money flying. His forearms were covered in weeping red sores, and his tortured eyes fixed me from a face twisted with pure hatred. I left the money where it was on the floor and added this to my now well-developed 'radar alert' of things to watch for in this crazy job.

The Metro beggars could really mess up your day. They went from carriage to carriage like we did, but moved a lot faster, whimpering and crying and cajoling the punters for a few centimes. Some had horrific disfigurements; one guy with only two fingers on his one remaining arm gave me a major outburst one day when we were playing on what he regarded as 'his' carriage. The most depressing were the gypsy women who had tiny, sickly-looking babies that never seemed to be awake. I wondered if they'd been drugged. The women would whine and plead like stranded kittens as they shivered their way through the carriage, and it was hardly worth the effort of going round with the hat after they had passed through, not so much because people had already given money but because everyone was so depressed.

Amidst all this we made enough money to survive and have a day off every three or four, which we needed. It was exhausting.

Garry went downhill fast. He had been putting on a brave face and talked of playing at the Pompidou Centre and getting gigs in bars, but we all knew it wasn't going to happen. I considered offering to play on the Metro with him, but I knew it wouldn't work – Simon and I were natural clowns, but Garry was a vulnerable loner. Twist and Shout really wasn't his thing. He came back to the hotel one day with a crappy nylon string acoustic guitar, having hocked his steel-string to pay the rent. He showed me the new instrument with a slightly manic smile and said he really liked the different sound and thought it would go well on the streets. To me the guitar sounded flat, sad and dead and I couldn't think of anything to say to him. Selling your guitar was like cutting off your hand.

One night I wandered into our room and found him lying on his bed with a needle and syringe still hanging in his arm. The syringe was full of blood and his pupils were tiny pinpricks in the stark white of the naked light bulb. This was where the rest of the money for the guitar went. Waves of emotion washed over me: anger, sadness and desolation. It was a tragedy. As if in a dream, I gently pulled the syringe out of his arm. He turned to look at me, and, almost in tears, I told him to break the needle and the syringe. I remember him saying softly, "You really care don't you ... you really do."

I dragged him downstairs to get him out of the solitary sadness of that scene, and insisted he play us a tune on his harmonica to try and bring him down. His mouth was so dry he couldn't get a breath out, and the tune came out like a dry cough. After a minute he just shook his head at me in quiet agony and melted back out through the door. He left a sad silence after him, and I struggled desperately with what the fuck else I could do. No answer came, and I left him to his lonely, desperate hit.

A couple of days later he appeared in the lobby with some wild-looking young girl called Briony. She had a lazy eye that would look past you as she spoke, and a strange intensity in the way she fixed you with the other eye that really freaked me out. While the rest of us partied, she spent the entire evening reading a monologue aloud from her diary, a vast saga of trivia about picking up her clothes from some squat she'd been thrown out of. Garry announced they were going to Corsica together, and he disappeared from our Paris life forever.

A steady tide of backpackers passed through the Nesle, apparently drawn by some entry in a travel guide that called the hotel "more of an existential experience than a place to sleep", but few were memorable in comparison to the long-term residents. Like Kastle the blonde punk, an in-your-face west-coast American who was exiled to France by her parents to get her away from her boyfriend. She ran away to Mexico with him at seventeen and married him 'cos it was a cool idea'. If she hadn't been so wired and wild, she would have been a plain and simple poor little rich girl.

Andrea was a hotel icon; he was all joy and happiness and everyone loved him. A passionate artist, he painted cars – expressive, organic-looking things that were almost cartoon-like, often with a gentle humour. He would paint on anything, tables, an old suitcase, tin cans, and of course our crazy mural of a bedroom wall. The hotel was littered with half-finished compositions on various bits of hardware. Andrea was never happy unless he was broke, and he was happy pretty much all the time. One memorable week he sold a painting for a considerable amount of money, and proceeded to buy everyone in the hotel food and gifts until he was stony broke again. I'm pretty sure he lived rent free, as Renée never seemed to pump him for the rent like she did everyone else. I presumed she fed him as well, because he never had a cent to his name.

My suspicion that Gillel, the Moroccan, was an ex-smack addict was confirmed in the first couple of days when I sang Neil Young's *Needle and the Damage Done*. He didn't say anything but got that soulful deep-eyed look and started rubbing his forearms. I could pick it in a second when I played that song on the streets. He and Barraq appeared to be semi-adopted sons of Renée; they were always at the hotel but never appeared to do anything approaching work. Both were difficult company at times, particularly after a hard day playing. They continually smoked heavy Turkish cigarettes with some kind of spice in them, which quickly overpowered the smell of the coffee once breakfast was over.

Renée's real son, Davide, was fifteen and had seen far too much of life for one so young. He had a permanent look of world-wise sorrow in his eyes that seemed strange in his young face. Renée would often leave him in charge of the hotel, and he would carefully vet those who wandered in every morning looking for a room. One day Davide turned down a couple who breezed in, when I knew one of the double rooms had just come free. When I asked him why, he shrugged and made a syringe mime into his arm. "No bags, Paris accent, they just look to steal things. They no good."

Renée was remarkable, the ultimate matriarch. She loved Simon and I, not just for ourselves and because we added so much to the atmosphere of the place, but because we were among the few likely to be able to make the rent regularly. Each morning at breakfast she would go through the books, taking the money, shuffling around in a heavy, intricately decorated wooden box for change, all the while making conversation in a voice that was like black silk; mostly in French, sometimes in Arabic and occasionally in very poor English. She was enormous, and always swathed in layers of cascading saris. I remember losing my balance once and holding my hand out to steady myself. It landed against her vast softness and just kept going. I regained my balance before I struck anything solid, and she just turned and gazed at me with those giant almond eyes like a sleepy leopard. It was difficult to work out with Renée how much was shrewd businesswoman and how much was soft matriarch. I am pretty sure that most of the artistic types got off paying the rent occasionally when times were tough, but given these people were what gave the hotel its wonderful bohemian atmosphere, maybe she knew that letting them stay would pay back in the end with the backpacker crowd, who just loved the feel of the place. She would often rent out a mattress on the floor for people going through a tough patch, but she rarely consulted with the occupants of said room. Plenty of times Simon and I would return to our room and find a mattress rolled out. This was a real hassle in an already cramped room, and we dealt with it by declaring that we would pay only forty francs instead of fifty if we had floor guests. This drew a wonderfully theatrical response from her, calling on our sense of justice and fair play for these poor backpackers that would otherwise have to sleep on the streets (or at least stay somewhere else and deprive Renée of some cash flow). But it worked – and we enjoyed a better relationship with our landlady in the process.

Then there was Albert, the geriatric cleaner. He had a magnificent, crinkled walnut shell of a face framed by a mane of grizzled grey hair and beard. He smoked rollup cigarettes because they were cheaper, but his hands were so arthritic he couldn't roll them himself. This was one of Andrea's daily tasks. He would sit for half an hour with the old man, either perched on the hotel's front step, or at their own special table at the Nesle bar across the road. The old man was as in love with Andrea as the rest of us, and he would grin toothlessly at Andrea's crazy gesticulations as he made conversation while trying to roll the cigarette at the same time. Theoretically Albert cleaned our room, but I don't think he ever made it beyond the third floor. Simon and I would occasionally protest to Renée about the state of our sheets, and she would throw us a clean one during breakfast. I complained once to her that I was getting bitten, and she carefully mimed that I should pull the bed away from the wall – apparently the fleas lived on the floor and climbed up the wall to bite me. If I pulled the bed out far enough, they wouldn't be able to make the jump. I didn't raise the subject again.

Hugo the German drummer/model was fascinating. Another ex-junkie, he told me he'd spent time with William Burroughs. This came up in conversation quite casually when I was talking about some Burroughs book I'd read, and he was so matter-of-fact about it that I think it was true. It was hard to tell with Hugo. Even talking about where to buy a coffee was an intense experience with him.

And then there were Nathalie and Rosene, the French girls. Simon was in virtual agony over the impossible china-doll beauty of Rosene. One morning when the door to our room was ajar, I watched Nathalie, naked from the waist down, casually wander out of the room, pee in the squat toilet without closing the door, then wander back into her room, completely oblivious to her audience. I was mesmerised.

One early morning I walked from Saint-Michel up to the Sacré-Cour in Montmartre, just as the street markets were setting up. It was a glorious day of ambling discovery, of sights, sounds and smells that captured the city for me, and made it live. Men lovingly arranging crabs and oysters and langoustine on beds of crushed ice. A shopkeeper hosing down the pavement in front of his shop, weaving the jet of the hose around the passers-by to avoid spraying them. The smells ... good coffee, bad drains, something frying in garlic, warm croissants, the fresh scent of yet another perfectly dressed girl breezing past, damp paper from a chaotic second-hand book stall where the books spilled off the stall into piles on the pavement. And everywhere people taking the time to enjoy and be part of the feel of the place.

Montmartre itself, winding up the narrow streets to the staircases that led you to the front of the cathedral, was the ultimate busking pitch. Here you could sit and watch a show played out on the flagstones between one downward sweep of stairs and the next, with the entire city as a breathtaking backdrop. I watched a strength and balancing act – a chunky man and woman wearing just enough gold lame to avoid getting arrested spinning and balancing on every part of each other imaginable. A wild puppet show under a chaotically dyed bedsheet twenty feet long, where masked heads and arms would appear and disappear through holes in the sheet. The whole city was spread out below me and I could pick the track I'd taken, the giant form of Notre-Dame leading my eye into the chaotic tangle of the Latin Quarter, framed on the left by the Pompidou Centre and the right by the green slab of Jardin du Luxembourg.

Another time I crossed the river, walked up past the vast facade of the Louvre and onto the Champs-Élysées, slowly winding through the endless stream of tourists to the Arc de Triomphe. The spectacle was magnificent but the feel of this part of town was not for me, all tourists and chrome and empty hurry and bustle.

I wandered from there over to the Eiffel Tower and spent a glorious couple of hours perched on a wall at Trocadéro looking across the river and watching skateboarders spiral and balance on the steps around me. I toyed with the idea of going up the Tower, but it was expensive, there were queues, and among the tourists I felt I was anywhere but Paris, so I didn't bother.

Another time I spent a glorious day wandering round the Musée Rodin, a slightly neglected garden dotted with masterpieces of sculpture, some covered in a damp blanket of moss, some burnished bright bronze, some mounted in the middle of little ornamental lakes. I had no idea how to look at sculpture but found that I became almost hypnotised by the bulk and the form and the detail, so massively solid and yet so subtle.

A favourite pastime with the central cast of the Nesle was to get a few bottles of wine and some food and sit by the Seine at the head of Île de la Cité, either during the dazzling March spring mornings or late at night when we'd be captured in the roving spotlights of the passing river cruises, dancing and howling till the boat moved on.

These were long, soft hours of happy drunken befuddlement, with much philosophising while sitting on the hard cobblestones of the wide path alongside the murky soup of the river. It was quite clear that we would all get famous, if not necessarily rich, and would be appreciated by the world for our various dazzling talents. Andrea was passionate about this. Money was nothing, but acknowledgment of talent by a world that needed art and music was everything. He would erupt into these gleeful, windmill arm exhortations of how much the world needed our talents, cheered on by our tattered group as we toasted his spirit with giant slugs of the plastic-bottled Villageoise.

Simon and I got to know the inner core of each other's beings from a thousand hours sitting on platforms waiting for trains, talking over endless bottles of Villageoise, and wandering through the Latin Quarter deciding what gourmet delight we could stretch to. The choice usually consisted of kebab, pizza, sneaking into the Sorbonne student café, or, if the weather was half-decent, getting the makings for a picnic by the river or in the Jardin du Luxembourg. On days when the money was good, we would indulge in a restaurant meal of couscous. Simon may have seemed difficult to deal with to some people; he was always 'on' and switching from one performance opportunity to another, but I found him good fun, intelligent and capable of some deep thought, particularly after half a bottle or so of the Villageoise. He was dreadful company, however, if he was trying to write a song. Then he would withdraw into a self-obsessed haze of cigarette smoke, staring with pinpoint pupils at whoever was trying to break his concentration. One time we were lying on our beds smoking and staring at the ceiling. Simon was making great hanging smoke stories above his head as he drifted into songwriting mode. He kept on smoking and, seeing that he was totally fixated on the glow of his cigarette, I turned the light off to see what would happen. He didn't move. By the light of his cigarette end I watched him chain smoke about a whole packet of cigarettes in the dark.

The next day, from somewhere between the brightening and waning glow of the cigarette, the curling of the smoke and some deep and meaningful musing on life and love, a song had appeared. It wasn't bad.

It was always interesting living opposite the two French girls, Nathalie and Rosene. Simon and I would squeeze past their doorway with our guitar in the morning. Clothes lying across the floor and the bed, a joyful "'allo" as we squeezed past them on the tiny spiralling stairs. The two of them sitting close together and intent as they absorbed our singing and theatrics, or sitting at cafes near Odéon drinking things that would take us a day on the Metro to pay for, playing film stars. They were wonderful.

One night we ended up in their room talking, smoking and drinking a bottle of gin. They had a bidet full of sand with hundreds of cigarette butts in it, and Nathalie constantly grazed these to make rollups while she talked animatedly of their plans to become famous "doing films, theatre, all s'things like that". Rosene might have had the looks, but Nathalie had the character, and did most of the talking. She described how they had come from some small town in the middle of France to find their fortune in the big city. They had been here for months, and were slowly getting some work, but, as she said, "many people in film business are fucking wanker bastards and just want to put us in their beds not their films ... is very hard".

I looked forward to another night of resurrecting my reviving schoolboy French and expanding my mind on a diet of alcohol, good company and the wicked rollups that Nathalie generated from the recycled stockpile. The tobacco was so tarry I think we were smoking rollups made up of rollups of rollups, with some dope mixed in too. I'd never drunk gin before, and this combined with the tarry cigarettes and dope traces meant I got very out of it very quickly. I found myself sitting next to Nathalie on the big bed, then the room being suddenly empty except for the two of us, all tangled up in each other under the big heavy quilt of the tired lumpy bed.

I woke up wondering where I was, suddenly acutely aware of Nathalie's sleeping form next to me. I waited for pangs of guilt and remorse about Kate to flow over me, but they didn't come. Nathalie stirred and slowly opened her eyes, and I detected a flicker of surprise that I was lying next to her. For a moment I thought we were going to have one of those 'How this could have happened' scenes, but she nuzzled into my arms with a big smile on her face and said something happy in that gorgeous heavy French accent. I felt wonderful – if you discounted the gin-soaked hangover and the taste of recycled rollups scorching my mouth.

We lay in bed for hours talking, and I got the first pieces of a jigsaw of a complex and troubled person. Dark tales of a drunken, abusive father who left them when she was eleven, and a stepfather who raped her within a year of arriving. She never told her mother, but instead retreated into drugs, smoking dope at ten and shooting up at fifteen.

Nathalie's father died when she was sixteen. She was smacked up when she found out by phone that he was dying, and by the time she'd come down enough to go across town he was dead. Her mother had been called in to arrange the funeral but bolted when Nathalie arrived. Nathalie and her younger brother slept in his dingy hotel room with the body for four days while the two of them were left to arrange the funeral.

She fell in love somewhere in all this, and thought the world had turned around for her, but it all turned sour and she left. He first tried to kill her then himself, confronting her in the street with his wrists ripped open and collapsing on the pavement in a pool of his own blood. All these stories came out in a very calm and matter-of-fact way. It was hard to believe she was still only nineteen.

She and Rosene had some small successes getting parts in films and would come back flushed and excited from wherever it was they were working. There was a tender closeness between them that was quite heartbreaking, and I was careful never to come between them. Nathalie and I never made love again; it became a relationship of words and tenderness and mutual encouragement, and I was quite happy with that. She gave me some modelling photos, a couple of shots with her glammed up and pouting on the back seat of some big old black car in a scrapyard. These were pretty but empty. In the shot that mattered she was looking through a broken window, with her hair down and tangled, a look of faraway loss in her eyes. I treasured it and still do.

My brief and shallow thrill of having a French film starlet girlfriend deepened quickly into compassion and admiration for a person trying to leave behind their darkness and stay in the light.

## 5 SOUS LE CIEL DE PARIS

She was so lost and yet so strong; younger than me and yet wise and old. And so vulnerable. She shined with a bubble and warmth of certainty that her dreams would come true. Except for the occasions she would slip, and I'd find her curled up and shivering under the big pile of duck down duvet with a folded sheet of silver paper beside her. Other times she would buy a bottle of cough mixture and down it in one, which she said was a substitute for the heroin hit. I tried it one glorious sunny day sitting by the Seine and spent four hours watching the light patterns on the water. It wasn't fun, and I didn't bother with it again.

We would lie for hours huddled under the covers in the giant sagging bed in that attic room. Listening to Waiting for a Friend and watching the April rain wash down the windows. Nothing to do but fall in love and talk for long, long hours about dreams and more dreams. Even now I revel in recalling the warm silk of her smoky voice seeping into my head like a warm drug.

I never felt so deeply for someone in such a short time or got more confused about what it was that I actually felt. I loved her not as a lover, but almost as a symbol of everything I was looking for that year. It was almost like she was put in my path to be everything I thought I was looking for. But God, I hated it when I came back and there would be that silver paper crumpled by the bed and the light would have gone out in her eyes. But that's when she really needed me. And it was the only time I didn't want to be there.

The distance she would get in her eyes when I sang a certain song would scare me. I would drag her back with smiles and touches and kisses and warmer songs. And she was happy to come. Until the next time, when I wasn't there, and she would go down to Saint-Michel and come back with the little pieces of folded silver paper and cry herself to sleep under the covers in that big, tired old bed.

It was all a million light years from the tedious grind of lecture theatres in Nottingham. And Kate. And then, in the dead of night, I remembered that I'd filled in a form at the dole office in Nottingham that said I would only miss one signing day, which gave me less than four weeks to get home and join that grim and depressing queue, all for fifty pounds a fortnight plus rent. This alone wasn't enough to go back, but the idea of having some kind of closure with Kate also came to me on those dark nights when I couldn't sleep. We'd had zero contact since I'd arrived in Paris, and it felt very much like we were through, but that conversation hadn't happened yet. It was my twenty-first birthday very soon and I'd arranged a joint party in Bedford with Sarah, Kate and Richard. I knew if I didn't show for this I would upset a lot of people that meant a lot to me. Sitting in the Nesle in Paris all these things seemed very irrelevant, but these were the friends who'd stood by me through my first few months of madness and supported me when I needed a floor to sleep on.

I decided to return to England for the party, with the firm idea that I would be in the UK for two weeks at most, and then return to the Nesle and Nathalie. I knew Simon would be fine playing the carriages on his own, and that in any case we were both looking for a reasonable excuse to split up to make more money in less time. Leaving Nathalie was harder. I knew Rosene was planning to leave Paris for some family event and Nathalie would be left on her own for a couple of weeks. Part of me yearned to stay with her and forget Kate and the dole office. But I decided to go back.

## 5 SOUS LE CIEL DE PARIS

And so it was that I was in the foyer of the hotel with my pack and my guitar, booked on the night bus to London. Nathalie, Simon, Rosene, Andrea and Kastle came all the way out to Place Stalingrad with me to get the bus. Nathalie lay her head on my shoulder and placed a hand on my chest to feel my heartbeat, and I wondered for the hundredth time if I was doing the right thing. It was dark and raining slightly, with diamond reflections in the hard fluorescent light of the bus station. I went through the motions of picking up my ticket, off-loading my pack and guitar, and then going round the group and saying goodbye. Andrea hugged me off my feet, close to tears. Simon made me promise to have a pint of Home Ales bitter and some fish and chips out of the paper for him the first day I got back. Rosene remained as perfect and unemotional as ever, and Kastle surprised the hell out of me by hugging me long and hard. Nathalie held me close and gentle, then stood back and gazed into my eyes for a long, long time, with that quiet smile on her face. I finally tore myself away and hauled myself up the stairs of the bus and into my seat. They all stood in the rain and waved as the bus disappeared. I pressed my face against the glass to keep them all in view for as long as possible.

Nathalie.

# 6 A SIMPLE TWIST OF FATE (2)

*He woke up, the room was bare*
*He didn't see her anywhere*
*Told himself he didn't care*
*Pushed the window open wide*
*Felt an emptiness inside ...*
Bob Dylan, 1974

For the entire journey home, I was completely miserable. The rain kept up and the night was black as coal. Over and over, I questioned what the hell I was doing leaving something so wonderful to go back for things that seemed to have no meaning for me.

While the bus did its usual two-hour wait at Calais, I stood outside, sheltering from the rain, breathing in the smell of diesel and saltwater and seaweed, watching the seagulls spiral in the floodlights. As I watched the French coast disappear into the night, I thought back to when Simon, Garry and I had done the same thing on our way to Paris, what felt like a lifetime ago now. The ferry journey was rough, damp and miserable, and many passengers were sick. I bought half a bottle of Southern Comfort, found myself a quiet corner, and drank it down.

The coach journey into London was a nightmare. There was a train strike, and the roads were clogged solid. I'd worked out that once the coach arrived at Victoria, I would have about six hours to get to Nottingham to sign on. This should have been ample time, but I hadn't factored in a train strike. I forced my way onto a coach, which moved at an impossibly slow pace across London. Every square inch of tarmac was choked with cars and trucks. There was nothing to do but wait. I tried to sleep, tasting the remnants of the Southern Comfort's sweet bitterness in my mouth. After three hours of crashing gears and jousting car horns we finally got to the M1. I'd toyed with the idea of hitching, but was glad I didn't when I saw the huge crowd at Staples Corner, desperately mobbing any car crazy enough to stop.

The bus finally rolled into Nottingham half an hour before the office closed. I relished the suspicious looks I got from the counter police as I queued up with my luggage. The air of tedious, desperate boredom in the dole office strengthened my resolve to sign off completely and get back to Paris as soon as the party was over.

Once the signing was through, I fulfilled my promise to Simon and bought some fish and chips, eating it out of the paper, then went to the buskers' pub near the Victoria Centre and drank a couple of pints for him. I enjoyed the beer and the cosy feel that only English pubs can generate, but these were small consolations. England felt safe and lifeless compared to Paris.

I walked across town, meeting up with several of the local crew and filling them in. This cheered me up, as even the likes of Mogs were impressed that we'd been playing on the train carriages. I thanked Ron hugely – without him we would never have found the Nesle and life would have been very different. No-one had heard from Garry, which surprised me. I'd thought he wouldn't last too long with the loopy Briony.

The final trip in what had been a very long day was bundling myself and my gear onto the bus up through

Canning Circus, down the Derby Road and finally to the house. I wondered what sort of reception was waiting for me – if anyone had remembered I was coming.

As I barged through the door, Rob had a bottle of home brew with the top off already, and a packet of Walkers cheese-and-onion crisps that he'd gone out and bought specially. I smiled for the first time all day.

I declared my intention to the lads to sign off completely and return to Paris within the month. This met with a mixed reaction, as it meant they would have to get someone else in for the room. But at the same time it was obvious that I'd outlived the house; everyone except Rob was immersed in a cloud of preparation for final exams and training for successful careers with companies like Jaguar and BP. I just didn't fit any more.

The party was only two nights away, so after a last night camped in my old room, I walked out onto Derby Road, stuck my thumb out, and headed south to Bedford.

I dropped into Sarah's house on the way home, and she was highly relieved and happy to see me. She was highly enthusiastic about the whole party organisation bit, and slowly got me revved up as well, especially when she modelled her costume, which was on the 'tart' side of the Tarts and Tramps theme. She did all sorts of Rocky Horror Show wiggles and writhes round her bedroom to show it off. I'd reminded myself a million times while staying with Sarah in York that she and I operated on a 'just friends' basis, and I had to remind myself again now.

Finally, after agreeing to various things to do with the organisation of the party, I walked the last mile and a half home. It was a funny thing about that walk; there were buses going up and down the Goldington Road every half an hour, but I don't think I ever took one, even when I was loaded up like a pack horse.

Thankfully I had the house to myself when I got home, and relished being able to relax in a long hot bath. I tried to phone Kate, but no-one was home. I think I was still in some kind of shock after leaving Paris and kept drifting away into some kind of dream state.

Once Mum came home all dream-like states evaporated. She greeted me with the usual fluttering joyfulness of having a son to pamper. All my washing disappeared into the depths of the laundry, and she fussed and flapped over the various things I'd been advised would be my contributions to the party.

I spent the next day and a half assembling my costume, dyeing my hair (which Mum insisted on overseeing, due to a previous peroxide overdose), doing my allotted tasks, and phoning Kate on a regular basis. I finally got through on the afternoon of the party. I knew immediately that something was wrong, and after a couple of minutes of stumbled conversation we wound things up. She rang back to apologise for being so 'weird', but that she was freaked out by all the things she had to get organised for the party. I'd gone beyond caring with Kate, and wished like hell we'd had a couple more days to agree we were over before we were 'on show'. A joint birthday party was the last place for a soft landing on a relationship that was past it.

Thanks to Mum's management, my hair wasn't nearly extreme enough for my liking, being a gentle dirty blond and not the peroxide whiteness I'd had before, but it would have to do. My costume was half tramp, half transvestite tart, and I thought I looked great.

The party was at an old water mill about ten miles out of town, and would be a sleep-over affair. I tried to arrange to see Kate before I went out there, or at least get a lift in the same car, but she made excuses and I ended up travelling out with Sarah and a scrum of others in Richard's latest car. I was jammed in the back between Sarah and Jane, who was wearing a costume that was at least as impressive as Sarah's. This did a lot to take my mind off Paris.

The party unfolded like some dream. The lads from the Nottingham house came down and solemnly presented me with a set of framed prints of late-50s American cars – an obsession during my first and second years at uni. My first reaction was how I would fit these in a backpack, but I was touched they'd made such an effort.

Kate showed up completely wired. A couple of times I tried the 'we need to talk' line but she just kept moving with a nailed on, almost manic smile. I gave up and concentrated on getting pissed, with some excellent assistance from Hatley, who came dressed as a monk complete with bottles of Bénédictine, port and some other concoction hidden in the folds of his habit, to avoid paying bar prices. As usual, drinking spirits did me no good at all.

It soon became apparent that Tom and Kate were back together again. In my drunken state I didn't cope with this well at all, to put it mildly. There was much drama between the three of us, and by morning it was very clear indeed that Kate and I were over. I was thankful Sarah and Helen were there to offer supportive hugs. Even at the time, my hypocrisy given Nathalie wasn't lost on me.

I spent another couple of weeks in Bedford after the party, celebrating my twenty-first birthday again on the actual day with a few close friends. Helen found a solemn, quiet moment to give me a St Christopher, to keep me safe on my travels. It felt very special, and quickly became my touchstone.

Kate and I breaking up was the big news for about a week but everyone, Kate and I included, got bored with it all after a while and I withdrew to plan my return to Paris. I grudgingly contacted the university to make sure they knew I hadn't completely disappeared, and was told that if I wanted to reapply I would have to be interviewed, but any interview would be at least two months away. This was fine by me.

I had done nothing constructive about my ultimate goal of getting to America, and I was in danger of letting it slip forever. The idea of going alone was much less daunting than it had been a few months ago, but the ideal would be to go with someone else. Simon was a distinct possibility – I could be Jack Kerouac and he could be Tom Joad. But the whole idea was to hitch on the open road, and two guys, each with a guitar, would be a hitchhiking nightmare. Nathalie I ruled out; she wanted to be a French film star, not an American hobo – and then there were the drugs. Kastle, the wild one from San Diego, would be going home sometime, but the idea of hitching with someone dressed in black with seven piercings in one ear didn't seem too practical either. It looked like I would go it alone, if I went at all.

I'd agreed with Simon that we would have a serious go at joint songwriting, and also learning some covers together to get some gigs in bars. The first commitment was selfish. I had a shocking track record in the songwriting department, with books full of scribbled one-liners, half verses and a few tunes either floating around in my head or hastily recorded by humming into the pin mike of a ghetto blaster. I had never finished anything to my satisfaction. I was keen to learn from Simon on how to get enough discipline behind the ideas to actually finish something. Learning cover versions together was more practical. The Metro was bearable but what little novelty it had was long gone, and we figured if we could get a gig or two in a bar it might pay well enough to give us a bit of variety. Also, playing five days out of seven on the Metro was quite relentless, and we figured a decent gig might give us an extra day off to revive our permanently croaky voices and sore fingers. All sorts of music books disappeared into my packing – David Bowie, Ian Dury, Pink Floyd (Simon hated them and I relished the chance to suggest it, just to see the reaction), along with Bob Dylan and Simon and Garfunkel (another Simon favourite – not!). I also took along some of my favourite books, and given I would be there at least two months, a wider than normal selection of clothes. All this would make great sense when I got to Paris, but the extra weight and volume meant I needed a second bag. I was weighed down like a packhorse.

Mum and Dad were both working on my final day in England, and there was no-one left in Bedford who cared enough about me to want to say goodbye, so I staggered out of the house alone, on foot, and lurched back up the Goldington Road looking like a Sherpa porter. I must have made quite an impression as without even sticking a thumb out a lady stopped to give me a lift. Her daughter was in the car, and the two of them were all questions about what I was up to on the drive to the station. When I told them what I was doing, it did sound pretty cool. I tried not to ham it up too much.

Another tedious grind of bus stations, ferries, ports and food stops in faceless places in the dead of night, and I was back at Place Stalingrad again. Immediately I set foot inside the Metro I was back in Paris mode, happier than I'd been for the whole time I was in England.

# 7 STRIKE ANOTHER MATCH (GO START ANEW)

*Leave your steppin' stones behind now, something calls for you*
*Forget the dead you've left, they will not follow you*
*The vagabond who's rapping at your door*
*Is standing in the clothes that you once wore*
*Strike another match, go start anew*
*And it's all over now, Baby Blue*
Bob Dylan, 1965

I plodded through the morning bustle from Saint-Michel, along Rue Saint-André des Arts, across the familiar labyrinth of back alleys to Rue Dauphine and into the Rue de Nesle, bursting into the hotel lobby during breakfast. I was looking forward to once again contributing to the drama of hotel life, but my return generated only a mild flutter. Simon had already left for work for the day, so Renée immediately reassigned me to my old quarters, smiling and blinking happily with those huge almond eyes. This was about as emotional as she got – except for when she was owed money. Nathalie gave me a beaming smile from the back of the room but left almost immediately for a job. Andrea and Gillel fussed and clucked, insisting on taking my heavy pack upstairs and saying how wonderful it would be to have *"toutes les deux buskers"* back again. Proudly showing me the new additions to the graffiti art on the wall in Room 17, Andrea, always the hotel gossip, gave me a rundown on some of the happenings while I'd been away, with many of his familiar *"quel monde, quelle histoire!*". He would break off regularly to celebrate some item I pulled out of my pack, each music book gaining a cry of approval and a loving stroke or kiss before being placed reverently on the bookshelf.

It seemed Rosene had never returned from her trip back home, so Nathalie was going it alone. Hugo and his girlfriend had disappeared from the hotel, no-one knew where. Briony, who'd headed south with Garry, had come back alone. Andrea knew nothing of Garry. Simon had been spending a lot of time with some Englishman called 'Seeeid', who smoked "many pots, maaany pots!" This I took to mean he did a lot of dope.

As usual after the journey I was dog tired, and after making the usual promises to Gillel and Andrea that Simon and I would put on a show later in the lobby, I crashed out for a few hours, joyfully breathing in the familiar smell of the room: the dusty blanket, some left-over Camembert simmering gently on the table, an overflowing ashtray, and the sweaty, metallic smell of the thousands of centimes that were slowly filling a sawn-off Villageoise bottle; too much trouble to count or spend. I fell asleep to the sounds of Paris floating in through the open window; shouts of market sellers, Renée and Gillel screeching at each other in Arabic over some crisis or other, Davide's drum kit just audible from the cellar six storeys below, cats mewling and purring in the tiny overgrown jungle of a garden, engines screaming and horns blaring and honking every time the lights changed just up the road at the Pont Neuf. I was back in heaven.

I was woken by Simon erupting through the door, guitar in hand, obviously returning from his morning stint on the Metro. He selected Sillitoe mode as he thumped his bag of money down on the table and propped his guitar carefully in the corner. I was 'young'un' back in town, gruffly missed but not to think I was that important that everyone couldn't get on without me, like. It was a good performance and I told him so. He replied by telling me I was a cheeky little shit and I could fuck off back to England. All said with a broad smile.

He then provided me with a more linguistically adept version of things that had happened while I was away. Nathalie had had some grief with a saxophone player. Having been to see him play a few nights in a row, he had thought he was on to a sure thing. She'd had to fight him off in some back alley and came home in tears, with clothes torn. When said sax player showed up at the Nesle, the police were called. Simon said that in my absence, he'd ended up being Nathalie's official comforter, spending the night in her bed – although he assured me nothing 'serious' happened.

I wasn't sure how to take this, so I countered by telling him about Kate and me and our spectacular demise.

Simon was his usual down-to-earth self. "Ay well, I considered the idea of telling Nathalie she could go and cry herself to sleep 'cos you were back in England seeing the woman you told me you were in love with until a few weeks back, but then I decided she needed something more helpful than that." The logic was hard to argue with, and we moved on.

He told me about his new mate, Sid from Leicester, who was indeed a heavy dope smoker, and "a pretty good bloke considering he's a fookin' student".

As if on cue, the man himself appeared. Sid was emaciated, almost skeletal – not in a hollow-eyed junkie way, he just didn't seem to have any fat or muscle over his bones. A shaven head gave him the appearance of a talking skull. He wore an almost permanent grin on his face, which was meant to be friendly but together with the skull thing gave me slight shivers. As we made small talk he rolled a whopping, elegantly shaped cone as matter-of-factly as I would have buttered a slice of bread. He was obviously an expert. Not yet midday, he lit up without batting an eyelid and hauled down a huge lungful, hanging onto it for as long as he could. He whacked down two or three more enormous tokes, burning off well over half the cone, and then offered it to me. I really wasn't interested at that time of day, but it seemed rude not to join a man in what was obviously a very cherished pastime, so I took a couple of token tokes and handed it on to Simon. Not only was it a huge joint but the gear was dynamite, and as my head started to spin I marvelled that he could even carry on a conversation.

Mind you, the conversation was pretty trippy stuff. Sid slipped into a Peter Cook and Dudley Moore sketch, which was surreal enough when Cook was driving it, but with Sid's added theatrical licence it became a saga of a dope-smoking ant marching into war armed only with enough mind-altering substances to turn the enemy into hopeless psychotics. Hauling away madly on the remains of the joint, Simon hung on every word, giggling until he choked. Not as stoned as either of them, I wasn't as amused, but Sid was harmless enough.

Simon suggested we get some bottles of wine and make Gillel's day by playing in the lobby. I was still tired from the travelling, and the dope hadn't helped, but thought maybe it would clear up the vague paranoia I was experiencing. For the hundredth time I promised myself I wouldn't smoke dope again.

# 7 STRIKE ANOTHER MATCH (GO START ANEW)

We strolled down to the little supermarket on Rue de Buci, past the toyshops and the cake shops and the flower sellers, the boulangerie and the impossibly expensive boutique shops that hardly ever seemed to open, and the little cafes and restaurants all trying to carve their own special niche on the face of the Latin Quarter. Simon was in great form, singing and gesticulating to the stall holders "*Il a retourné, Monsieur Guitar L'Anglaise, il a retourné!*" It was hopelessly naff and we laughed and laughed, holding onto each other for support as we staggered along in fits of giggles. My spirits soared; I loved this place, and these people.

We bought an armful of bottles of wine and some good pâté and bread and headed back to the hotel to play. It was a wonderful session that ambled through the afternoon and into the night. Everyone was close on hysterical that 'the band was back together', although in reality Simon and I knew few songs together. It didn't matter; the feeling was there.

Nathalie appeared in the doorway, giving me a warm smile, and I grinned back as we played. But I was caught in the great trap of being a musician; I had to keep playing to keep the spirit of the evening going, so I couldn't stop and talk to her to clear my worries. She swayed in the corner, almost in a trance, smiling at the two of us. When someone suggested we move the party down to the river, it was all rush and chaos while more provisions and bottles of wine appeared. In the confusion I didn't see Nathalie leave. Presuming she must be waiting outside for me, I walked out the front door to see her leaning back against the bonnet of a car, Simon leaning up against her, the two of them engaged in a deep and passionate kiss.

When she saw me, she pushed Simon away. He stared straight at me – not aggressive, not guilty, just neutral. I stood in the road, guitar in hand, the wronged man. As the party mob erupted from the hotel behind me, the three of us stood our ground. Finally, Simon spoke.

"Let's go down the river and talk this through, eh? – there's a few things need to be straightened out."

Numb, I allowed myself to be swept along with the now considerably subdued crowd. Gillel would have his party no matter what threatened to make his two beloved musicians want to tear each other's heads off.

Somehow, we ended up down on the towpath below Pont Neuf, sitting on the cobblestones, our backs to the park wall, looking back across the river at the Quarter and the old wooden barges moored up along the Left Bank.

Simon offered me a cigarette, lit one himself, took a long drag and started talking. Nathalie sat next to him, huddled up, looking completely miserable, staring at the cobblestones and chewing her bottom lip.

Simon calmly went through the points. I'd told Nathalie that I was going back to England to see my girlfriend. I'd also told her I didn't love her as a girlfriend but more as a friend, and she had no idea if I was ever actually going to come back. Added to this she'd been abandoned by her best friend to make her own way and assaulted by someone she thought was a friend. It was inevitable that she would need someone to lean on, and things had just kind of developed from there.

In a state of mild shock, I talked out my first reactions, saying I couldn't stay there, and I'd be moving on in a couple of days. Everyone – Simon and Nathalie included – howled I couldn't go, this was my home, I was needed here.

"Look," explained Simon. "If you'd been here, she would have turned to you, but you weren't, and if things

## 7 STRIKE ANOTHER MATCH (GO START ANEW)

had worked out for you in England we probably never would have set eyes on you again. I feel like a bastard, but that's the way it is, and you'd be bloody daft to leave 'cos of this. We all love you."

Gulping down the Villageoise, as desolate as I felt I also knew deep inside that this was great theatre – the wronged man getting drunk because his best friend stole his woman, even while they still loved each other so much they couldn't break the bond between them, all set against the backdrop of the magnificent River Seine, the lights of the Notre-Dame towering into the night sky just down the river. I admit to milking it for every ounce of comfort and compassion possible, but deep down I was really hurting. And still today, the image of Nathalie and Simon on the bonnet of that car is one of those memories that stays sharp and clear.

I don't remember exactly how the evening ended, but I presume that with the help of my friends I staggered back up to the room and collapsed on the bed. I woke next morning with a dreadful head and a mouth like an ashtray. Simon was already downstairs with the guitar. He looked up at me as I entered the lobby with my guitar, and we nodded in a mutual agreement – we would be playing separately from now on. We both knew that my words about leaving were hollow; it was all too good, and I didn't want to leave. That day on the Metro I had an amazingly good day. On a whim I played David Bowie's version of the Jacques Brel song *Amsterdam*, a wonderfully passionate song known by the French. I was in such emotional turmoil I sang it superbly – it's a song you must do full-on or not at all. It made me the best money I'd ever made, and became my staple 'go to' song.

Life and love had certainly taken a few unexpected twists and turns in the past month. Going from two girlfriends to none in the space of a couple of weeks had been a major knock, and I spent several days in a haze of mild depression and shock. Equally bad, or even worse, was my changed relationship with Simon. He was spending most of his time with Nathalie, so the long hours she and I had lain in bed reflecting on life and staring at the ceiling in the fifth-floor room was at an end. And the plans Simon and I had dreamed up about writing songs together and getting gigs in bars evaporated, at least for the time being. I missed them both.

It was a strange time. I still adored everything about the city and the hotel, but there was an aching emptiness where my two closest friends had disappeared. Simon hadn't yet sorted out a separate room, so he and Nathalie slept in the tiny washroom off the big fifth-floor room. Our room was still the main venue for parties, and now that Sid was around, these involved major dope smoking as well as the traditional wine guzzling. Sid didn't have a bed in our room, but almost always crashed out there. So there were at least six people sleeping in a room which officially had room for three – not to mention the half dozen or so who would gather each night for revelry. This couldn't go on. The night it all blew up in our faces was when some poor American backpacker, who had paid good money to sleep in the third bed in the room, walked in to find it packed with people drinking and smoking, either sitting all over his bed or bedding down on the floor. Luckily, he complained to Gillel and not Renée. An agonised Gillel dragged us down the road to a café to implore us to get

## 7 STRIKE ANOTHER MATCH (GO START ANEW)

our act together or we would all be out of the hotel, and he would be out of a job. Simon agreed to get a separate room with Nathalie after that, and we got rid of the hangers-on, including a lovely Swiss-German couple who'd been sleeping on our floor. When we told them they couldn't stay there, they just smiled sweetly and walked off in the direction of the river to sleep under the bridges. We never saw them again.

Inevitably, Simon couldn't make enough money to support both he and Nathalie, so she 'officially' moved out, so she didn't have to pay rent. The charade involved Simon making a big show of walking her to the lobby each evening and waving her off down the street. She would camp in a café for a couple of hours then sneak back in the dead of night. She'd leave at dawn before coming back to spend the day there. All this required scouting trips up and down the staircase to make sure the eagle-eyed Renée was nowhere around, together with the occasional baksheesh packet of cigarettes or a bottle of something for Gillel and Barraq, both of whom knew full well what was going on. This was a time consuming and exhausting process, not helped by Nathalie's increasing lapses back onto the smack. She was putting less effort into finding film work, relying on Simon to keep her fed. It wasn't hard to realise Simon's American plans were as good as dead. He barely had enough money to survive on, let alone to also support Nathalie. In contrast, my funds were steadily growing now that I was playing solo, and I had no ties or obligations to anybody. I could set my sights wherever I wanted. But I also had only myself to blame if I went nowhere!

Briony, the English girl who'd taken off with Garry, was back at the hotel and was a regular at our parties. She was still strange. Her eyes, though mostly covered by her long, wispy auburn fringe, were shy – kind of distant, kind of friendly. Like a kaleidoscope, always changing. A T-shirt, ragged denim jacket, denim shorts and a pair of artistically enhanced baseball boots were pretty much the only clothes she ever wore – maybe the only ones she owned. She travelled light. During our parties she would sit hunched up over her diary, scribbling stream-of-consciousness notes onto the purple pages in wild coloured pens – snapshots of our conversations and moods, a crazy avalanche of words. She could keep this up for hours, and after a big night, we would gather in the lobby for breakfast the next morning to find out what we'd been raving about. She filled pages and pages with a huge looping scrawl that sometimes crossed over itself so much you lost track of which line you were on. Most of her conversation consisted of reading back parts of the diary, and it was hard to get her to talk about very much else. She spent a lot of time with the older buskers at the Mazet, who I tended to steer clear of because they spent all their time giving me advice I didn't want on how to improve my busking, or talking about the wild drugs they were doing, had done, or were planning on doing. I found I could never really relax with Briony and so tended to avoid her, until one night in my room when we somehow started massaging each other, and she ended up crashing in my bed.

Neither of us were sure what to do about this in the morning. One thing I was sure of – and thankful about – was that I wasn't in love with her, nor she with me. After the emotional traumas with Kate and Nathalie this was a very appealing situation, and we became a kind of high school couple, nothing too heavy either physically or emotionally. I thought spending time with her might dilute her weirdness a bit. I was wrong, she really was out in a space all on her own!

Briony's story was an interesting one. She was the youngest by a long way of a family of six kids; her father was in his sixties when she was born. She'd already faced a lot of challenges in life. Her balance was terrible, and she'd had a few operations on her eyes because they 'didn't work the same as everybody else's'. Her brain seemed to be wired slightly different to most; sometimes the simplest things took forever to get across, while at other times she could be almost telepathic.

She had been banished to Paris to get her away from some guy she'd been 'manically obsessed with' (her words), sleeping outside his house and following him around everywhere he went. Technically she was in Paris to study, and her father had provided six months' worth of accommodation in travellers cheques. But Briony preferred to keep the cheques and lived in a squat for three months until it was shut down. She showed it to me one day. It was in a rundown part of the city, and the whole building reeked of mushroom dampness and urine through the barred windows. Briony's take was that it had been totally worthwhile; she was a couple of thousand francs ahead, and had met up with the Mazet buskers, who provided her with a small income for collecting for them. She took me to the Mazet a couple of times, and I swapped war stories with the other buskers. It was a desperately depressing experience. There I was with a girlfriend I had no feelings for, drinking in a bar I didn't want to go to, with people I didn't like. A long way from what I'd planned for my triumphant return to Paris.

I was curious to find out what happened to Garry. It seemed the trip fizzled out halfway through France; Garry had no money, no real plan, and didn't seem to want the added responsibility of another person to take care of. Briony was only eighteen, and Garry would have been coming up for thirty.

It turned out that Briony was a keen and regular hitchhiker, and, amazingly, would regularly hitchhike on her own. She had gone to some posh boarding school near the famous festival town of Glastonbury, just outside Bristol, a convenient hitch from her parents' home in Cornwall. Inevitably my big plan of hitching across America came up, and she brought up the idea of us going together. I was very unsure about this. Briony felt too crazy and eccentric to be a good choice as a hitching partner for a few months on the far side of the world, and at only eighteen years old seemed too young. But the idea took root.

Having gone to school near Glastonbury, Briony had naturally gravitated to the ragged community of musicians and artists there, in obvious preference to her well-groomed school chums. This meant she had an early education in a wide spectrum of drugs. About a week after we got together, she announced she was off to Les Halles Metro to try and score some acid. It wasn't a Paris drug then, but this didn't deter her.

Hours later she returned, with no acid and minus a significant amount of money. The dealers had strung her along and ripped her off. She was distraught. The only solace available was vino and dope. I bought a couple of better-than-usual quality bottles and we climbed the stairs to Room 17. Briony didn't normally drink much, preferring the dope hit to the alcohol, but this night she took a bottle to herself and

## 7 STRIKE ANOTHER MATCH (GO START ANEW)

necked it straight in big gulps. Soon a gaggle of the others showed up and it turned into one of the wildest nights we ever had. People were climbing from window to window and up on to the roof, five floors up, pissed and stoned, howling at the moon. Simon was in magnificent form, in a stoned frenzy of word jumbling and mixing that had me in stitches.

The evening blurred. More and more bottles and joints appeared. Somehow, Briony and I ended up back in her room, and our prior unspoken agreement evaporated.

The next morning I awoke with an utterly crashing hangover. Kastle, wide awake in the bed across the room, looked at us in sharp-eyed disbelief. There wasn't much I could think of to say, so I just shrugged and smiled. Kastle laughed and did her usual whirlwind exit with flashing eyes and a stream of 'fucks' and 'assholes'. When Briony finally awoke, she was clearly as hung over and surprised as I was.

Neither of us could really think of anything to say. I'd been slack on the busking for a couple of days and knew I had to get back to it, to avoid breaking into my rainy-day fund. I also needed time to process what had happened. Briony totally got this – when money was tight the playing came first, for any busker. I sensed she also wanted time to work out what had just happened, so I struggled back up to Room 17. Since Simon had moved out I was now the only official tenant. The place was in chaos, with people wrapped up in a jumble of blankets and bedclothes that had been ripped off the beds and onto the floor. A light rain drizzled in through the open windows. I picked my way through the wine bottles, ashtrays and drug paraphernalia to my guitar, thankfully still in its case, and escaped to the Metro.

I worked the carriages on autopilot. There was a big part of my brain that was saying this was a very bad idea, with the reasoning roughly equal between caution learned after my recent disasters with Nathalie and Kate, and, while I had been able to persuade myself that Nathalie and Kate had been soul mates, I knew full well that this was not the case with Briony. I decided I would go back, confess it was all a big mistake.

In the end, that didn't happen, and Briony and I found ourselves almost by default in a clumsy and difficult relationship, one that neither of us really understood nor desired. But we decided that, if things stayed even halfway tolerable, we would go to America together and see what happened.

We began calling the bluff of the endless stream of backpackers coming through the hotel who said, "If you're ever in the US, look us up." A couple of times this offer evaporated into thin air when it became clear we might *actually* show up, but most of them came good with an address. The problem was we either didn't want to stay with them or they lived in some place that was nowhere near anywhere we had any desire to go. A big exception was Jerry, a New Yorker who – rare for an American – really tried to be a part of Paris, rather than just an onlooker. He struggled to converse in French, but kept at it. He would wander out into the tiny jungle that was the hotel's back garden and sing soulfully to the moon in pretend-French, agonised eyes to the sky. He was great, and when the offer of a place to stay came up we warned him not to make it unless he was deadly serious. New York was the one place we were certain we would go (if we got anywhere!) as all the cheap flights landed there. Being Jerry, we knew he meant it.

Life in the hotel was getting stale. Briony and I made an effort to go and see some other parts of the city and one day ended up at the Museum Of Modern Art, overlooking the

## 7 STRIKE ANOTHER MATCH (GO START ANEW)

Eiffel Tower near Trocadéro. There were huge installation pieces laid out on a wide gallery floor: fabric and cushions, bits of scrap metal, and a particularly quirky one involving lots of pieces of spherical rocks, from a metre across down to tiny pebbles, all cascading off each other and making a very pleasing jumble across the floor. Briony got her starry-eyed furtive look and proceeded to steal one of the rocks, roughly the size of an apple, declaring this would be our talisman, if and when we got to America. I wasn't sure how stealing a small and missable piece of art stacked up against doing a runner with the Mona Lisa, but figured it was unlikely to get us a life sentence.

Once Briony and I became an item it seemed no time at all before, amazingly, Kastle and Andrea got together. I thought this was mere coincidence but got strong hints from Briony that the occasional bursts of affection from Kastle had been as near as she would get to declaring a serious interest in me. This was no more confusing than anything else that had happened in the last few months in terms of my weaving path with women. So there was a period when everyone seemed to be in couples – Simon and Nathalie, Andrea and Kastle, and Briony and I, until suddenly Andrea had something to go to in Elba. Amidst a huge swirl of emotion from the whole hotel, he left with about two days' notice. He bequeathed all sorts of half-finished pieces of work to various people – he had paintings on everything from litter bins to chocolate tins and mirrors, not to mention a decent portion of the wall in Room 17. He gave me a hand-drawn sketch of a collection of his beautiful sad-happy cars in a junk yard, which I carefully placed behind the felt padding of my guitar case; an item to be treasured.

The day he left was awful. Renée was distraught and, along with the rest of us, implored him to change his mind. Andrea's sense of theatre was as magnificent as ever, and, declaring he must go, like some bad scene from a black-and-white war movie, clasped Renée's hands, staring into her eyes and declaring, "You must go's where your spirit pulls you." Those gathering for his goodbye were in near hysterics of emotion on the tiny pavement outside the Nesle. He finally left in an enormous green wreck of a car driven by some chain-smoking guy, gear overflowing out the windows. As the car reversed down the road, he clasped his hands to his head in mock despair, laughing and crying at the same time before disappearing around the corner. We all missed him like crazy for a couple of days, but life moved on. There were daily pangs of wonderful memories every time we saw some offering, painted on a mirror, a wall or a table. Simon and I received a postcard from Elba, simply inscribed "*Je vous attend a L'ile d'Elba. Tout les deux avec les guitarres*" (sic), and seriously discussed the idea of leaving Paris behind us – out of the earshot of Nathalie and Briony of course.

My busking had become almost robotic by this time, and I was able to go through each four-minute performance appearing to be wildly enthusiastic, while daydreaming about some crazy hotel happening or other. There was nothing more I could learn about the Metro. I knew which carriage I wanted to play, I could radar just about any hassles before they erupted, I could weave my way through a crowded carriage with my hat out for money and the guitar round my neck without barging through too many people, and I could time it perfectly so the hat swooped past the last gaggle of punters just as the train was drawing into either Montparnasse or Odéon. It was by far the easiest way to stay alive busking in Paris, but day after day of playing the same song on a train that was literally taking me from nowhere to nowhere started to take its toll. My take slowly slipped, and, with my occasional nights down at the Mazet and my increasing drinking and drug taking at the hotel, somewhere in the back of my mind I knew I was turning into the very creatures I'd seen when I first arrived and known I should keep clear of. I yearned for the endless, spiralling conversations with Simon, sitting on the orange bucket seats, solving all the world's problems.

Weeks went by with nothing changing. I was restless. Every day it seemed I would chat to another player on the Metro who was heading off somewhere, and I was still grinding up and down the same four stops playing the same song thirty times to make ends meet.

So many times that year, I got a sense of when something big was about to change. I had this feeling now, although what did happen was the last thing in the world I would have expected, and it put me in a position of needing to make one of the hardest decisions I would ever have to make.

Yeolmbridge House, Yeolmbridge.

# 8 TANGLED UP IN BLUE

*The only thing I knew how to do was to keep on keeping on
Like a bird that flew
Tangled up in blue*
Bob Dylan, 1974

I was running through a new song up in Room 17 one afternoon when Nathalie came charging upstairs, breathless. My dad was on the phone, and it was urgent. I flew down the stairs three at a time – I couldn't even remember telling Mum and Dad the name of the place I was staying at, so it would have been a major exercise to track me down.

The payphone was in the lobby and the usual crowd was there, all looking expectantly at me as I took the phone from the table.

I listened, dumbstruck, while Dad explained what had happened. I mumbled a couple of things, promised to phone him back soon, and put the phone down.

The university had written, saying if I wanted to go back at all I had to attend an interview in in Nottingham – in four days. If I didn't show, they would assume that I was not interested in returning to complete my degree, and I would be struck from the records. I explained this to the room and a collective groan went up.

I slumped down on a chair, lost in thought, and somehow the room turned into a debate of what I should do, revved up by the inevitable Villageoise that appeared from somewhere. I poured a large glass and knocked back the acrid powerful mixture, as always loving the sour hit at the back of my throat and the fire going down to my belly. I contrasted this with my vision of what it would be like to sit in those tedious lecture halls again. No musicians or artists or actors or ballerinas there.

Going back to the sterile university was the last place on earth I felt like going, and to leave somewhere like the Nesle was too bizarre to contemplate. I expected the jury to come out very strongly in favour of me letting the university go in order to follow my other dreams. I was wrong; the room was divided. Barraq became quite eloquent as the wine and the dope got into him.

"The most important thing in your life is that you have a choice. To be able to choose is everything. If you go back and get through the interview you can choose whether or not you want to go back to your college. If you go back and get your piece of paper, you can choose to use it or not use it. You now have no piece of paper, you have no choice, my friend. Me, I never had the chance to study, so I have no choice, the hotel is my life, and I have no choice. Choice is *everything*."

Predictably, Simon was highly vocal about me following my dream, making music my life and leaving the dead academic life for those who had no spirit to them. (Ironically, he was the only one of us who actually *had* a degree!). Kastle couldn't understand why there was any need to discuss the issue – I wouldn't go and that was it. Briony and Nathalie seemed as undecided as I did. Nathalie started off enthused about the need to follow your heart, but was moved by Barraq's passion and spent a lot of time staring blankly out of the window, talking to herself.

The conversations flicked from English to French as the emotion ran high; French winning over when the hearts got the lead, English when the heads were speaking.

The talk wandered back and forth for hours, and I was no nearer to working out what I wanted to do. Finally, in a daze of alcohol, dope and confusion, I declared that I needed to get away from everyone and make up my own mind. I walked out onto Rue de Nesle and headed east towards the teeming night hordes around Saint-Michel. Everywhere were the sights, sounds and smells that I loved. The glorious closed-down boulangerie with the memorial notice in the window to the dead baker: "*He gave us his bread and pastries for his whole life. He was a proud man of Paris and he is remembered and loved. When you smell warm fresh bread think of our friend the baker.*" The smell of the Greek restaurants on the Rue Saint-Séverin, on the other side of the Boulevard Saint-Michel, and the nightly drama of the men trying to cajole the tourists through the front door. The bright lights of the bookshops that stayed open so late, with the gorgeously scarfed and perfectly perfumed French students from the Sorbonne pouting their way through the posters. The pavement artists and fire eaters who staked out the pavement under the fountain in Place Saint-Michel. And around the edges and under the surface, the parts I now knew as well: a vacant-eyed busker pulling nervously on a cigarette, the twisted smiles and glazed eyes of the junkies who had the money for a fix, and the shivering, desperate, hollow terrified ache of the ones who hadn't. And the clochards. More than anything else that night, I remember a clochard propped up against a steel roller door between two Sandwich Grec counters, alternating between begging, screaming and crying at the universe while slowly and ostentatiously masturbating inside his giant trousers held together with safety pins. He was drinking a bottle of Villageoise, taking huge swigs and spitting and dribbling it down his chin as he raved at the world.

All the passionately argued points on what I should do jumbled around my head. I'd gone out to remind myself of all the reasons why I should firm up my resolve to stay, but Barraq's words kept coming back to me – choice was everything. Something else that had become clear as the debate raged was that the younger people who had somewhere or someone to go back to were saying I shouldn't leave, but those with no choices left were saying I should go back. I knew that in the last few weeks I'd realised that there was only so long that I wanted to keep on being a busker – the wreckage in the Mazet each night was a great example of how you were likely to end up if you played on the streets for ten years. Simon's idea of following his dream and being a musician was, in fact, not my dream. I knew that I was enjoying playing less in the last couple of months, because I had to play to stay alive, and it was becoming just another tedious job to get by. I didn't have Simon's passion and ability to write songs, although I was certainly starting to get enough of life's experiences under my belt to write something worth listening to. My dream to travel was more about getting the restlessness out of my body. Paris had held me for longer than anywhere else that year and I had been genuinely happy, but Andrea leaving had shown me that the one thing worse than leaving was being left behind. I'd fixated on America as the ultimate fix to end my wanderlust.

## 8 TANGLED UP IN BLUE

Spending another couple of months in Paris drunk and stoned, albeit happy, was unlikely to get me there. Who was to say I wouldn't end up like the Mazet crowd, or even the sad crazy clochard sitting on the pavement? I came to my decision as the clochard finally fell asleep with his head on his chest, the wine dribbling out of his mouth and his other hand still inside his trousers. I would go with choice. However crazy that moment of decision felt – standing in the middle of Paris watching a drunken tramp fall asleep with his hand on his dick and puke dribbling from his mouth – I knew what I had to do. I would go back. I would go back to Nottingham and take the interview.

That decision initiated a whirlwind. I booked my ticket and prepared to say goodbye to the Nesle again. While I packed, the walls of Room 17 seemed to shout at me that I was doing the wrong thing – all those inspired artistic creations and heroic scribblings and quotes of adventurers and romantics, and there was I ignoring it all to go and do the safe and sure thing. The only thing that kept me going was looking beyond the simple interview to that magic word of 'choice'. I didn't dare to think about the details of my return to Nottingham; if I had there is no way I would have gone.

In an attempt to cheer me up, Briony organised a bizarre night excursion to the park at Île de la Cité for some passion beneath the stars. We spent hours lying on our backs while I pointed out all the stars I knew. I even gave her a star; I'd only ever given away one, to Helen. Briony was touched. It was a wonderful idea and should have been a magical moment, but as usual there was a fumbling uncertainty during our lovemaking, and the feeling it was all a big mistake.

As we pondered the stars and the giant floodlit bulk of Pont Neuf with Notre-Dame rising behind it, we saw torches and flashing blue lights stop on the bridge. We threw our clothes back on just as a gaggle of gendarmes appeared, and I had visions of missing my interview in Nottingham due to being in a Paris jail for doing whatever it was we were doing wrong to get all this attention. I heard one gendarme say "*Putain, Ils sont habillés*" – fuck it, they're dressed. The gendarmes obviously weren't interested in arresting us, and it turned out they were there because someone had reported seeing what looked like a body getting thrown off the bridge into the river. We made it clear we were busy on other things when the incident occurred, and the gendarmes loved it. They were fascinated by the idea that we had a nice warm hotel room to go back to, and yet were out here in the park. With much humour, they advised us we should go back to bed in our hotel before the 'crazy' who had thrown the person off the bridge came and found us. It seemed bizarre to me that while this went on, we and the gendarmes knew there was a pack of clochards sleeping in nooks and crannies on the river tow path. I didn't see any of them getting woken up and quizzed over whether they had thrown anyone off the bridge – but then that wouldn't have been half as much fun as talking to us.

The next day I went round the hotel again to say goodbye. I knew I wouldn't be back any time soon. Nathalie was difficult. It was becoming clear that the film thing was unlikely to happen, and I could see Simon was on the way to burning out trying to make a living for them both. The only film offers Nathalie was getting were borderline pornography, and I had this feeling in the pit of my stomach that she would have to make the choice soon between doing something in this line or getting out of Paris. I didn't like to think about it much. At all. Our final words were at the door of the tiny room she shared with Simon. I tried to make it not awkward but failed. I drank in those deep troubled eyes one last time as she smiled her tired smile, leaned her head on the door frame, and wished me good luck.

In spite of Barraq's huge influence on my decision, I don't think I found him to say goodbye. Renée was gushy and fluttery but, in classic form, very careful to make sure I was up to date with the rent.

Finally it was time to go. Briony and Kastle came with me to the night bus at the desolate Place Stalingrad. I was weighed down with all the books I'd staggered over with, most of which I'd hardly touched. For some reason the Metro was packed so we had to stand for most of the way. It felt quite strange to be standing on the carriage as a passenger. A busker stuck his head in the carriage at Les Halles but withdrew because there was no spot to stand – out of habit I was standing, with my huge pack and guitar case, on the exact spot he would have stood. Even amidst the turbulent and difficult feelings, Briony and I managed to break out laughing.

Once part of the everyday background, my decision to leave had seemed to tune me into the plight of the clochards. One was sprawled out on a seat just down the carriage, unconscious. He had pissed in his ragged stained pants, and his face seemed to writhe in some internal torment. I was haunted by the same feeling that I could end up there; it almost seemed as if he were placed there to urge me onwards and upwards on the emotional rollercoaster journey that was my departure from Paris.

The wait at the bus station was as awful as ever. Briony and I struggled our way through. She said she would be back in England in a few weeks. We both knew this was far from being a certainty. After a fumbled hug, I was on the bus. The pain was physical as the bus pulled away. I might not have been in love with Briony, but I sure as hell was in love with Paris.

The journey was the same as ever: buses that smelled like ashtrays, ferries that reeked of diesel and puke, only marginally relieved by the salt tang of the sea, and the screaming tedium of waiting while customs and immigration at either end checked we were fit to leave or enter the country. Once again I arrived exhausted and desolate at Victoria Bus Station in the middle of morning rush hour, hardly an uplifting way to return to England. Mum and Dad would have liked me to drop into Bedford on the way but there simply wasn't time, so I ground my way through the hordes with my mountain of gear, buying tickets, boarding the bus. For once I slept for most of the way, and as the bus pulled into Nottingham, I actually felt a stirring of positivity as we wound our way through the one-way system into the centre of the city. Late spring was turning into summer and there was a warm softness in the air. Nottingham was still a good place. I would have loved to take a wander round the streets and catch up with the other buskers but lugging all that gear around was just too ridiculous to contemplate, so I staggered across to Slab Square and caught the bus up the Derby Road.

In an almost unbelievable fluke, Rob had phoned the Nesle the day after Dad had, so he knew I was coming back. I made my way wearily through the familiar jungle of the garden and into the house, to be immediately surrounded by the lads. It felt strange to have this attention, as we'd grown apart – me living on Paris streets while they slogged on with the studying. But now we had something in common again. In less than twenty-four hours I had to present myself at an interview where it was all or nothing to re-enter uni. They allowed me a quick coffee and a plate of beans on toast before all yearning for Paris disappeared in a frantic and intensive exercise of interview grooming and coaching.

There wasn't much about my appearance that was right. I was never going to look like someone who wanted to work for BP. The one and only suit I'd ever owned might have fit me at seventeen, but not now. It was re-consigned to my wardrobe. The sharpest two dressers in the house, Richard and Dave, were destined for jobs at BP and Jaguar, so their clothes were very much in sharp executive mode. After much fussing and debate I was bustled into various items of clothing and catwalked round the room. It was decided that Dave's charcoal grey pinstripe suit and Richard's blue shirt and sharp tie were the best choice, though I felt a complete idiot in them. Shoes were a real headache. The only person who had the same size feet as me was Rob. Dave's feet were two sizes bigger than me, but he had the better shoes. It felt like I was trying to be James Bond, but not bringing it off. My protests were ignored. As Dave succinctly put it in his flat Wigan accent: "If you've shagged all the way back from Paris for this, you might as well play for a win, and believe me, the clothes matter – and you never have a fucking clue about what to wear, ever." I gave in.

The next part of the process was psychoanalysing the people who would be interviewing me. One was Rob's

Head of Department, who Rob got on well with, not least because they shared a passion for messing about with English sports cars. An interviewer that had time for Rob's somewhat unorthodox approach to life would at least give me a fair hearing, which was reassuring. This was in sharp contrast to the other person, one of my own former lecturers. I am sure that Dr Mecklenburgh was one of the few people I have ever met that might be classed as a genius, but this was diluted significantly by his almost complete lack of ability to communicate with anyone who he considered less than genius. Almost everyone dreaded doing his courses because you were permanently immersed in a sea of partial differential equations and mathematical squiggles that mere mortals like me found impossible to follow. I'd never passed an exam in his subject, although I was far from alone there.

The coaching squad then moved on to what I should say. This caused a lot of heated debate. A couple of the lads thought that any mention of busking and living it up in Paris would be disastrous, and that I should make up something more conventional. I refused point blank, as this was the whole point of taking the year out. So the challenge was to come up with what I'd learned during my 'gallivanting around' that would be useful as a student studying for a degree in Chemical Engineering.

"I've learned that it's a tough old world out there, and buskers don't end up as rock stars. Having a degree gives you a lot more choices in life and I now really understand how important that is."

The coaching squad were impressed by this, and as we discussed all the other questions that might come up, I realised that, ironically, my experiences and the friends I'd made at the

Nesle had given me the substance of a solid reason to come back to university – the last thing on earth I would have expected when I first made my way up to Room 17.

Finally, after hours of grilling we'd covered everything we could cover, and I was allowed over to the pub for couple of beers and to catch up with Mick the landlord. After drinking cheap red wine for the last three months, it took a couple of pints before I got the taste for bitter and White Shield back. The boys hustled me out of the pub after a couple of drinks to ensure I didn't rock up for the interview with a raging hangover, and I spent the night in my forlorn and empty old room, shivering in a borrowed sleeping bag on my damp old bed, trying not to think too much about the Nesle, the interview, or anything at all really. It was a long and lonely night.

I got to the university early and sat in the engineering faculty café in my borrowed suit and shoes, nursing a grey and tired coffee – the insipid powdery liquid nothing like what I'd got used to in Paris.

When it was time to go in, I rustled upstairs in my sharp suit, knocked on the door, and skated across the enormous space in my huge boat shoes. It all went smoothly. The questions were reasonable and asked with at least some warmth, and it was clear that the coaching and clothes bullying from the boys was a very good move. Nothing came up that we hadn't at least tossed around, and I could see my core reasoning obviously scored a hit with both my interviewers. Another irony hit me in that room. All the reading of body language and faces I'd been doing to determine whether or not I could get some money out of a passing punter, I could now put to use in reading my interviewers like a book. They stretched the exercise out to something like an hour, but it felt a mere formality and I got the sense that even they saw the ridiculousness of the situation. Towards the end they even started asking questions about how one went about staying alive playing the guitar on the Paris Metro, to which I responded with complete honesty.

After it was over, I went up to the union bar to catch up with Chris the DJ and a few other people, feeling relaxed and comfortable. I was nearly certain I was through, and if I wasn't, I knew I could never have made up a story that would have satisfied them. Two hours later I was informed I'd passed, so had a few more beers. Chris was presenting the lunchtime show on the university radio station and he kindly played Phil Collins' *Against All Odds* as a small token of his view on me getting back in.

So that was it. I had an end point to my wandering round if I wanted it, five months down the track. I hung around in Nottingham for a couple of days after this, but I was feeling restless, and, despite the huge amount of effort the boys had put in, I became something of a spare part in the house again. I wasn't paying rent, and they were all studying hard for exams while I had complete freedom to do as I pleased. I simply didn't fit.

I was acutely aware that I no longer had a sense of where I belonged. I ached for the golden days of talking for endless hours with Simon about whatever came into our heads, and the warm glow of quiet conversations with Nathalie about her crazy film star dreams. But that was all over, and I knew going back to Paris was a bad idea. I had no desire to go down to Bedford to see Mum and Dad, even though I knew I should, and London was closed to me because of the saga with Kate. I phoned Sarah in York, and hitched up easily in the lengthening days to spend a few days with her there. But I knew I was just marking time.

Eventually I did get back to Bedford to see Mum and Dad. While they were suffocatingly glad to see me, they were careful not to be too overjoyed that I had passed the interview. I felt like a complete git for stalling so long before coming home to see them. But I was feeling in a very alienated space. Ironically, despite all the self-doubt and confusion, the only place I felt really at home was playing on the streets, and wandering down to the pitches each day, wherever I happened to be, was the only time I felt relaxed and comfortable with life. Not only was I 'bomb-proof' as a result of doing the Metro in Paris, I had experienced enough of love and life's more jagged edges to put some genuine guts into the songs, while still having a naive, twenty-one-year-old face to tug at the punters' heart strings. I got confident enough to change a few keys in some of my staple songs, and change some words round so I really 'owned' them. *Tangled Up In Blue* went to a new, higher, more tortured key, and I played it over and over again, belting it out in an almost trance-like state and changing the words to fit my own saga around that of Mr Zimmerman's restless and love-damaged hero. It worked a treat and I made good money everywhere I went.

After a few days of self-reflection in Bedford I realised that, just like in *Tangled Up in Blue*, "the only thing I knew how to do was to keep on keepin' on", and the only place left to go was America. Somewhere in the back of my head it scared me that once I focused on a new place to aim for, I felt a lot more comfortable with life again. The idea when I started all this was to get rid of the restlessness – not make it the essence of who I was. But there was no going back.

But how to make it happen? Briony was the only person I'd come across all year who was interested in going with me. It was already May, and I had no time left to meet up with anyone else. It was either go with her, go alone, or not go at all. Huge warning bells kept ringing in my head about getting into something so extreme with her. I never seemed to get near working out what went on inside Briony's head. All I ever got right was that I would get it wrong. She would go through periods when she would pick a behaviour or emotion for the day and act it out, not even convincing herself that it was how she was really feeling. It almost seemed that when we first got tangled up together, she was in a 'relationship' act for the day, and never got up the nerve to tell me that was all it was. But she wasn't an actor like Simon. She had a very sincere and warm side. Briony would have to be the hardest person I met that year to describe. And yet she was the one I was potentially choosing to hitchhike across a continent with. Smart move! However, I knew hitching across America would only ever really work with a woman, and busking would only work with someone who regarded hanging around on street corners as a reasonably good day out. Briony fitted the bill for both.

I looked at what paperwork we would need to get into the US and it was significant. Even to get a tourist visa required either about fifty bucks a day for every day of your visit, or a guardian for the duration of your stay. If you were under twenty-five, you needed a guardian, regardless of how much money you had. Briony was eighteen and I had just turned twenty-one. On paper it looked more promising if I tried on my own. Briony was due back in England very soon, and I needed to know what I would say to her, both about our clumsy relationship, and about America.

When she did ring, she said she'd broached the idea of us hitchhiking across America with her mother and father. They weren't completely comfortable with the idea and had expressed a desire to meet the person who had put this idea in her head, and could I come down to Cornwall as soon as possible. The prospect of this was more than a little scary. Briony's descriptions of her father had been vivid – he sounded like a tough old bastard. She'd dropped some dark hints about him escaping from eastern Europe at the end of the Second World War, bringing stuff out with him that was later converted into large amounts of money after a change of identity. He was in his seventies, had Parkinson's disease and was confined to a wheelchair, so perhaps not so scary now. Briony's mother was much younger than her husband. She had a job up the road in Exeter, but the roads in Cornwall were so impossible that she only came home at weekends. A brother and a sister had the task of looking after the invalid father during the week. I suspected that Briony's parents would flatly refuse to let her go, and that my visit would be just a formality.

However, I'd never been to Cornwall in my life, there was nothing new happening anywhere else, and I had nothing to lose except a potential travelling partner. I gathered my belongings, got a lift from Mum and Dad to a good hitching spot on the M4, and stuck out my thumb to hitch to Cornwall.

The hitch was a tricky one, as you had to get around Bristol and Exeter. Major cities were always a hassle; a lift that dropped you at some minor junction on the wrong side of the city could mean hours waiting to get the next lift.

So it was six hours after I started that I got dropped off about ten miles away from Briony's family home. I phoned up to give them the opportunity to offer me a lift for that last ten miles only to be told I should get the bus. The next bus wasn't for a couple of hours, so I tried my luck busking in the bus station, with little result. Once I got into Yeolmbridge I rang again, and the phone was answered by a frightfully plummy chap who turned out to be Briony's brother, Jonathon. He said he'd "nip dain" and pick me up in the Rover.

Somewhat to my surprise, Briony came with him. We had our usual scene of not really knowing what to do when we met each other. We sidled around for a second or two then fumbled a kind of mutual peck on the cheek; this was watched with considerable amusement by Jonathon.

Both Jonathon and the Rover proved impressive to look at. He had that Battle of Britain fighter pilot look that women seemed to die for, all tight wavy hair and perfect teeth. He was frightfully friendly and chatted away pleasantly as we headed out to the family abode – Yeolmbridge House, Yeolmbridge.

At first sighting, it was a funny looking place, and the more I got to know it the wilder it became. There was a separate summer house out the front, which, like the Rover as it turned out, was more impressive from a distance than up close. As we parked outside and I got out of the car I could see the skylights and lots of the windows were broken, and there were dead leaves and pigeon shit all over the ripped and rotting green baize of the vast snooker table. Shiny red, yellow and green snooker balls still rested on the table. The vividly coloured balls and dead leaves on the torn green baize, with the ink-black slate beneath it, was a surreal image.

I shouldered through the massively solid front door with my pack and guitar, to be greeted by a room so entirely filled with furniture that there was only enough room left for a passage through to the rest of the house. Getting to the curtains was a major effort and obviously no-one bothered, so the room was in a brooding semi-darkness even though it was a bright sunlit day outside. The next room was exactly the same, and even my untrained eye could see a lot of this furniture was serious antiques. There were doors off to the side of these rooms that I never got to see, but I imagine they were chock-a-block too. Yeolmbridge House was not a small place, and it was stacked just about to capacity with 'stuff'. As we moved through the house, my attention was firmly focused on the fact that Briony's father could be sitting behind the next door. I wasn't looking forward to meeting him.

I was ushered through to the living quarters, and there he sat. The Father was as impressive and memorable as the house. A large but crumpled-up man, he sat in his wheelchair with a tarry looking cigarette between his fingers, dripping a large snout of ash. The first two fingers on his left hand were nicotine-stained, mahogany coloured from the fingernail to the second knuckle. His fingernails were curved talons, more than an inch long. He perched forward in the wheelchair to look at me; I thought uncomfortably of Edgar Allen Poe's *The Raven*.

Two packs of Players Navy Cut sat on the table beside him, together with a mug that would hold about a pint of coffee. It appeared to have the congealed remains of a brew a few hours old, and as he turned to get a better view of me, he took a long swig. God knows what it must have tasted like. He raised his head, took a long draw of his cigarette, then exhaled slowly through his clenched teeth. The effect of that smoke curling out past those teeth and claw-like fingernails, with his piercing eyes sizing me up in that dark room, was frankly terrifying.

"So he got here then?" he said, looking at me but talking presumably to either Jonathon or Briony. His steely voice was chafed and cracked from all that smoking, with a strong hint of eastern Europe or German. Jonathon said something cheerfully to that effect.

"And how long is he planning on staying?" I think Briony fielded that one. It was apparent that The Father was not going to engage in any direct conversation with me at all.

"And it's this one that you plan on travelling across America with ..." pause for drag on cigarette, "... hitchhiking?" He virtually spat out the last word in a cloud of smoke and glistening talons.

Briony went into nervous body language mode, dropping her chin, curling up a lock of her hair and flicking vacant sideways glances and sucking her lip, and came out with a very small "Yes".

He bored into me with those piercing eyes, staring out of his creased wreck of a face for long, long seconds. His giant brooding presence completely dominated the tiny room. Then he grunted, settled back in the wheelchair with another huge pull on his cigarette, and looked out of the window. It seemed our introduction was over.

Briony ushered me upstairs to my room, and we sat down to talk things over. I was still coming down from a state of mortal terror, and it took a while to get my breath and head together.

I wasted no time in saying I thought it was hopeless and there was no way her father would ever let her go. Briony, remarkably, seemed quite relaxed and confident about her chances, and I slowly began to work out why. It seemed The Father applied the same philosophy to his children as he did to his wild cats. They weren't fed, but left to forage in the fields around the house. A forlorn mewling from somewhere up on the roof indicated a stranded kitten. It seemed the family principle of survive or die extended even to this unfortunate.

Strength lay in running your own life and testing yourself against challenges; being of strong character was everything. If Briony was crazy enough to want to go to America, it would be against his principles to stop her, even though he might hate the idea (and, equally, I surmised, the person who put the idea in her head). But it was the money issue that Briony thought would prevent her from going, even if he gave her permission. "They all think I'm flat stony broke, and Daddy will say that if I want to go, I will have to pay for it all myself. He'll be thinking that'll stop me – but what Daddy doesn't know is that I still have all those luvverly travellers cheques from Paris, don't I?"

I listened to the forlorn mewling of the abandoned kitten on the roof as I digested this. The logic sounded good – not all that common for Briony – but at the same time the sound of the kitten seemed to be a message of what could happen if you pushed this 'testing yourself against the challenges' thing too far!

Briony's sister Rachel was their father's main carer. She maintained the frosty attitude she'd greeted me with. I think she regarded Briony and I – and Jonathon for that matter – as carefree freeloaders who got in her way while she was stuck in a decaying house caring for a dying man. Which of course was correct.

One morning Briony sneaked into my room and hopped under the covers for a cuddle. Rachel radared what was going on and appeared at the door, knocking and whispering in near hysteria that if The Father got any hint of what was happening, he would without any shadow of a doubt kill us both – or words to that effect. We weren't up to anything, but Briony made it worse by hiding under the bedclothes and refusing to move, so when Rachel opened the door she only saw me in the bed, with Briony under the covers. I gave her an apologetic smile and a shrug. She wavered for a moment and I thought she was going to faint, but she repeated her dire warnings, threw a look of complete contempt and hatred at me, and slammed out. I figured I wouldn't be on her Christmas card list for a while.

I never met Briony's mother. She rang a few times, and I was called to the phone to say hello. She was remarkably friendly considering I was planning on whisking her eighteen-year-old daughter off to hitchhike around the USA.

The dreaded confrontation with The Father never happened. I was present at a couple of conversations where he gave Briony a bit of a grilling about the trip, but she managed to evade anything too uncomfortable, and played dumb on any details. His approach of never talking to me directly meant he couldn't focus his intensity on me; if he had, I think I would have curled up and folded on the spot.

We stayed at Yeolmbridge House for about a week. I'd never been to Cornwall and it was good to explore somewhere new. We had no car so had to walk most of the time, and the house was a fair way away from anywhere. After a couple of days, I started to really enjoy this; it was like being lost in some time warp. Going to the local pubs was a strange experience. This was 1984. Punk music had been and gone, and Frankie Goes to Hollywood, The Smiths and Echo and the Bunnymen were all happening. However, Briony's friends were all still wearing flares and denim jackets with Deep Purple and Black Sabbath on the back. They would gather round the juke box in the pub, put some heavy metal song on and stand in a circle lashing each other with their long hair while they headbanged away through the song. They all drank Scrumpy cider too, which probably explained a lot. I was forced to drink this horrible concoction while I was there, as anyone that drank anything else was regarded as beneath contempt. The stuff was opaque green with a heavy sediment, and after two pints I was ready to go and lie down in a cowfield and count the clouds. All the pubs we went to were tiny little places that seemed to be about five hundred years old and, other than the strains of Status Quo and Black Sabbath, were rather quaint.

A week or so of this and we were restless. It was time to move. We took a trip to Glastonbury, where Briony had gone to school and home of the biggest music festival in the country. Naturally we would hitch; we figured it would be a good test run for America. It seemed an easy run, though two of us with a pack and a guitar would limit the number of people who would want to pick us up. After assuring Rachel we'd be staying in separate houses (Briony with a family friend, me with a bloke called Barney), Jonathon dropped us off at the hitching point, gave us an encouraging thumbs up and puttered off. If he wasn't wearing a yellow Biggles scarf, he should have been.

There wasn't a huge amount of traffic, and what there was consisted mostly of families on holiday. In my experience, families just about never picked up hitchers and to be fair, most cars that passed us would have had no hope of fitting the two of us and all our gear. Plus it was Saturday morning, normally a bad time for hitching. After an hour and a half with nothing going past, we decided to split up. I was sure that Briony would have no problems alone, so she took most of the gear, including my guitar. She gave me Barney's phone number and the number of the family she was going to stay with and moved fifty yards up the tarmac. Ten minutes later a truck pulled up with a squeal of air brakes, and she was away. But I wasn't.

I kept my thumb out and tried to look relaxed, but my mind was racing. I was in a terrible spot, the traffic was much too fast, and there wasn't anywhere for anyone to stop. When the truck stopped for Briony, it had caused a minor traffic jam while she hauled herself and the gear up into the cab. I decided to start walking backwards, still hitching, as somewhere in the mist of the next hill I thought I could see a lay-by. It took over an hour to get there, and another half an hour to wait, but finally a couple pulled over. I resisted the urge to jump for joy, loaded my gear in, and was on my way. They were German, and had hitched a lot themselves, not an uncommon kind of lift. They were very friendly, but they only took me twenty miles up the road, and what's more the A-road was closed for maintenance, so we wasted more time on a back roads detour. They dropped me at a very quiet-looking junction and I thought I was stuffed, but less than ten cars later I was on the move again with a lift from a single woman, which was most unusual. Desperation had made me much less fussy than normal; she was driving into Exeter and would drop me on the 'dead' side of the city. Again, I thought I was in trouble, but an elderly lady in a tiny car who I hardly bothered raising my thumb to pulled over after half an hour or so. She was only going down the road, but, critically, could drop me at the start of the M5, and, from my map, at a major junction. I was in business.

Except I wasn't. She dropped me at the junction, but it was a road engineer's dream of two high-speed roads merging while hardly having to slow down. Anyone having the inclination to stop would take a very long time to do so, and no-one was inclined to anyway. The one exception to this was a friendly police car that stopped to check my ID and my reason for being. I was silently begging them to take pity on me and give me a drop off somewhere more promising, but this clearly wasn't on the agenda, and they disappeared. So I waited. And waited. And waited.

Finally, after 7pm, with nothing coming past me except cars full of screaming kids and camping gear, I decided I had tried for long enough and would get a bus or train from Exeter. It was a good five-mile walk, and by the time I found the bus station, I'd missed the last bus by fifteen minutes. Clearly my guardian angel had taken the day off. My final option was the train, so I walked another two miles to get to the train station, to find I'd missed the last train by about fifteen minutes. At this point I lost my sense of humour and had a major meltdown on the platform, with a cohort of British Rail passengers as my bemused audience.

There was nothing for it but to walk back into Exeter and try and find somewhere to crash for the night. It was after nine o'clock now and getting dark. I rang Briony to let her know I was in difficulty but not actually dead; however, she hadn't arrived at the house, and the family didn't even know she was meant to be coming.

I was exhausted and starving, so after a feast of cod and chips on a park bench I took stock. I had no idea where to look for a hotel, and wanted to get moving by first light.

What I needed was somewhere warm, safe and dry to hole up until dawn. There was an enormous multistorey car park behind me, and I reasoned the further up this I went the less people I was likely to come across, so I got the lift to the top floor, found myself a nook at the top of a stairway and rolled out my sleeping bag, using my pack as cushioning from the cold concrete floor. I was asleep in minutes.

Voices in the stairwell beneath me jolted me awake. Heavy footsteps were climbing the stairs, and a casual conversation was going on. To scramble all my gear together and run was impossible. I waited in the half-light of antiseptic neon drifting in through the stairwell door, holding my breath as the voices climbed and climbed. Finally, two heads appeared coming out of the stairwell, and I didn't know whether to laugh or cry when I saw two policemen's helmets.

They were most amused to find me there, but not particularly surprised. It seemed my lair was a favourite among locals who had no place else to go, and this was a regular part of their Saturday night beat. In gentle west country accents, they explained I had two choices.

"You can either book into a noice little 'otel, or oi can book you into one of our comfy little cells for the noight. In either case, woi can give you a chauffeured lift to the accommodation of your choice. It's up to you, moi young friend."

I seriously toyed with the idea of doing a night in the cells just so I could say I'd done it; it would be considerably more comfortable than my current lodgings. However, I needed to be sure I could get going early in the morning, and the possibility of getting a black mark that could affect my chances of getting an American visa also loomed large. I decided to take up their 'koind offer' of a lift to a hotel.

## 8 TANGLED UP IN BLUE

They dropped me at the entrance to a very homely looking place that they said did an excellent breakfast and was used to admitting people at silly hours of the night on the recommendation of the local constabulary. They bid me good night, watching to make sure I went inside. I don't remember how much the hotel cost, but it was worth every penny, and the proprietor was wonderfully relaxed at having a guest turn up in the dead of night under a police escort. The room was all lace trimmings and pink roses, and the bed, after several hours on the concrete floor, seemed the most sumptuous luxury I had ever encountered. I was asleep again in five minutes, breathing a silent prayer of thanks to the good humour and common sense of a couple of friendly English coppers.

My idea for an early start didn't eventuate, partly because I didn't wake up, and partly because of the enormous breakfast. I made the trek to the train station again – which was just as far in daylight as it had been at night. I consulted the times, worked out the next train was in an hour or so, and settled down to wait. A train came and went, but it was too early to be mine. But when no other train showed up, I realised it was Sunday, and I'd been reading the wrong timetable. I should have got on that earlier train, and now had another two hours to wait. For the second time in less than a day I had a major 'wetty' on an Exeter station, cursing God and my guardian angel and Briony and British Rail and the heartless British public who wouldn't give a poor guy a lift, and, last but not least, myself for getting into such a stupid lifestyle and not being able to read a bloody train timetable.

Eventually a train hauled in and took me to Barnstaple, where after more tedious walking, I got a bus that dropped me off in Glastonbury. I reflected that somewhere there had to be a happy and sensible land where the bus and train people got together and put their stations next to each other, but that happy land certainly wasn't England. It had taken me over twenty-four hours to go less than a hundred miles.

Getting to Glastonbury wasn't the end of my woes, as I still had to find Briony. I phoned the host family again and got the same negative response, and this time they were genuinely worried, especially as the last time I'd seen Briony, she was climbing alone into the cab of a truck. However, I had a feeling Briony was OK, and said I'd ring back once I heard anything.

I sat on the steps of the ancient stone cross in the middle of town and called on the ancient druids. Despite all the trials and traumas of the last twenty-four hours, I was finally enjoying myself. The sun was out, the town was a fascinating mix of west country market-town tweedy types and crazy looking hippies. If I was back in Nottingham doing what I was meant to, I would have been cramming for some exam on how to build an oil refinery. Things were pretty good really.

Finally, after about an hour, Briony appeared, wandering dreamily down the street, without a care in the world. I crept up behind her and pounced. She didn't bat an eyelid.

"Oh, there you are, I was wondering how I was going to track you down. Where did you get to last night?" I looked closely to detect whether she was taking the piss, but she was for real. I explained that single guys found it more difficult to hitch in deepest darkest Cornwall than single girls, that I had got stranded, narrowly escaped a night in the cells, phoned the place where she said she would be staying but she'd never showed up, and there wasn't a whole lot more I could do. All

I got in return was an exasperated response of "Why the fuck did you phone them? They'll be worried sick now and Mum and Dad'll find out I didn't stay there."

"I phoned them because YOU fucking told me to and because I THOUGHT you might want to know that I WASN'T going to get to Glastonbury ... where we were MEANT to be going TOGETHER and where you SAID we would have NO fucking problem hitching to. Does that make SOME kind of sense to you??" I felt my third meltdown in under a day brewing fast. My tirade vaguely broke through the layers of other-worldly mist that periodically enveloped Briony's brain, and she changed the subject. It turned out she'd run into some hippy friends when she arrived, learned that some guy she knew had just died, and got into a memorial smoking session for him at some café. To Briony, this constituted a perfectly reasonable excuse, and she couldn't see what all the fuss was about. I closed with an ultimatum.

"I want to make one thing very clear – IF, and right now it's a very big if, we end up going to America together, under no circumstances whatever do we split up while hitching. We stay together until we starve to death or die of thirst. That's the deal. Agreed?"

She blinked in startled surprise, got her hunted-rabbit look, and, when I asked again, finally nodded.

"Thank you. And now, could you please, please reunite me with my guitar?"

"I sometimes think you care more about that guitar than you do about me."

"Spot on, baby. Absolutely spot on."

All in all, things were looking very encouraging for two months or so travelling across America together.

The Glastonbury experience was a collision of two very different worlds, and gave me a bit more of an insight into Briony's somewhat unusual perception of the universe. We alternated between extreme hippies, drug dealers and alternative lifestyle types, and Briony's old school mates, who came from serious money. My only recollections of them are of lots of chaps wearing tweed jackets and expensive-looking shirts and shoes, and lots of perfect-skinned girls wearing designer frocks who made bitchy comments that went completely over Briony's head. Briony herself lived in a denim jacket, a pair of jeans that she periodically redecorated with sparkling nail polish (her left leg currently had an RIP message for the guy who had died) and a pair of shocking purple hiking boots. She was about as far from being a Laura Ashley public school gal as you could get.

While we were there Briony insisted on taking me to visit the parents of the guy she'd been obsessed with before being exiled to Paris. She sighed nostalgically at the spot where she'd slept on the lawn outside his house. The parents treated her like a creature from another planet, but they let us in and gave us a nice cup of tea in a frightfully British way. The poor guy who had been the object of her desire arrived home unexpectedly, and after a polite hello was bundled through the kitchen and away from Briony. I cringed through the entire bizarre exercise, wondering yet again how I could be contemplating going to America with this crazy girl.

Meeting the alternative community of Glastonbury was a lot more fun. Barney, the guy Briony had arranged for me to stay with, was a significant dope dealer in town, but seemed to regard it as a community service rather than a money-making exercise. He was very mellow indeed, and spent his whole life in a marijuana haze that I quickly became enveloped in. While a little odd, Barney was a good-hearted and fun guy, and I was grateful for the space on his floor.

Between Barney's and the local café – the main drop-in and gossip spot – I managed to meet most of the alternative lifestylers of Glastonbury. One night a party was held for some guy who was leaving town to become, of all things, a truck driver in the US. It was a wild affair, with some highly exotic people and too many drugs for my liking. I remember one guy with a mirror around his neck wandering around offering lines of coke and speed. He had a gorgeous but tragic daughter who was about six. Dressed in her little party dress that was all bows and frills and glitter, she kept doing little spins and turns around him the whole night to try and get his attention. He mostly ignored her and would occasionally flare up and tell her to go and find someone to play with. It was sad, and gave me a different perspective on the seemingly carefree, alternative lifestyle.

There was plenty of music going on and I had a great time jamming with various people, though it all degenerated towards the end of the night. Everyone was so full of their favourite poisons that no-one could string a song together. I was just as bad, as I'd been taking a toke or a sniff of most things that came past throughout the night. The café owners were recording the music, so I started a Neil Young song but in the wrong key, far too high. I got through it in a falsetto soprano voice, but it sounded bloody awful. I cringed the next day when I thought about someone having to listen to it.

In between parties, meeting people and chilling out at Barney's, Briony and I walked miles through the soft green valleys surrounding Glastonbury. One of the reasons the music festival began there was because the place was meant to have ancient significance. There was a lot of talk about ley lines and druids. It could just have been the talk – and all the illegal substances we were doing – but to me the country around Glastonbury certainly had a very special feel. There was an air of ancient and patient waiting, a feeling that big unseen things were going on at an imperceptibly slow but remorseless pace in the fabric of the soil and air, of secrets hanging somewhere just beyond what could be seen. I tried to describe this to one of the party people and they just gave me a quiet nod and said "Why do you think we live here? If you can feel that my friend, you should stay". I found it confusing and not a little sad that the same people who drew sustenance from this very special feeling still wanted or needed to do so many drugs.

During our walks we sketched out plans for the US. We would have to go to the US embassy in London and present various credentials to get issued with visas, which could be complicated by Briony's 'little drug conviction' that was sitting in a police file. One night at Barneys she'd produced some unmistakably Paris dope that she'd walked through English customs with 'for a laugh'. It was probably worth about five quid and wouldn't last a night. To risk getting sprung for this seemed crazy to me, particularly as it could knock any US plans on the head but, yet again, I came back to the mantra that Briony and I looked at life in very different ways.

We both needed to do some serious paper shuffling to find birth certificates, get proof that we had something to come back to the UK for, and get letters of support from people we knew in the US. The only chances of this were the

Americans who had come through the Nesle who had given us their addresses. However, Briony found she'd mislaid the addresses somewhere between Paris and London. This triggered yet another debate on whether going with each other was a good idea. Luckily, I still had Jerry's details. The only other possibility was an aunt and uncle in Canada. I didn't know how much this would count for, but figured it couldn't lose us anything.

We needed to get back to our respective parental nests and start pulling all the red tape stuff together. Briony still had the worrying task of getting her parents to agree to letting her go, bearing in mind she was still only eighteen and classed as a minor under American law.

And so we walked out of Glastonbury together and then parted, with me hitching north to Bristol and from there to Bedford, and Briony back to Yeolmbridge. Our plan was to meet up in either London, Bedford or Nottingham – or possibly not at all, depending on whether we could get the paperwork together, whether her parents came to the party, and whether a couple of phone calls to the embassy would establish that Briony's little slip-up in the past would cost her a visa.

The following weeks were a blur. I was back and forward between Nottingham and London at least three times, and Bedford in between, chasing down the paperwork, keeping the visa wheels turning, and going to various university celebrations in Nottingham. I don't think I slept in the same place for more than three nights, and it was often just the night.

One time, hitching south to Bedford, I arrived at Junction 25 of the M1 to find it was solid with guys who didn't look like the normal hitching crew. They were too serious, too sombre, and in some cases too old. I walked past them and ended up way down on the entry ramp, mystified at where all these unusual people could have come from. A Black Maria police van appeared at the top of the entry road and pulled up by the first hitcher. I knew I was sunk. There was nowhere to run to, so I watched grimly as they slowly went down the line, unhurriedly putting the men in the back of the van. When they reached me, the copper said, "You don't look much like a fuckin' miner, lad," and left me where I was. Once my relief passed, my blood boiled. It was 1984 and the miners' strike was in full swing. Over the next few years the mining industry in the Midlands became a pale shadow of its former self, and whole towns ended up on the scrap heap. It was heartbreaking.

Twice in Nottingham I woke up in a strange house with a girl next to me, wondering quite how I got there. I was quite open with Briony about these happenings, and she would ring me to agonise and sigh about Tristan, the guy she'd met on the ferry with whom she seemed quite besotted. At the same time, we were still sleeping together. Neither of us spent too much time analysing the situation for logic.

I never got the details of how she got past her parents, but she managed to get a letter from them saying all the things the visa application wanted them to say, and we added it to the pile of papers we would have to present.

The boys in Nottingham threw a farewell cocktail party for me. My status at the house was now such that while I was expected to pay my share for the grog, my bed was being used by people from out of town. I needed to find somewhere else to sleep. For some reason I put up with this crap, but it soured my final parting with them.

## 8 TANGLED UP IN BLUE

Briony came up for the party. It involved lots of games in the park across the road, and Briony had a terrible time of it, being picked last for softball and never even seeing the ball, let alone hitting it. She tried to cover up the things her body didn't do very well at. One day we were fooling around and I swung her round in a mock romantic circle like some couple in a chocolate advert. She lost her grip on my hands and flew back onto the ground, with her head snapping back onto the concrete with a sickening thud like a melon hitting the ground. I thought for a second she'd fractured her skull, but she made light of it and insisted it was all OK. It was scary to watch; none of her 'saving' reflexes kicked in when they should have – her hands never got anywhere close to breaking her fall.

I lost the St Christopher that Helen gave me at that games party. The ball came spiralling out of the sky when I was sitting on the grass talking to someone, hitting me on the neck and breaking the chain. It couldn't have flown more than six feet from where I was sitting, but Briony and I spent hours and hours searching through the grass and never found it. This gave me a cold feeling in the pit of my stomach; it had become a kind of talisman. We took it as a bad sign for our trip.

I seemed to be in a perpetual, self-induced whirlwind of moving on, feeling more lost and rootless than ever. Rob and Helen were there for me, but I'd lost the last traces of rapport with the lads in the house, and felt distanced from some other good friends as well, including Martin in Bedford and Chris the DJ. The only time I felt really relaxed was standing on the street with my guitar round my neck watching money trickle into my case. It was a scary feeling. I would lie awake at night staring into the dark, wondering if I would ever lose the hollow need to be somewhere else tomorrow. I had become a real gypsy.

Slowly we accumulated the papers we needed for America. The university was, as usual, a complete pain in the arse. I rang and asked for a letter of confirmation that I was attending and the letter that arrived said something vague like 'eligible to recommence studies if present on the day of re-enrolment'. One of the more important bits of the red tape jigsaw was a letter saying you had something to go back to, to prove you wouldn't overstay. The letter didn't exactly have a ring of certainty, and after several heated phone calls, I hitched up there, marched in with the wording I wanted, and refused to leave until it had been typed up and signed by someone important. It took two days.

Still missing were any letters of support from anyone in the US. I had a letter from my uncle in Ottawa (which looked pretty close to America if you looked at a small enough map, but I wasn't sure immigration would agree). Jerry hadn't written back, which was a big disappointment. I'd had faith in him and was surprised that he'd let us down. But time was moving on, so we decided to take the plunge and front up at the American embassy. The English weather had finally decided it was summer, so of course we hitched down to London. We'd reached Junction 25 on the M1 and I nipped into the bushes for a pee. When I came back Briony was rolling a joint by the side of the motorway in broad daylight, while being eyed off with some alarm by the other hitchers. This was very risky, as the police stopped regularly to check on people hitching. When I started to make a fuss Briony said cheerily, "It's all relative – this little piece of dope was quite a bit bigger and in my pocket last week when I hitched down to Glastonbury using that sign that said 'Vibesville, man'. Now *that* was risky!"

We hitched down in a couple of hours, a good run, then spent two hours grinding across London to get to Briony's brother-in-law's place in the East End, where we'd be staying.

Roger was, like everyone in Briony's family, a difficult package to work out. He had bought a house off the Mile End Road in an area that was about to 'move', making him a plummy, almost-middle-age yuppy living in the middle of an Eastenders set; a fish out of water. He was renovating the home for the family to move into, and there was a nursery for the two kids down on the bottom floor. Briony and I slept there, pushing the two little beds together. We lay together, nervous, talking little, knowing the next day would probably be make or break on our crazy, magnificent plan. Eventually we made love in a half-desperate way, as if one of us would be leaving forever in the morning. It was a strange experience in the little nursery beds, with Tigger mobiles wafting over our heads.

Afterwards I lay looking at the ceiling, trying to work out how I'd ended up there, asking myself why I was sticking with the idea of going with Briony when I knew it would mean trouble somewhere along the line. But I was too scared to contemplate going it alone, and I had no other plan to get rid of the driving emptiness inside me.

The embassy was a huge, echoing place with lots of marble and smoked glass. We joined endless queues and answered endless questions to endless numbers of Americans.

What do you plan to do in the US? How will you support yourselves? Tricky – I was pretty sure that hitchhiking and busking wouldn't get the result we wanted. I'd grilled Briony for days beforehand not to say anything wild and blow it. We were separated most of the time and didn't talk much when we were together; there was always someone official looking within earshot.

I put all my concerns down to paranoia – until I got called into a separate room by a very large, very senior-looking Afro-American guy.

He gave me a penetrating look.

"Sir, I want to make a few things clear regarding the issue of visas for you and the young lady who is accompanying you."

I gulped and nodded. This sounded bad.

"Firstly, the young lady is eighteen years old. She is classed as a minor under state law in many places in the United States. You are twenty-one years old and so will be regarded as her legal guardian. You will be responsible for her safety, and for her actions."

I nodded and gulped a couple more times.

"Are you aware that the young lady has a current conviction for possession of marijuana?"

The nodding and gulping were getting a bit tedious but I couldn't think of anything else to do. He gave me that penetrating look again.

"Sir, I really recommend that you have a good think about your responsibilities and obligations regarding the young lady."

Nod, gulp, faint smile. The smile was a mistake.

"Sir, I fail to see the humorous side of this conversation." I nodded and gulped and apologised, saying the reason I found it funny is that I had been thinking of little else for a good long while. This was a good shot, and he puckered his lips and even raised a glimmer of a smile back. He moved on.

"Sir, we try to ensure that people we issue visas to are in a position to support themselves while in the United States. We advise that people have at least fifty dollars for each day of their stay, or someone who will provide a written declaration that they will support that person while in the United States. You do not appear to have either of these things." He sat forward across his desk and drilled into me with his eyes. "This is of concern to me."

It was time to do something more than nod and gulp. The only card up my sleeve was Jerry. I said he'd given us a verbal commitment and we were expecting the confirmation letter any day.

"Yes sir, the young lady has mentioned Mr Jerry Hoffner to us. I note that you met Mr Hoffner for a period of about two weeks while staying in a hotel in Paris. That is correct?"

Nod and gulp. It was his turn to smile a little.

"I should highlight that citizens of the United States can be a little generous in offering accommodation to people who they meet while on vacation. It is perhaps optimistic to be relying on an offer like this to guarantee your safety while in the *United States*." He always said the United States and he infused it with an aura of reverence. He was very impressive. I did my ghost of a smile back.

"Sir, we have promises from perhaps seven people for accommodation in the United States." It was infectious! "I have not mentioned these other people because I think they were behaving in the way you describe. Mr Hoffner was different. He meant it."

He leaned back in his chair and gave me that penetrating look again, obviously considering his decision.

"I will be candid with you sir. You cannot currently demonstrate that you will have a place of safety in the

United States, you are being accompanied by a minor who has a current conviction for possession of a restricted substance. You *believe* you will shortly receive a letter from a person you have known for only a short period of time who will be prepared to support you. The only support you can currently claim is in Ottawa Canada, and you are planning to fly into JF Kennedy Airport, New York." He leaned forward to emphasise his point. "New York is a long way from Ottawa, sir, and take my word for it, New York City is no place to be without adequate funding or friends you can rely on. Am I making myself clear to you, sir?"

I was out of saliva to gulp with, so I just nodded. He looked long and hard one more time, then sighed and seemed to make a decision. I was electric with tension.

"Sir, we will issue the young lady and yourself with visas. However, you need to be aware that your documentation will be scrutinised on entry to the United States, and a decision will be made at that time whether you will be granted legal entry to the country, and what length of time you will be allowed to stay. It would be very much in your interest to either have that letter of support from Mr Hoffner, or be in possession of adequate funding for the duration of your stay. If you do not have these things, I would advise you to think very hard about flying to Canada rather than New York. Good luck, sir, take care of that young lady, and, if things work out for the two of you, enjoy our beautiful country". He extended a huge hand across the table, shook my hand, and gave me a smile.

So, we had the visas, but we weren't necessarily in. Although the victory wasn't complete, we celebrated with Roger that night, and the next morning split up again to get organised.

## 8 TANGLED UP IN BLUE

Staples Corner was chock-a-block with other hitchers. I walked up beyond most of the others and unfolded my well-worn 'Bedford' sign. Ten minutes after I got there a truck thundered past and the driver pointed at me and stuck up his thumb. It turned out to be one of the strangest lifts I'd had. The truck was carrying some kind of industrial waste on the way to a landfill just out of Bedford. The Ouse valley was considered a great place for dumping nasties because it was composed of clay a couple of hundred feet thick. This apparently meant you could chuck anything you liked in the ground and it would be safe for the next million years. The security at the landfill was so tight you had to have photo ID, and as I didn't have it, the driver had to leave me. He'd come back and pick me up.

He disappeared over the horizon in a long line of other trucks that were also dumping nasties into the ground. The trucks were surrounded by mobs of seagulls, and there was a dirty blue-brown mist clinging to the side of the hill in the warm summer rain. It was a forlorn and highly depressing image. As I waited, I realised with a shock that although I would recognise the driver, all the trucks looked identical and I couldn't tell which one was his. He had all my gear on board, including my guitar and my passport with my hard-won American visa. If this was some kind of elaborate rip-off trick, I was in very deep shit indeed. After twenty minutes I was starting to panic, but finally saw a figure waving at me from an advancing truck. He was a really nice guy, and it depressed the hell out of him that he was doing something so grim and destructive for a living but, as he said, you gotta eat.

He gave me a lift to within a couple of hundred yards of Mum and Dad's house in Bedford – not a bad effort for one lift all the way from London.

Thanks to Richard Branson's new Virgin Atlantic airline, return tickets to New York were only a hundred and ninety-nine quid. We booked a two-month trip, and using the embassy equation of fifty bucks a day, we had enough money to last a bit over two weeks. I tried to work out a plan, but I didn't really care where we went, as long as we went a long, long way. Nothing on the tourist trail really stirred me up, except maybe the Grand Canyon. Fortunately Briony felt the same – we were in it for the journey. I bought a backpacker guide that had a list of cheap accommodation in major centres, but even they didn't look cheap enough for our budget. We would need to meet a lot of people to stay with, or I would be doing a lot of playing on the streets. This didn't worry me half as much as Jerry. We still hadn't heard from him. Every time I rang his number there was no answer.

My Canadian uncle wrote a letter full of well-meaning advice and warnings, the first being that under no circumstances try and hitchhike anywhere near New York City, followed by "nobody, but nobody does a favour for nothing in New York City".

I had a phone number for Kastle's parents in San Diego, and, on a hunch, rang it to see if she was there. She answered the phone herself and shrieked and screamed when she heard my voice. I explained the crazy plan and she immediately said we could stay as long as we liked if we got to San Diego, and it all sounded 'really cool'. She gave me a brief rundown on the Nesle. Simon had left for Nottingham, Nathalie had been thrown out by Renée because she couldn't pay the rent, and Gillel seemed to be having some kind of breakdown. That was all I had time to find out, bearing in mind the phone rates. It felt good that we had one person we could rely on, albeit three thousand miles from where we were flying in.

The news about Nathalie worried me. I would lie and stare into space and think of her, hoping she'd given up on her dreams and gone back to be with Rosene, while knowing this would be the last thing she would want to do.

I managed to track Simon down in Nottingham, and the news was all very sad. Gillel had gone crazy, smashing one of the huge ornate mirrors in the Nesle lobby and was arrested after Renée called the police. No film work had come along for Nathalie that didn't involve taking her clothes off, and she'd started using what little money they had to buy smack. Simon suspected she was injecting again. He finally gave up and came home. It was depressing to hear about how little time it had taken for the life I'd known and loved in Paris to disintegrate completely.

I felt a bit smug telling Simon that the nebulous plan of going to America was now a reality. He was satisfyingly impressed, but gobsmacked that I was going with Briony.

"She's fuckin' bonkers that one – you'll need to watch her." I thanked him for his sage advice. We had a wild night out in The Garage, the coolest club in Nottingham. I'd never managed to get through the door while I was a student but had no trouble with my weird hair and Simon by my side. We drank and drank and reminisced about Paris and shared woman troubles and somewhere during the course of the evening I fell headfirst down a staircase into a basement full of goths and punks who I thought were going to eat me, but who turned out to be very sociable.

The day Briony arrived in Bedford, packed and ready to go, was the Bedford Regatta. It was a good day out, sitting by the river drinking beer, watching some other poor

Briony.

bastards killing themselves. We spent a carefree day with Richard and Mike and Sarah and a gang of others. Helen dropped over to wish us luck and, after an hour of trying to see if I was wearing the St Christopher, walked over and opened my shirt. We had to explain what happened, and we all made light of it, but I caught the reflection in Helen's eyes of my own feelings of bad karma.

I had more tangible reasons than this to be worried. I hadn't told Briony or my parents, but on the morning of the regatta I'd phoned Jerry yet again, and the number had been disconnected.

The chances of us having somewhere safe to stay in New York were now close to zero – if they let us into the country at all.

## 9 THE CITY THAT NEVER SLEEPS

*These vagabond shoes are longing to stray
Right through the very heart of it
New York, New York.
I wanna wake up
In a city that never sleeps*
New York, New York. **Fred Ebb, 1977**

We spent our last night in the UK at Roger's place. My dad insisted on giving us a lift down to London. I knew his mind must be racing with things to say to us, principally, I imagined, about forgetting the whole thing, but he kept the conversation very relaxed and low key. I reflected on the conversation we'd had in the Nottingham pub on the day I told him I was dropping out of uni. So much had happened since. I felt like a different person, about a hundred years older.

Dad dropped us off, spoke briefly with Roger, then it was time for goodbyes. Before he drove off, he just squeezed my shoulder, looked deep into my eyes, and wished us luck.

"Do it well, son, do it well," was all he said. I wondered what The Father's last words were to Briony.

I spent most of the night staring at the ceiling in the little nursery room, putting together a plan for what to do if we couldn't find Jerry in New York. I decided we would either put our gear into a Left Luggage somewhere and book into a hotel or get on a bus and head out of town.

Next morning, we farewelled Roger and set off for Heathrow, battling our way right across London on the Underground, from east to west. In terms of clothing, we were travelling very light, with everything for the two of us, including two sleeping bags, crammed into one large rucksack. This was to make up for the guitar – hitching with two packs, the two of us *and* the guitar would really restrict us getting lifts. We still took up a hell of a lot of room, but the guitar was our food ticket, and it wasn't staying behind.

I'd never flown before, so the airport was a novelty, particularly as we were flying with the trendy new Virgin Atlantic airline, who seemed keen to impress. The crew made a big fuss about the guitar, allowing me to carry it on to the aircraft myself and making sure all the strings were slackened off to avoid damaging the neck before they spirited it away somewhere safe.

I strummed away in the departure lounge for a while, partly to help me relax and partly to see if I could snare some friendly New Yorker on his way back home who might offer us a bed for the night, but no luck.

As a distraction, we bought a very naff touristy Union Jack shopping bag, with the idea that we could display this while hitching across America, to make us more interesting. It turned out to be a wise investment.

I was so preoccupied that I hardly noticed Briony. She was particularly insecure and jumpy-eyed and spending a fair bit of time talking to her trusty rock. She was much more sociable on the flight, wandering up and down the aircraft chatting to people while I slept. She was clearly also fishing for someone who could give us a bed for the night when we arrived.

## 9 THE CITY THAT NEVER SLEEPS

My guitar was hand delivered to me at the other end, which was jolly nice, and then, with a deep breath, we headed to immigration.

As we shuffled slowly to the front of the line, it was obvious that some people got an easy run while others got a grilling. They definitely weren't just rubber-stamping people in. This was bad news. When it was our turn, the guy looked through our passports, flicked an eye over the supporting letters we had, and asked to see what funds we had. I knew we were in trouble.

"Sir, the letter of support you have is from your relative in Canada. Canada is not in the United States, and our job here is to check that you will not be a liability to the citizens of the United States or place yourselves in danger by not having an adequate plan in place to ensure a trouble-free vacation. I see nothing here that will allow me to let you into the United States for two months. Can you help me here?"

I came out with the same old stuff about Uncle Barry, but this cut no ice at all.

"Sir, your funds are such that you will not be able to support yourself for any length of time in the United States, and your declared guardian is in Canada. I am therefore going to give you one week to leave the United States. In this way, you will be able to see New York City, and will be at your relative's house before your money runs out."

We both howled in protest and started into lots of ifs and buts. He cut in very quickly indeed.

"This is not negotiable. I counsel you to not cause any further delay. There are a lot of people waiting here. Have a safe stay in New York. Good day." Firm, final, and only slightly less than disastrous. We had to be in Canada within a week. Fuck.

We caught a bus to the Port Authority bus terminal on 42nd Street. On the way we had our first view of Manhattan. It looked exactly like it did in the films and TV shows: yellow taxis driving past people trying to flag them down, limos driving past ragged men and garbage cans, and above all else, movement and energy – an amphetamine dream.

I made sure we were first off, to grab our gear. There were a lot of people hanging around in the dark depths of the bus station who I didn't like the look of.

We found a Left Luggage counter in the bus station. We also found a lost sheep; a short blond guy who Briony had talked to on the plane. He was weaving his way up to the counter at the same time as us. He was very obviously pissed, having made the most of the free grog on the flight. His name was Colin, and he was on his way upstate to do some kind of postgraduate study, but right now he had no place to stay, no plan and the beginnings of a raging hangover. He was very relaxed about all this – except the impending hangover – and he lightened up my mood considerably. I was really feeling the weight of responsibility. Using eye language, Briony and I agreed to invite him to join us; there would be safety in numbers, and we could split a room three ways. The only thing that would make Colin a liability was if, by some miracle, Jerry only had room for two.

As I checked the guitar into the Left Luggage, the guy on the counter raised his eyebrows.

"You be careful taking this out, you hear – this is not something I would be carrying around on the streets in this neighbourhood." This did wonders for our paranoia.

We weaved our way through the enormous Port Authority building and out onto 42nd Street, Manhattan's centre of sleaze. Peep shows, bars and porn shops lined the street, hookers and pimps of both sexes lounged in doorways, calling for trade. Within a minute of us hitting the street, a fat businessman muttered at me, asking whether I wanted to sell my ass. It was only about a two-minute walk from the bus station to the Times Square subway, but it was memorable. My warning radar was off the scale, and everywhere I looked I saw sharks circling, ready to pick off the unwary. Amidst all this mayhem, the only sign of any police action was a cop writing a ticket for double parking. Bizarre.

The subway was confusing and just as scary as street level. Ironic, really, considering how much time Briony and I had spent below ground in Paris. But the contrast between the brightly lit art deco chrome of the Paris Metro and the dim, decaying dilapidation of the New York subway – circa 1984 – was huge. We'd caught the back end of rush hour and the trains were packed solid. We watched as several trains heading north passed us without stopping. Hopping on the first train that stopped, we figured it would be hard to get lost with all the numbered streets. We were at 42nd Street, Jerry's place was on West 71st. Simple! The doors closed and the train powered off, passing through station after station without stopping. It flew right past 72nd. I suddenly became aware that we were the only white people on the train, and we were getting some strange looks. An old black guy moved close to us and spoke under his breath.

"I think you guys are on the wrong train." I tried a smile and said we'd meant to get off at 72nd.

"Well, you sure are on the wrong train – this is an express, goes all the way up to 125th before it stops." I must have looked blank.

"125th is the centre of Harlem. You don't see many white folks up there." Oh, joy! We'd managed to get ourselves into a no-go zone within ten minutes of leaving the bus station. Fortunately, the guy turned into a saviour.

"You just stick with me, when the train stops we'll just cross over the platform and wait for the next express back downtown." And that's exactly what we did. When the train stopped there was a sea of black faces on the station, with lots of heads turning to see the curiosity – us. Our guardian escorted us across the line, calling out as he did so that we were with him while gently opening a path through the crowded platform. A quite surreal experience. In a beautiful deep gravelly voice, he gave a short lesson on how the subway worked.

Apparently, you ignored the signs on the train itself, and concentrated on the big decaying displays above the platform, which in theory had lights next to the station you wanted. He spoke quietly as we waited, his eyes flicking round the crowded station, checking on people passing and looking, and occasionally fending off with a nod and a smile, saying "These folks are with me."

After what seemed an age, but was only about five minutes, our train came, and we clambered on.

"You folks get back to where you belong and have a good time in New York, OK?" We shouted our thanks as the doors closed and whisked us away from Harlem. Without him, my radar told me we could have been ripped off or mugged. Or both. In reality, it was probably a low risk, but it felt like a narrow escape at the time. I breathed a silent sigh of relief that the guitar was safe.

We finally got to our desired station, walked to West 71st and found Jerry's building. Unlike anywhere we'd seen so far, this area felt like serious money. How did he afford it? The button for Jerry's flat had the name 'Dee Dee Irving' next to it. I pushed the bell and waited. Nothing happened for ages, and we were starting to think no-one was home when a male voice answered. We asked for Jerry, explaining who we were. After a pause, the voice said, "I'll be down in a second, just stand away from the door while you wait." We did as we were told, mystified. I was quickly concluding that New York was a much more alien environment than Paris had ever been. I had spent my whole time so far in the city wondering what the hell was going on.

A South American-looking guy appeared. Ushering us into the lobby, he explained he was Jerry's ex-flatmate. He was obviously nervous and appeared relieved when the elevator arrived and was empty. He was acting very strangely, and I was far from comfortable.

Once we were in the ninth-floor apartment he started to talk quickly, and our jet-lagged senses struggled to keep up with the torrent of information. His name was Victor. The apartment was in the name of Dee Dee Irving, and, when she had originally taken on the lease it had been a very rundown area. In an effort to get the area on the 'up', leases had been given to people on a lifetime basis at what, at the time, had been a reasonably high but affordable rent. This was twenty years ago, and while rents elsewhere had gone through the roof, rents here had stayed at a fraction of what it would normally have been. Dee Dee Irving had been dead for years, but her husband had continued the lease in her name, renting the place to a succession of people at ten times what he was paying under her name. While Jerry was away in Paris, the building's owners had called in private detectives to sort things out. All sorts of nasty writs were being served on anyone they could prove weren't legal tenants. They'd also been intercepting the mail of anyone under suspicion for months, which is why Jerry had never received our letter.

Given that Jerry was a stockbroker and Victor a lawyer, any kind of conviction would be bad. They both moved out over a month ago – which is why my phone calls were never answered. Eventually the phone was cut off.

What was truly bizarre was that Victor was there for the first time in weeks to pick up the last of his personal belongings, and he wouldn't be back. The chance of us turning up at that precise moment was so slim as to be ridiculous, but that's what happened.

He suggested we stay in the apartment but warned us to be careful of who we spoke to on the way in and out, as the building's owners were trying to collect information on illegal tenants. Given we were getting thrown out of the country in a week, the odds of getting sued didn't seem high.

We helped him carry the last of his gear down to a pickup truck parked out the front of the building, aware that he was jumping at shadows all the time. He gave us Jerry's phone number, a bottle of wine he'd left in the apartment and the keys to the place. We asked what we should do with the keys when we left. He shrugged and told us to just give them away or throw them in the river. And then he was gone, and just like that we were the proud and ridiculously lucky tenants of a fully furnished apartment on the Upper West Side, two minutes from Central Park and a block from where John Lennon was shot.

We explored the flat and couldn't believe our eyes. Dee Dee Irving had been an opera singer, and there was a baby grand piano, a serious looking reel-to-reel tape recorder, and a gorgeous retro-looking big chrome mike on a heavy stand. There were two spacious bedrooms, a comfortable lounge, a fully set up kitchen, sheets and towels ... everything you could ever want – even wardrobes full of clothes.

## 9 THE CITY THAT NEVER SLEEPS

And we had the keys. To ourselves.

It was plainly impossible, but there we were. We opened the bottle of wine and toasted each other and our good fortune. Soon, jet lag and exhaustion took over. Briony and I chose what we dubbed the 'Wedgwood Room' as it was decorated in eggshell blue with white trimmings on the mouldings. We let Colin have the master bedroom, as we felt uneasy about sleeping in the bed where this woman we would never know, whose space we were invading, might well have died.

I woke often through the hot and humid New York summer night, listening to the sound of the streets; a bit like Paris, but more gruff and brash. Briony slept beside me, snoring gently with a half-smile on her face. I watched the shadows on the ceiling slowly move towards the dawn, marvelling over and over at how we could have got to this place.

The sense of unreality was still with me the next morning, but the apartment hadn't disappeared like a mirage, so I kept on believing. Given we had a week to get to Canada, I thought I should alert my uncle and went down to the street to find a payphone. Manhattan in daylight was just as intense, an urban avalanche of the senses. I spoke to my uncle and tried to sound enthusiastic to all the excited twittering about how we could visit all the places I'd heard about from my grandma. But Canada just wasn't on the list in terms of my big American dream.

After buying basic provisions from a nearby corner store, it was clear we would quickly run out of money at these prices. Ditto when we went out to a diner for breakfast; we got a really hard time from the waitress when we didn't leave a tip.

Over breakfast we decided to wait till the next morning to get the gear out of the bus terminal, thinking that hoodlums weren't generally early risers. We also talked through what to do about our lack of a US visa. Colin had agreed to provide us with a guardian letter for our time there. He was a British citizen on a temporary student visa, but it was a start. We came up with a couple of possible plans, including heading for Vancouver instead of San Diego and trying to cross back into the US at Niagara Falls. Staying with my uncle hardly got a mention. We would go it alone somehow, somewhere.

As we had such limited time, we decided to do some of the tourist things – the Empire State Building and all that. We quickly got ourselves into an uncomfortable situation trying to get the most out of the strange New York bus ticket system. Every ticket was valid for a second journey for a couple of hours after you bought the ticket. We used half a ticket to see the Hard Rock Café, which was on Briony's list for some reason. We walked in, looked at the prices, then turned around and walked out. Using the second half of our ticket, we asked the driver to drop us off at the closest point due north of the Empire State Building. As he pulled up, he asked us to be careful, saying to Briony, "They might think you're a queen walking down there, lady." We learned quickly that New York was a city where you could walk into a different universe within a couple of blocks. We went from nondescript apartment blocks to burned-out buildings and derelict car lots within the space of less than a hundred metres. Grim-looking groups sat on packing crates in wastelands of rubble behind crumbling facades of what used to be buildings. A drunk lay comatose in the gutter, the plaster cast on his broken leg shattered and broken around him, shaking his head and mumbling. The car lot owners sat sweating in cheap folding chairs at the front of the lot, looking at us in disbelief. For the umpteenth time in a couple of days my street radar was off

## 9 THE CITY THAT NEVER SLEEPS

the scale. New York seemed a crazy place to be in, if you wanted life to be safe.

Later I looked up the area, and learned it was the Bowery slums.

We'd managed to contact Jerry and were relieved at how glad he was to hear from us. He visited us at the apartment, echoing Victor's suggestion that we stay there. He gave us a few more warnings about New York: always carry your wallet in your front pocket, never use a Left Luggage locker at the Port Authority bus terminal as there were lots of counterfeit keys around. Never go further north than 100th Street, never go into Central Park after dark, and never stop to talk to anyone trying to get your attention on the street. It was ironic that we'd broken most of these already and got away with it! We also learned that we weren't quite as lucky as we'd thought with the apartment. Jerry told us that the eviction lawyers were getting access rights to the apartments, breaking in and changing the locks. If you thought you had a case to retrieve your gear, you had to go to court to argue it. With these sage words of advice he left, taking his academic qualification certificates that were on the wall with him, to avoid any trace of names.

The plan was that one of us would have to be always in the apartment. I also jigged the fire escape exit so we could open it in a split second, and we stored our gear next to the door. As no-one else would be taking anything from the place except the lawyers, anything we wanted was ours. I knew the big tape recorder and piano were out of the question, but the steel microphone was portable. There were also wardrobes full of clothes of all descriptions, and the three of us paraded around the flat in a bizarre array of paraphernalia, Colin in a huge sombrero and cheesecloth kaftan, and Briony wearing psychedelic harlequin patchwork pants.

Jerry had told us we should take the Staten Island ferry from the Wall Street end of Manhattan, as this gave magnificent views of Manhattan and the Statue of Liberty for the princely sum of twenty-five cents. Briony and I set out, with Colin happy to stay in the apartment with a bottle of wine or two.

The Statue of Liberty looked exactly as we expected it to, but knowing it was a gift from the French after some war or other, we wondered how Gallic pride could have coped with donating something so iconic to a race that the French, and particularly Parisians, regarded as inferior.

I liked Staten Island. After Manhattan, it seemed a different planet. We walked past the rusting hulks of older-generation American cars and felt like we were walking through a Bruce Springsteen song. On the ferry back we heard wafts of live music. We followed the sounds and came across two buskers hard at it, singing some early Beatles stuff in scarily tight harmony. I'd heard lots of buskers belting out Beatles songs, but these two guys were nailing the harmonies and at least some of the 'unknown chords' that make the songs so brilliant, and for a muso, addictive. This was far more exciting than the views and we watched them the whole way back. They only played the Beatles, which I thought was highly unusual, being in America. We got talking to them, and they were cautious until they realised we were English, at which point we suddenly became highly interesting because we came from near (in their eyes) the mythical Liverpool, home of the Beatles and all things musically wonderful. Their names were Josh and Jonathon, which I thought would make a great name for a band, but they didn't get it.

The now-empty ferry was starting to fill up with people going back the other way and I wondered if Josh

## 9 THE CITY THAT NEVER SLEEPS

and Jonathon would play again, but it was obvious their shift was over. A gaggle of South American musicians with pan pipes and drums were hovering, and Josh and Jonathon quickly shuffled their guitar cases aside to let them set up. Local protocol at work. I'd discovered an insight into the New York approach to busking, in the last place I would ever have thought of looking.

As we walked off the ferry it was obvious that Jonathon wasn't well. He could hardly lift his feet off the ground and stared ahead as if blind. I was amazed that he could belt out the songs so strongly.

They were obsessed with the Beatles and riveted by our Englishness, asking lots of questions. They were under the impression it was still 1965 in England and everyone had Beatles posters on their walls. I tried hard to avoid shattering their dreams, partly through selfishness – as I wanted to make sure we met up with these guys again – and partly because it was so obviously a core part of their being that somewhere there was a mythical land where people still lived and breathed the music they played.

We talked briefly about my chances of busking in New York but it quickly became apparent that it wasn't going to happen. They confirmed that busking on the streets in New York was downright dangerous. As for the ferries, like London, I'd have to pass my 'audition' and, like Covent Garden, be good enough to pass the audition. That just wasn't going to happen in the time we had.

We talked for half an hour or so then exchanged phone numbers and addresses and a promise to meet up again. When they found out we were staying a block from where John Lennon got shot, they regarded this as an omen. They disappeared off into the gloom of the subway, Jonathon shuffling along like a man of eighty.

Briony and I talked money on the subway back to the apartment. We could survive in New York now that we were rent free, but with busking looking impossible we would struggle for the two months. Also, we would have to catch a bus to put some serious distance between New York and ourselves before we could think about hitching – it just seemed too dangerous.

When we got back to the apartment a woman was standing in the foyer. She asked us straight out if we lived there. Bearing in mind Jerry's warnings about private detectives and lawyers and changing locks, we just put on our best English accents and acted confused. This seemed to work; she smiled and said for us to enjoy our stay in New York. We all three got in the elevator and instead of pressing 'nine' I pressed the seventh floor, staring Briony into silence. We hopped out at the seventh, waved goodbye and raced up the fire escape to our floor, making sure the coast was clear before opening the door. Living rent free in the Upper West Side was good, but I knew that by the end of the week I would have had my fill of having to go through all this just to get inside.

Colin clearly had had no such issues. He was lying naked and unconscious on the big double bed, a one-and-a-half litre bottle of Botticelli wine beside him, almost empty. So much for our faithful guard dog.

That night we were enjoying a very acceptable meal cooked by Colin, washed down with the other bottle of Botticelli, when at 10pm all the lights went out. I went down to the street and managed to find a place open that sold candles. I bought a whole box full, prompting the

## 9 THE CITY THAT NEVER SLEEPS

storekeeper to make some wry comment about not making the power bill this month.

We made the best of it – you really could do a lot worse than eating by candlelight with a half-decent bottle of wine, good company and the glow of Manhattan coming in through the windows.

After dinner we decided to hit the streets, and to make life more interesting we wore our crazy foraged outfits. I looked the most sane, with my trusty busking hat being the only thing out of the ordinary. Briony put on the harlequin pants, a big feather boa and a spangly opera-singer headdress. Colin got the award for the wildest look, with the giant sombrero, the translucent cheesecloth kaftan and a hot pink singlet underneath that he could just squeeze into. We looked entirely bizarre, which would probably mean we would fit in on the streets at night in New York City. We headed for Broadway, about a five-minute walk away. To be on the safe side we took no money with us, although we did take a glass of wine each. We felt that would finish off our image nicely.

We felt a frisson of daring as we stepped out, getting the giggles at the image we presented. Broadway was just another big street for the first few minutes, but we soon came across a strange scene that grabbed our attention. In a tiny corner park about a hundred people were walking around in the same direction. We made our way to a park bench in the middle of the circling horde to try and find out what was going on. We got more than a few looks, doubtless because of our wild appearance, but as soon as we sat down, the looks became more hostile looks. We were gestured to keep moving but were in a crazy mood by this time and decided to sit it out and see what happened. After a couple of minutes one of the circle walkers came over, an angry looking Puerto Rican. He asked us what the fuck we thought we were doing. It was time for the plummy English accents again and we innocently said we were out for an evening stroll and were just taking a breather. The accents, coupled with our wild appearance, threw him off balance and he changed immediately from threatening to bemused.

"You guys are crazy – just crazy." Colin, helped by a full day of slugging down wine, answered with an excellent Noel Coward impression. "No dear boy, we are British, frightfully British."

The Puerto Rican's grin widened, and he laughed out loud. We had graduated from being crazy to being 'cool'. He returned to his laps around the park. We continued watching and realised we were witnessing a drug buying and selling exercise. People would wander out of the night, mingle with the circulating throng, mutter about prices and products, little plastic bags and wads of notes would change hands and the person would disappear back into the night without anyone stopping or sitting down. It turned out that sitting down could be construed as loitering and gave the police grounds for picking you up, but if you kept moving, the odds of getting busted were much smaller. This seemed even better than the guy getting a parking ticket outside the brothels of 42nd Street – it was okay to sell heroin on the street as long as you didn't sit down while you were doing it.

The word quickly passed among the circulating dealers that we were crazy Englishmen and therefore exempt from the normal protocols of late-night drug trafficking on the streets of New York. A few came over to hear our weird accents. When he'd finished his glass of wine, Colin circled the park, looking magnificently crazy as he strolled along in the kaftan, the enormous brim of the sombrero bobbing in time with his footsteps.

At the time it didn't feel strange that mingling with heroin dealers on a New York street, dressed like a carnival sideshow, would make me more relaxed about life – but then I was in a strange headspace.

We arranged to meet up with Jonathon one night and had a strange time of it. Being English, we automatically proposed the idea of going to a pub, which in New York meant a bar. We spent a dreadful two hours sitting in some dark neon-drenched hole with music pounding out so loud none of us could talk to each other. The only other people there seemed to be hookers and sad rich businessmen who didn't want to go home. We salvaged the night by going back to Jonathon's place in Greenwich. His place was obsessively spotless and clean and there were steel shutters over the windows, even though he lived three floors up. We started playing. Jonathon began with his obsessive Beatles renditions before moving on to his own stuff, which was heavily derivative of early Lennon/McCartney. I hate sitting through people playing their own songs and then having to endorse them, but it was harder than ever with Jonathon, partly because of the Beatles echoes and partly because he really was so very unwell. He could hardly see and moved like a man crippled with arthritis. He talked at length about trying to find a doctor who could make him see and walk again, and of how his insurance had already run out twice. He was desperate to try some different kind of treatment.

AIDS was something we'd heard of, but it wasn't yet the scourge it became. I will never know for sure if Jonathon

Briony in Times Square.

## 9 THE CITY THAT NEVER SLEEPS

had it, but in hindsight he probably did. He was a gentle and kind guy who just happened to be living in a time warp. After a couple of hours he tired and suggested we should see some of Greenwich Village while we were there. The Village was wonderful. Bob Dylan had walked these streets and played at cafes here in the year I was born. We did a couple of coffee shops and got a whole new feel for the city. If I was staying in New York for any length of time this is where I knew I would end up; like Saint-Michel, it felt like home. The presence of music was everywhere. I even saw a busker, but he looked lost and desperate planted on the pavement with cars going by three feet away, and I knew this wasn't a spot I would try either.

Jonathon had also told us to check out the street life at Washington Square. At last, something approximating street performance! There was a comedian with a portable PA doing some stand-up routine with an audience of a couple of hundred, and a few mime and juggling acts with lots of fire and dazzle. It was almost midnight and there was a large press of people. I kept a close hand on my wallet. Briony and I would separate, wander around soaking up the atmosphere and then meet up again. I was enjoying it immensely, but a couple of times Briony came back looking tense.

"I'm being followed and groped by some old bastard, and I'm getting scared." She meant it. We stuck close after that. Any further exploring hands quickly disappeared when she turned and yelled at them.

We didn't leave Washington Square until after 2am. It was still pumping. At this time of night the subway was even more oppressive and threatening, but we got back to the apartment without any grief. I slept soundly, feeling we were finally getting under the skin of this crazy city.

We woke the next morning to the sound of water being thrown out of the window from the apartment above, and when I went to the bathroom, I discovered we were flooded. Something had blocked in the pipes below us and all the water from higher floors was backing up through the bath plughole. Briony and I spent the morning bailing water and keeping guard on the apartment while Colin went out to see something of the city. On his way back in, it was his turn to get the third degree from someone in the foyer. What with no power, water coming back at us out of the drains and people asking awkward questions every time we wanted to go in or out, the apartment wasn't really feeling like a good place to be. But it was free rent.

Briony and I knew we had to make a decision on how we were going to get out of New York, so we headed back to the bus terminal yet again. On the way we went to 72nd Street and found the doorway where John Lennon was shot. There were poems and messages scribbled around the door and painted on the pavement. It was very sombre and sad and completely at odds with the hot sunshiny day and bustle of the city.

We spent a depressing couple of hours at the bus terminal, queuing up to ask questions, doing sums, looking at maps to find the best and cheapest way out. I was sitting glumly out on the pavement when a very hairy and happy guy wandered past and asked if I had a light. When I said no, he smiled and said, "Damn it, how am I gonna set myself on fire, man?" He took another look at me. "Hey man, don't look so down, Neil Young is still makin' music and life is GOOD." I smiled back at him. He told me his name was Sonny. When Briony returned I introduced them and went back to continue our research. By the time I got

## 9 THE CITY THAT NEVER SLEEPS

back the two of them were putting some money together to buy a 'nickel bag' of dope and some Thunderbird liquor. Sonny disappeared with the money and neither of us really expected him to come back. We were oddly contented to get ripped off by such a laidback and nice guy, so were amazed when he came back ten minutes later with the dope and the bottle of Thunderbird. We decided to take some time out and retired to a back alley to drink the booze and 'smoke reefer', as Sonny described it.

It turned out Sonny was the very person we needed to have met at that moment. He was Canadian and had been travelling round the US and Canada for the last three years, mostly hitching. He'd hitched north out of New York several times and told us the way to do it was to walk to the Lincoln Tunnel and get a lift right there. When we asked about dangerous lifts he smiled. "Well, there's a traffic cop in a booth about fifty feet away from where you're standing, so if things look mean, just holler at him. But you can normally tell if the guy picking you up is some kind of axe murderer. I've been travelling three years and I've never had a problem yet."

This all sounded very reassuring after the nightmare letter from my uncle and Jerry's dire tales of mean old New York. Even better, Sonny gave us his address, which was somewhere on the west side of Canada. He was on his way back there and expected to be home in about two weeks. If we blew it getting back into America again, we could drop in to see him. He even talked about resurrecting a car he had and the three of us driving across Canada. We decided on the spot that we would take his advice and hitch out, as the bus thing was all too depressing and hard and completely at odds with what we'd come here to do.

We spent two hours with Sonny in the alley behind the bus station, sitting in the sun smoking dope and drinking the Thunderbird. It felt wonderful. A marvellous discovery was finding out his real name was Cyril Thistle. Cyril was the last name in the universe you would pick for this giant gentle bear of a man. We gave him an English pound note as a memory of our time together and bade him farewell. I had a feeling we would meet up with Sonny again in Canada, as I had little hope of getting back into the US.

We walked all the way back to the apartment, feeling on top of the world. We bought a road atlas and hung out in Central Park for a couple of hours, basking in the sunshine and tracing our fingers across the route through upstate New York to Canada. We tried not to look too hard at the wide-open spaces west of us where we might never be allowed to go.

When we arrived, Colin was getting ready to leave for Ithaca. We couldn't face the idea of going to the bus terminal again, so we bid him farewell on the sidewalk, watching him weave his way through the crowds, showing the effects of the latest bottle of wine and his heavy pack.

The next problem was what to do with all our stuff. We still only had the one pack between us and had nearly doubled our clothes from ransacking the wardrobes. I also couldn't leave the microphone behind. I phoned Jerry to ask if we could store stuff at his place. After telling us we were mad to be hitching out of New York City, he obliged, if we dropped it off. So, working in the warm glow of candlelight in the now ransacked flat, we got down to packing what we regarded as our bare minimum. The guitar added a huge amount of bulk, but I knew I'd have to start busking at some point for us to stay alive, so leaving it wasn't an option.

# 9 THE CITY THAT NEVER SLEEPS

I ran all the way to Jerry's. It was dark and carrying an expensive-looking bag towards the Harlem end of the city didn't seem very safe. I found Jerry's place, and tried several times to explain to the old Puerto Rican concierge who the bag was for, but it was impossible to know how much he really took in. I had no choice but to believe it was all going to be OK.

I then ran all the way back to the apartment, not so much through fear this time, but excitement. It felt like this was the start of the real trip.

Our last night in the apartment felt very strange. A lightning storm somewhere off the mainland flickered silently on the ceiling, and thunder rumbled quietly. With no power, the apartment was very quiet. Any sounds seemed magnified – the dripping of a tap, the creaking of floorboards as someone walked around upstairs, a cockroach skittering behind a skirting board somewhere. I thought of the dead opera singer's things around us. The evidence of our rifling was evident in the opened cupboards and things lying around on the floors. Half-burned candles dotted almost every flat surface in the apartment. On impulse I removed all the deadlocks from the fire escape door in case we had to make a run for it, and, irrationally, lay awake for hours listening for any signs of the lawyers trying to break in. Briony, on the other hand, slept like a log.

Next morning we crammed down the last of a loaf of bread and scanned the apartment one more time for things we might still be able to take. There was a sense of reluctance to leave our sanctuary, but at the same time we were eager for the road. We closed the door behind ourselves for the last time and made our way down to the street, breathing one last 'thank you' to Victor and Jerry.

For about the sixth time, we took the bus to the Port Authority bus terminal. From there it was a five-minute walk to the entrance of the Lincoln Tunnel – not easy going with all our gear. We stopped halfway to smoke the last of the dope that we'd bought with Sonny. My head went into an instant spin; it was 7.30 in the morning.

The Lincoln Tunnel was exactly as Sonny had described it. A confusing maze of traffic cones attempted to make sure everyone drove where they were meant to, and a uniformed man sat in a small glass-sided booth on the roadside just before the tunnel dived underground. He watched us weave our way through the cones with a look of mild disbelief on his face, but armed with Sonny's good vibe advice, we didn't waver. Making sure he saw our Union Jack bag, we gave him a friendly nod and a wave, turned our back on him to face the oncoming traffic, and stuck our thumbs out for the first time in America.

This was too much for him and he came out for a closer look, sauntering over to us with a half-official, half-amused air. I sized him up and thought that the innocent English tourist act would work. I was right. He became very relaxed and friendly and asked if we could move about fifty feet back towards Manhattan so that we were out of his jurisdiction. We were happy to oblige, and he returned to his booth a happy man.

After less than ten minutes a tired-looking black hatchback pulled over and the young driver offered to take us to the other side of the tunnel. We were off and, as Briony put it, we'd done New York and it hadn't done us.

Our first lift was over almost before it had begun. Ten minutes after we got in, we were through the tunnel and out again and dropped off on the New Jersey Turnpike, giving

## 9 THE CITY THAT NEVER SLEEPS

us the chance to start 'counting the cars on the New Jersey Turnpike, as we've all gone to look for America', just like in the Simon and Garfunkel song. Fortunately, we didn't have time to count many, as we soon caught another lift in a big, sleek Chrysler to the wonderfully named – but very ordinary looking – Hackensack, where we were dropped off in the main street.

Another car soon pulled up and my heart sank as I saw a policeman in uniform driving. He leaned across and asked if we knew that where we were hitching was illegal, then offered to take us somewhere better. On the way he gave us some books about how we needed God in our lives, and gave us a bit of Jehovah's Witness philosophy, which we were quite happy to listen to in order to not get fined. Fifteen minutes later he dropped us back at the New Jersey/New York state line. Confusingly, we realised we were going back into New York State.

"Two states in less than an hour – not bad!" quipped Briony. The cop dropped us at a tiny truck stop on Interstate 87, which he assured us was legal. It may have been legal, but it was an awful place to hitch. We decide to hump our way up the interstate to what looked like a more promising intersection. By now we were close to the edge of the vast urban sprawl surrounding New York City, and hoped we'd catch a decent long ride. And so we did. Our next driver took us thirty miles up state. He'd hitched from Tucson to New York himself a couple of years back and was keen to educate us. His two main themes were to never stop walking in the direction you wanted to go – which, loaded like packhorses as we were, I knew we would be keeping to an absolute minimum – and to never travel without water, which seemed like a very good piece of advice. Ironically, two minutes after he dropped us off, we realised we'd left our water bottle in his car.

We took time out to have a breather and take stock. Four lifts in an hour and a half were better than we would have dared to dream, and we were dazzled by how easy it seemed to be. I was euphoric at finally setting off on the dream that had sat inside me for a whole year. It was a great feeling, but it was hard work to keep moving. Loading and unloading the gear eight times really rammed home how heavy we were travelling. It was almost embarrassing how we loaded up a normal size car when we got all our gear and ourselves in.

This wasn't an issue for our next lift, a huge utility truck, with more than enough room in the trayback to swallow up our gear. We sat three across on the big bench seat, Briony in the middle. Our driver was a very sociable racehorse owner called Jim, who drove us north for a good two hours and insisted on buying us a burger and a beer for lunch. We were flattered by his hospitality, but also frustrated at his laidback lunch approach. It was well over an hour by the time we'd ordered and he'd chatted to the barman and had his second beer. In retrospect we were still living on frantic New York time and Jim was very much in chilled upstate mode. Maybe that was what we needed to start unplugging us from the mania of Manhattan. Whatever the reason, once we took off Briony ran out of steam and fell asleep with her head on Jim's shoulder. I watched out of the corner of my eye as to how Jim would take this, but he just kept driving with a wise old smile on his face. He was a nice guy.

He dropped us at a shocker of a truck stop at a place called Albany North and disappeared with a relaxed wave.

Our next lift was at the opposite end of the nice person spectrum. I don't really understand why he picked us

## 9 THE CITY THAT NEVER SLEEPS

up as he spent most of his time slagging off hitchhikers, musicians and the English, but as long as we kept moving north neither of us really cared. We told him we were going to Montreal and from there to Ottawa and couldn't believe our ears when he said they must be small places because he'd never heard of them. It was our first real taste of America being the entire universe to Americans.

We drove north with him for well over two hours through the eastern side of the Adirondack Mountains. It was beautiful country. By the time he dropped us off, there was a hint of evening in the air. We were still only about two-thirds of the way to Montreal and at least two hundred miles from Ottawa. The interstate was devoid of traffic, so we decided to stretch our legs and prepare ourselves for sleeping under a bridge somewhere. It was warm, with no hint of rain. Just then the first car we'd seen in ages appeared, and we suddenly started windmilling to the road with arms flying and just about parting company with the guitar and pack in our efforts to get their attention. Amazingly, they stopped. They were French Canadians and were going all the way to Montreal. The bad news was they were coming back from a bike race and had two bikes on top of the car and loads of gear in the back. It was almost physically impossible to get both of us and all the gear in, and I could see they were on the point of saying it was all too hard. But we somehow managed to squeeze ourselves in, and, sprawling across the pack and the guitar, we gave them a cheerful smile from the back. They shrugged their shoulders, laughed, and indicated in sign language that if we were happy then so were they. We were very happy – it was too good a lift to knock back – but trying to fit ourselves round all the gear was hard work!

They spoke little English, and their French sounded bizarre to our ears, used as we were to the Parisian accent. We couldn't understand much of what they said, which felt strange after our time in Paris where we could understand virtually everything.

They were happy for us to stay quiet in the back, and we were very happy to be still travelling north. The Canadian border would be coming up soon, and I was thinking they would drop us off there, as it would take much longer to get through immigration with us on board. But we really wanted Montreal.

The border eventually appeared and what I had been thinking obviously just occurred to the French Canadians. As the customs officials worked their way down the line, they had a hurried conversation, then whispered back to say that if asked, we were with them. It seemed we had our lift to Montreal.

It took well over an hour to get through customs and immigration. Canadian immigration was very laid back after our experience in New York, and my Canadian uncle's letter of guardianship really helped.

When we finally emerged from the other end of the bureaucratic mill, our Canadian chauffeurs were sitting in the car with the engine running trying their best to look cheerful. We shrugged apologetically, snaked our way into our respective nests in between the gear, and drove on into the dark and moonless night.

As well-lit built-up areas started to flash past the window, I sensed we were coming into Montreal. It was well past ten o'clock, and my mind was again racing with what we should do to get through the night. We had used up more than our share of goodwill with our drivers. Sleeping rough in the city

## 9 THE CITY THAT NEVER SLEEPS

was bottom of the list, ringing Uncle Barry and begging for a lift to Ottawa was top, but I doubted he'd be impressed. We might have to find a cheap hotel room somewhere.

The offer of a bed option evaporated as the car pulled over at a Metro station. With a smile and a wave from the rear-view mirror, the message was clear. We unloaded our gear, trying not to think about them going to a house that probably had enough room on the floor for a couple of freeloading Brits with nowhere to go.

We entered the Montreal metro. It was a different universe, shiny and new, with stainless steel, neon, and inane piped music that had me wanting to rip the speaker out of the roof within two minutes.

We asked about finding a cheap bed for the night and were given some directions. We emerged onto a street that felt like a mini–Latin Quarter and 42nd Street rolled into one, with an unmistakably French feel to it and some light-hearted sleaze as well. It felt good and we decided to book a place for the night. We rang my uncle to let him know we were alive. Barry sounded very relieved to hear from us, and amazed that we were in Montreal. He suggested getting a bus to Ottawa, as we were only about 125 miles away. It was so late this hadn't even occurred to me, and in any case, it had been a long day and we'd just about run out of steam. Barry didn't give up easily though, and the next minute was saying he would drive over and pick us up. I stepped out of the phone booth with mixed feelings, and when I told Briony what was happening, she seemed to feel the same. Montreal felt like a good place to spend a bit of time, and I was sure I could make some money busking here, but it was not to be. We knew we had a while to wait and so took it in turns strolling down the one-street Latin Quarter of Montreal while the other guarded the gear. It all felt very small-town after New York, which suited us just fine. We even had time to get on the Metro again and took a picturesque ride around the edge of the large lake that Montreal sits on; the lights of the city reflecting on the water through the enormous picture windows.

The bus station was the cleanest I'd ever seen, a different universe to the vast brooding hulk of the Port Authority bus station in New York. I was amazed to see that buses left for Ottawa every hour throughout the night and thought of Barry doing a two hundred and fifty-mile round trip when we could have just hopped on a bus – but such is life.

Close to midnight, Barry finally pulled in, in the huge old wagon he'd described to us. I recognised it straight away – I could see my grandma perched in the back seat, all fired up and ready to welcome one of her brood. We were enveloped in lots of pecking on the cheek from aunts and grandmas and back-slapping from Uncle Barry. This all felt very weird indeed after all our adventures, and both Briony and I had problems taking it all seriously. For the eighth time that day we loaded our gear into a car, but this time, knowing we had a bed at the other end, let our exhaustion take over. We were both asleep within ten minutes.

We woke as we bounced into the driveway of Auntie Jill's and Uncle Barry's home. I had been seeing photos of it since I was four years old. It felt very surreal – my cousins Jeanette and Richard saying hi, a friendly dog, cups of tea and lots of fussing that we really weren't used to – and weren't really looking for. But at the same time, it was relaxing to be able to turn off my street 'radar' for a while and not worry about getting through the next day.

## 9 THE CITY THAT NEVER SLEEPS

Briony was sharing a room with my cousin Jeanette, and I was in the basement at the opposite end of the house. We had crispy clean sheets and big fluffy towels, hot water in the shower and a fully stocked fridge that we had free access to. Even though it wasn't what we were here for, it would be easy to get used to. I drifted into sleep after a long hot shower, still vaguely marvelling at the fact that we could get from the middle of New York City to Ottawa in a day, a distance of over four hundred miles, crossing an international border in the process. It took around eighteen hours in total. Not bad for a first day, not bad at all.

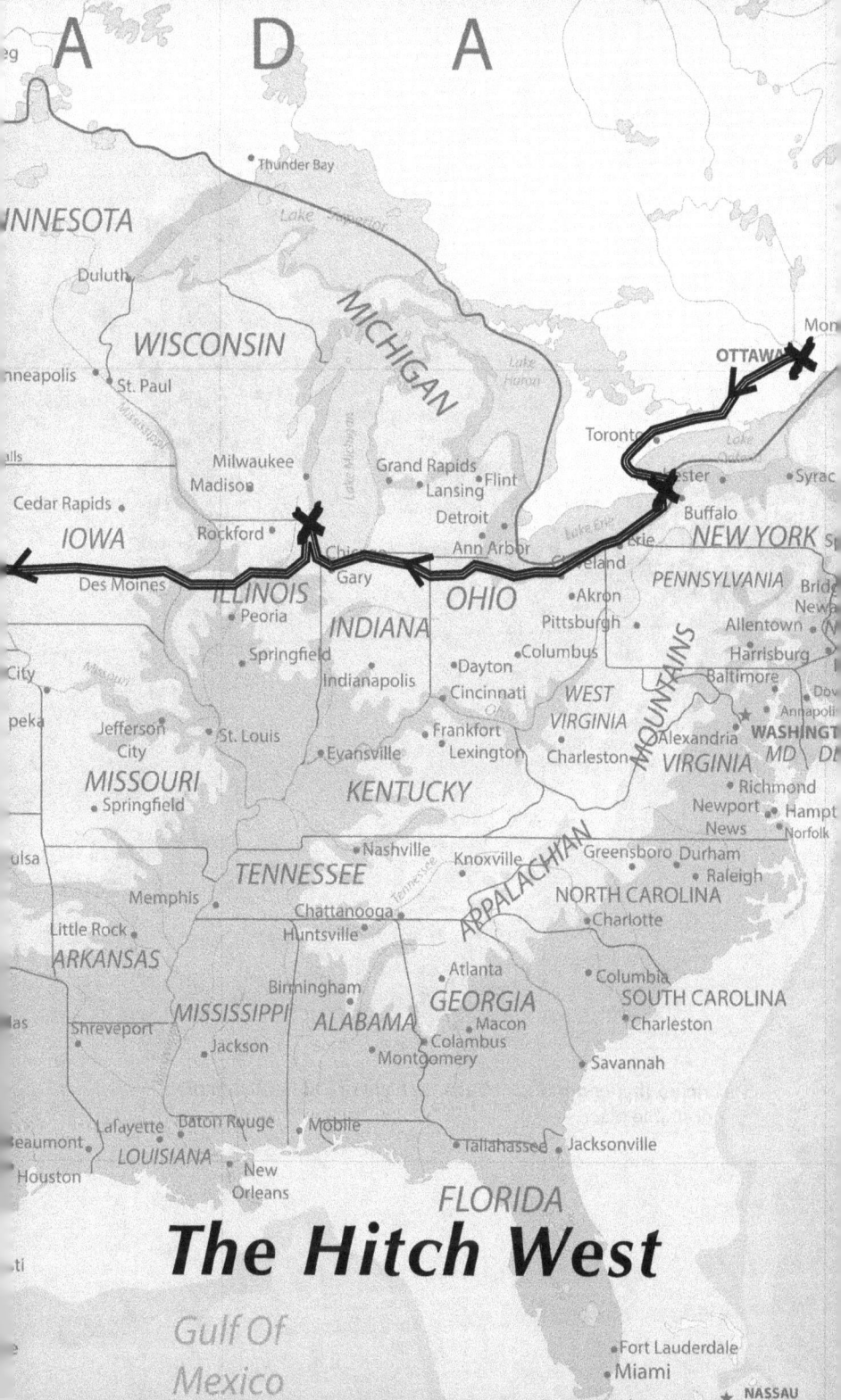

**Hejira** [hej-er-*uh*] *noun, Arabic.* A flight or journey to a more desirable place.

# 10 HEJIRA

*I'm porous with travel fever
But you know I'm so glad to be on my own*
Hejira, Joni Mitchell, 1976

We were quickly immersed in the all-embracing hospitality of aunts and uncles and cousins and grandmas. It was a strange experience. I wasn't used to the 'big happy family' vibe. They were cautiously hospitable to Briony, but carefully avoided any talk about what we'd been up to, concentrating instead on organising the standard tour all my family members did when we visited 'the Canadians'. I had no desire to go, and neither did Briony. We didn't say anything as we'd just arrived, but one thing I was certain of, even if we couldn't get back into the States there was no way we could stay here for the whole two months.

Briony and I were getting on well, but it was, as always, a strange relationship. We were becoming aware of all the difficult places we didn't go in conversations to avoid any hassle, and I knew I showed my irritation at some of her crazier antics too easily, but after an intense day like we'd had travelling from New York to Ottawa, followed by the full-on rellie experience, we realised that we had a whole lot in common – enough to keep going, anyway.

Then everything went to pieces. We were taking a bike ride beside the Ottawa River on a gravel path when Briony lost control of her bike going down a shallow hill. She went headfirst over the handlebars and all those saving reflexes failed to work again, and she landed face first, sliding several feet along the gravel. As I picked her up, blood streamed from her face and her forearms were a real mess, but she was still smiling and shrugging apologetically through the mask of blood. I'm ashamed to say the first thought in my head was how the hell we would ever be able to hitch with her looking like she'd had her face ripped off.

We got her to the hospital, making sure we took along all the paperwork showing her travel and health insurance. Briony insisted on taking the faithful rock as her security talisman. Getting through the hospital administration was bizarre; they insisted she keep signing bits of paper to make sure they were financially covered while all the time blood was pouring out of the wounds on her face and arms. She never cried and hardly seemed to show any signs of pain. They took her away and, as she described it afterwards, used what felt like a scouring pad to get all the dirt out of her wounds, taking a good deal more skin off in the process. They put a couple of stitches in her chin, which seemed to have hit the ground first. She looked a lot better when she finally re-emerged from casualty after a couple of hours, but her face was red raw like sunburn, and she was obviously now in considerable pain. I gave her an awkward encouraging hug, and we travelled in silence back to the house, she still clutching the rock and staring straight ahead, tears in her eyes and biting her lip but refusing to give into the pain.

The next day her face was quite swollen and was starting to scab up. She looked terrible but seemed to be feeling better, so we went to see the sights of downtown Ottawa. It was all very touristy with big government buildings, men in silly uniforms, and of course the Mounties. However, given what had happened, a bit of inane wandering around suited Briony quite well for the day. I was trying to hide my frustration at what I saw as the end of our plans of doing the wide-open road thing but she knew what I was thinking and made a point of telling me that this wouldn't change anything. She was still as keen as ever to go for the big hitch. That was all very well, but she still looked as if she'd had a cheese grater run over her face, and I couldn't believe it would do anything for our chances of getting a lift.

As it turned out, we did a lot of touristy things with my relatives, canoeing around lakes and windsurfing and messing about in sailing dinghies. Probably the most memorable thing we did in Ottawa was go to a drive-in movie. It felt like the most real thing we'd done since we got there, buying popcorn, sitting in the big old Dodge and watching the youth of Canada going through their courtship rituals while *Ghostbusters* unrolled on the enormous screen. I also found a copy of the *The Grapes of Wrath* somewhere in the house, and devoured the stark, vivid writing of Steinbeck, knowing that I wanted to do the same journey the Joads did across the mountains to California. I loved the brutal, naked honesty of the book, and the unbreakable guts and integrity of the family. It was my escape from the cotton-wool inanity of living in suburban Canada.

Finally, after a week, Briony seemed well enough for us to get going. We'd decided to head for a place called Oshawa, which was on the way to Niagara Falls. We'd chosen this as our point to try and get back into the US, partly because it was west, in the direction we wanted to be going, and partly because, averse to being tourists as we were, the Falls was something we actually wanted to see. We also had the offer of a lift there from a cousin's boyfriend.

The family was very gushy at our leaving and worried about Briony, but she'd made it quite clear that she wanted to be away as much as I did. We left in a flurry of being handed toilet rolls and sun cream and mosquito repellent and a nice lunch and though it was all very kind, we were just about screaming by the time we finally got out of the driveway. The best gift by far was that they were happy for me to take *The Grapes of Wrath* with me.

The journey down to Oshawa was quite enlightening. Canada seemed to be one huge pine forest, and we drove for hours without seeing any real sign of civilisation. We were dropped off at a hitching point west of Oshawa, and got a good run of lifts that took us through Toronto, round the west of Lake Ontario and on into Niagara Falls. Our favourite lift was in a vast sixteen-wheeler Dodge truck with a guy who reckoned he'd dodged the draft for Vietnam. It felt wonderful hauling ourselves up the steps to sit in a cab from where you could look down on everyone else on the road. Niagara wasn't what I expected – lots of neon, naff honeymoon hotels and gangs of aimless teenagers wandering around looking for something to do.

We'd travelled over 500km and needed somewhere to sleep. We were exhausted. I played guitar for a while to some of the kids and tried to work out if there was anywhere we could crash in the park. We weren't particularly bothered about getting a hotel. As I played we watched two cops wander into the throng of teenagers and arrest one for no reason we could work out. If we slept rough, I had the feeling we ran a high risk of the same fate – not ideal the day before we planned to try and get back into the US. So we found a little bed and breakfast place next to the river, which at twelve bucks each was a wonderful deal. Once we had the gear somewhere safe we made our way up to the Horseshoe Falls. It was a remarkable sight: a vast bulk of water rolling ponderously and silently off the canyon's edge, then exploding loudly when it hit the river at the bottom, spray and spume fogging the river back up the Falls and creating phantom rainbows everywhere. Sadly, the impact was vastly reduced by all the concrete and hype that had grown like a running sore around it. To make something so awesome and powerful seem clichéd took a fair bit of effort, but the tourist trade had managed it and we felt no desire to be there for very long.

As we headed back to our b'n'b we got talking to one of the teenagers who had been in the park when the police showed up. He asked if we had all the paperwork to get across the border. When we admitted we were not confident of getting in, he told us that we should get there as near to nine o'clock in the morning as possible, as this was when the shifts changed and the guys were much more inclined to do a rubber stamp job so they could go home.

We thanked him for this useful bit of advice. Our elation at another good day's travelling was slowly being taken over by thoughts of how important the next twenty-four hours were going to be for the future of our adventure.

The next morning we were ready to leave at eight. I got out the map to check directions, but Briony started on about the vibes thing again and I lost it and said, "OK, tell me which way the vibes are telling us to go."

She got her hunted-rabbit look, and after thirty seconds of contemplation starting walking in completely the opposite direction of where we needed to be going. I lost it even more, knowing that if we blew the timing this could torpedo any chance we had of getting back into the US. After a short sharp row Briony retreated into her shell and I went back to the map, vibes or no vibes, and in twenty minutes we were at the footbridge over the twenty-mile canyon that ran between Lake Ontario and Lake Erie. It certainly formed a most effective border. The bridge was an amazing contraption, a suspension bridge less than six feet wide, strung a couple of hundred feet up in the air at a point where the river was around three hundred yards wide. The border checkpoint was on the far side. It was a dramatic walk; strung out across this enormous breathtaking river gorge, with an impending showdown with the border guards at the other end. Real high adventure stuff. I felt like we were in some James Bond movie, timing our walk to make sure immigration were off their guard. We'd watched the bridge for a good ten minutes before we started out and no-one had gone ahead of us, so we were pretty sure the guys would be sitting there just watching the clock. We set out at a quarter-to-nine and made a big show of looking over the side and pointing up and down the gorge and generally dilly-dallying around so that we arrived at precisely three minutes to nine.

The immigration guy looked the part for the James Bond movie. He was a big guy and was fairly bursting out of his uniform, with an enormous peaked hat perched on top of his head. He exuded an aura of quiet efficiency and I was scared witless we weren't going to get in. But he actually smiled and said he'd noticed how excited we were coming across the footbridge and hoped we'd enjoyed our stay in Niagara. He then started through our paperwork, looking very hard at our money situation and at Briony's age. When he got to Colin's flowery letter about us staying with him in Ithaca I could see alarm bells going off.

"Could you please run through what your plans will be while in the United States, sir?" He eyed up the guitar and Briony's scratched and scabbed-up face. Trying to sound light-hearted, I explained that we planned to stay with Colin and do some sightseeing in the Adirondacks, and possibly team up with him to go on a drive to somewhere yet to be decided.

The tension was unbearable, made worse by the fact we were trying to hide it. He pushed back his cap to scratch his forehead with the tip of a pen, obviously weighing up whether to let us in or not. I nearly lost it when I saw him glance at his watch. It was by now past nine. I saw the slightest hint of resignation come into his stance before he gave us one long, last thoughtful stare, then stamped our passports, and wished us luck.

It was hard to stay calm until we were out of sight of the customs booth, but once we got around the corner we were whooping and hollering all over the pavement. In a moment of clarity I checked the dates to make sure we were covered until our flight home and confirmed that, yes, we had the run of the country until Virgin Atlantic took us away.

We had a celebratory burger and Sprite in the best American fashion, then turned our thoughts to what we would do next. We'd toyed with the idea of staying on the American side of the Falls for another day to see if it felt better from this side, but the view wasn't half as impressive as the Canadian side. It was almost like the Americans had turned their back on the Falls because someone else could do it better. Buffalo, the town on the American side, was small-town US industrial with hardly a trace of interest in the Falls. So we decided to head west.

We found the local bus company office and asked for a bus that would take us as far as we could go south in the direction of Interstate 90. The guy at the desk took a minute or so to work out what we were on about and then said, "Ah, now I see what you want to do," and suggested a bus that was leaving in about ten minutes. We stayed on the bus until the bitter end of the trip, then asked for directions to the freeway, which was about a ten-minute walk. It was not particularly good news when we got there – the freeway had an express tollway running down the middle and local traffic lanes on either side. Anyone in the lanes close to us would probably only be going a couple of junctions, but hitching in the long-distance middle lanes would have been suicidal. We waited less than half an hour before we were picked up, and a young mum gave us a lift just out of town, which was fine, but also dropped us on the wrong side of a tollbooth, which was disastrous. We stood for ten minutes or so on this deserted windswept junction with not a hint of a car in sight, then decided to walk back out onto the freeway. The guy in the tollbooth saw us coming and came out, shouting that it was illegal to hitch on the interstate and we would get arrested if we tried. So we retreated, but after half an hour without a single vehicle coming past, knew we had to try something else.

We could see a bridge over the freeway off in the distance and decided we would walk to this, cross back to the right side of the freeway, then climb down and hitch from the hard shoulder. The plan was good in theory, but it was a lot further than it looked to the bridge. We could feel the eyes of the tollbooth man drilling into our backs, and wondered if he would work out our plan and call the traffic cops. It took us twenty minutes of hard slogging to get to the bridge, and by the time we crossed the bridge we were sweating and straining with all the stuff. We climbed down and took refuge in the shade of the bridge to cool off for a few minutes. While we were cooling off, we realised that there was no hard shoulder or breakdown lane, so anyone stopping would have to do so on the slow lane of the freeway itself. Standing on the road was a death wish, so we had to hitch balanced precariously on the crash barrier. If our friend at the tollbooth had called the traffic cops I dreaded to think what the fine would be for doing what we were doing – it was so stupid it probably wasn't even in the books. But we didn't have a lot of choice.

We took it in turns for twenty minutes or so, praying that we would get picked up before anyone official saw us, when finally a van pulled up. It was one of those vans that they use to set up live TV broadcasts and was chock full of gear, but we got everything in somehow. The driver was completely taken by our Englishness and very sociable. He only took us a few miles but got us to a spot where there was at least a pullover lane. We'd learned not to get the wrong side of the tollbooths, but it was hair-raising stuff asking the driver to stop on the freeway. However, apparently our Englishness was so quaint he was happy to oblige, and as a parting gift he gave us a whole smoked fish that was going to be his tea. It was about two foot long and we knew it would only last about an hour before it would start to stink in the sun, so we ate as much as we could then stashed it in the coolest, most shaded spot we could find. We were clear of the city now and could hope for a decent lift. After only ten minutes an enormous truck pulled over, and a small guy with a ginger moustache and a big leery smile looked down on us. We asked where he was going and he shouted, "Chicago, make your mind up quick buddy, I'm in a hurry and you're standin' in a crazy spot." We had no idea where Chicago was, but figured it must be in basically the right direction so, with a couple more jibes from our driver, we hauled ourselves and the gear up into the truck and met Steve the Trucker. It would be an interesting experience.

Steve was big on rules. As he ground the gears he was already telling us what the drill was. He reckoned he was doing some kind of scam where he was two different drivers on the tachometer and so could drive twice as far as any other driver in a day. For some reason this meant that all stops had to be timed and on schedule. "We stop when I say we stop, we go when I say we go, you take a piss when I say you take a piss, and if you're not there when you should be, I'll go without you." I was wondering whether this was going to be worth the obvious grief he was going to put us through but when I looked at the atlas I realised that Chicago was several hundred miles west, and we would be with him for at least a day. It was a dream lift as far as getting us across the country, but he was hard work. He alternated between telling us his life story, wild things he'd seen on the road, and describing the set-up he had up in Minnesota: "Eighty acres, two horses, two Dobermans and no assholes." He reckoned he'd run away from home at sixteen and travelled the roads for a couple of years until he met up with a truck driver who took him under his wing and helped him get his ticket. "I been driving ten years now, and I've seen everything on these roads. Couples going at it driving down the road. Hell, I seen guys doin' it with other guys drivin' down the road in the middle of the night. I damn near drove them off the road they made me so mad." He talked a lot about guns and told us there was a 47-Magnum under the bunk in the back, for if we started to get any funny ideas – or anyone else for that matter.

He kept up the bluster for several hours but it didn't take long to work out that underneath it he was a reasonable guy who was lonely, needed a bit of company and was trying to make himself sound a bit more wild and interesting than he actually was. We were happy to play the wide-eyed youngsters who could learn a lot about the world from him, for the sake of a lift of over five hundred miles. After six hours or so we stopped at a fast-food place and he made us stay in the cab while he went and bought the food, shouting us both a chicken and chips, eating it in his lap and starting to drive the second he finished eating.

And we rolled along all day. The speed limit in the US was a soporific fifty-five miles an hour, and so the miles seemed to take a very long time to disappear. As the day drew on I worked out that we would either hit Chicago in the middle of the night or he would pull over for a sleep. Whatever happened we would either have to sleep with him in the truck or take our chances in the dark wherever we decided to part company. If it was the middle of Chicago this didn't sound like fun at all. It would have been really good to be able to talk it through with Briony without him being in earshot, but we didn't stop all day long and talk was impossible in the cab. However, there were weighbridges every couple of hours along the interstate to make sure trucks weren't overloaded, and each time one of these came up we had to hide in the bunk at the back of the cab. I managed a short conversation with her during one of these when Steve had to get out to talk, and she seemed relaxed about the idea of us staying with him through the night. I wasn't so sure, as his eyes were all over Briony, even though her face was such a mess.

We rolled down the south side of Lake Erie, through Cleveland and Toledo, and then struck out due west for the south end of Lake Michigan. The miles rolling under the big wheels of the truck felt wonderful, and I knew I was getting a taste of what I'd come here to find – a place where you could just keep going and going while the travel fever slowly worked itself out of your guts.

As dark came down I wondered what he would do, and he just kept right on driving. Eventually Briony had to call for a toilet stop, and he made the most of the scene. "God damn it, I only go once every two days, and I don't have time for you to delay me here. You got three minutes, and I'll only stop if I see you running, and I want to see YOU running naked!" This to Briony. I thought I might as well take advantage of the stop, figuring that Briony would take longer than me but when I got back out she was already back in the truck. Steve was revving the engine. I played his game and jogged across the tarmac, but didn't play hard enough for Steve.

"God damn it you little prick I said for you to RUN, you hear me! One more trick like that and I'll drive away and leave you behind, and take your little woman and that shit-box guitar with me!"

I decided I wouldn't be sad to see the back of Steve.

The truck finally rolled into Chicago in the middle of the night. Steve ordered us into the bunk, indicating that we had to stay out of sight while the truck was unloaded. We climbed into the back, and he disappeared. It was stifling in the bunk with the windows up and the air con off so I sneaked forward to inch down the windows, scared stiff that I would be spotted by some security guard and we would get thrown out in the middle of God-knows-where in some industrial estate in Chicago. At about 4am we heard the back of the truck lower and fork lifts and heavy boots started to transfer the load out to the warehouse. This went on for two or three hours, but by now we were beyond exhaustion and I slept through most of it. Steve appeared back in the cab and without looking around he said, "You guys cosy in there? Don't even think about trying to find that Magnum by the way, you gotta know where to look." A shiver went down my spine – to while away the hours I'd been hunting under the mattress to see what the big Clint Eastwood revolver looked like in real life.

"I'm heading for Minnesota now, so if you're going to San Diego you gotta get out. I'll drop you at a spot where you can walk up to a truck stop, but don't take too long getting out or I'll drive away with your stuff." By now I was over all the threats and just nodded tiredly at him, which didn't go down too well. Ten minutes later we ground to a halt on a busy interstate, and he pointed at a truck stop up some branch of the interstate that he reckoned was right for us. Then, without a wave from either him or us, he was gone.

We were perhaps a third of the way across America.

We slogged our gear to the truck stop and hunkered down while I got my bearings from the road atlas. I worked out that we'd taken a big detour up through Chicago with Steve, going almost as far as the Wisconsin state line to unload, then coming back through the western side of the city. The truck stop was a reasonable spot if you wanted to head south, but not good for going west. We needed to walk another mile or so to intersect with Interstate 55 for the long haul west. We sat for five minutes then started grinding our way along the tarmac, the air sucking in and out as trucks thundered past, nearly knocking us off our feet. As we plodded down the highway a part of me was thinking we should stop and take a look at Chicago, but it felt good to just keep moving, and it would have been a lot harder to work our way into the city and find a place to stay. Briony hadn't even mentioned the idea of stopping. Better to just keep moving on.

And move on we did. I made a sign that said 'Denver', a city roughly halfway across the country. We had a run of short lifts that took us right across Illinois and through Moline, and got dropped at a truck stop in Walcott, just across the Illinois border in Iowa. The entrance to the truck stop had a weird one-way system that meant that every vehicle passed us twice, once when it left the interstate and once when it went back on it. This meant we could wave our sign at trucks coming off for a stop and give them time to think about picking us up while they were having a coffee and a stretch. We'd been there half an hour when a truck came grinding up to the entrance ramp and pulled over. A grinning bearded face with a black leather cap leaned out, removed a pair of mirrored wraparound sunglasses, and shouted "I'm glad you're still here, I was hoping you would be. I can take you all the way to Denver."

And so we met up with Al Dobson. We climbed aboard and stashed our gear in the sleeping cabin and waited to see what our new companion was like. We were a little cautious after our experiences with Steve. It was about 900 miles to Denver, and I hoped we would get along with this guy. It would be a very long couple of days if we didn't. He didn't hurry the introductions, in fact Al didn't really hurry anything, and over the first few hours it became obvious he was a very different creature to Steve.

He asked questions that went below the surface of the usual hitching chat – the "where are you going, where have you come from" that usually occupied a lot of air space in the hitching universe. He was about the first person to ask *why* we were doing what we were doing, which Briony and I had never really tried to work out, other than it just felt right. This triggered more than a little internal soul searching, assisted by some gentle but acute questioning from Al. It became obvious to me that we had little interest in where we were going, as long as we just kept going. We'd missed all the things you were meant to do in New York and Ottawa, skipped through Niagara with the briefest of looks at the Falls, and passed off the chance to see Chicago. Al listened, his eyes fixed on the road but his mind obviously turning over what we were saying. After a couple of unhurried hours gazing at the hypnotic ribbon of tarmac disappearing under our wheels, he shrugged his shoulders and said, "Guys, it seems simple to me. It's the journey that's important, not the destination. It's a Buddhist thing."

And just like that, he captured our whole rambling analysis in one sentence. I had done a lot more talking than Briony, but she seemed to agree with my struggle to put into words what was pushing us onwards.

Al's cab was a different universe to Steve's. He lent Briony his little radio Walkman, and when she tried to give it back after an hour or so, he shook his head.

"No, you hang onto it for now, it gives me pleasure to watch you enjoy listening to it, and I can listen to it anytime." I couldn't imagine Steve saying something like that.

And so Al and his cosy cabin became our dream hitch. All through the day we rolled across Iowa, through Des Moines and then into Nebraska. The country slowly opened out into one giant corn field, flat as a billiard table as far as the eye could see. After a few hours my eyes started to ache for something to relieve all that flatness, but precious little appeared. The Nebraska interstate was straight as an arrow, and made of huge concrete slabs rather than tarmac. The big truck tyres made a thud each time you crossed a join between slabs, generating a hypnotic, train-like rhythm to back up our conversation, which rose and swirled and curled like smoke from a friendly camp fire. It was a mesmeric experience, helped by the hash pipe Al passed around every couple of hours. Each time we stopped to stretch, Al would come back with a small gift for us, a beer or a candy bar or an apple, smiling disarmingly and fending off our thanks. "You really don't need to do that, guys."

We established early on that Al and I were both Mad Max nuts and Al would inject a hint of Mel Gibson at the wheel to liven up the atmosphere. "I'm a burned-out shell of a man living beyond the edge of civilisation, and gee I love leather."

Night came down slowly, and we finally pulled into a truck stop. Al insisted on buying us food and lent us his key for the truckers' shower block and a clean towel each. The shower was wonderful after sweating away on the road for two days – I was wearing pretty much the same clothes as when we'd walked back into America.

Once it was dark, Al delved into a storage locker hanging under the truck and pulled out some fireworks

## 10 HEJIRA

and we had our own display right there in the truck park, with little rockets fizzing into the night sky and Roman candles spluttering on the tarmac. It was hilarious, and we got rounds of applause from the other truckies wandering to and from the diner. There was a pinball machine in the truck stop and I demonstrated one of the few things I'd actually learned proficiently at university, winning several credits and impressing Al no end.

We sat outside the truck looking at the stars for a long time after that, sometimes talking, sometimes just lost in the sky, a comfortable silence hanging over us as we breathed in the smell of the big truck – hot metal, oil and diesel.

Al exceeded his gentlemanly status by insisting that Briony and I share the bunk while he slept in the driver's seat. We protested, but he would hear nothing of it, meeting our protests with the same easy and unmoveable smile. He even kept the truck engine on idle all night to keep us all cool. I hate to think what it would have been like perched on that driver's seat all night with the truck shuddering away, but he never murmured.

We hit the road early and the next day unfolded very much the same. I'd worked out that if I sat on the bunk of the sleep cabin I could play my guitar without pushing Briony out the window and taking Al's head off with the neck of the guitar, so every couple of hours I put on a bit of a show, alternating between Neil Young, Janis Joplin, Bob Dylan and Bruce Springsteen, all familiar territory to Al. He'd never heard of The Jam, The Clash and Joy Division. Belting out *That's Entertainment* as we rolled across the corn fields of Nebraska was a surreal experience.

As we crossed into Colorado, the Rockies reared in front of us, a huge relief from the eye-aching emptiness of the corn belt. After nearly two days, about fifty miles out of Denver, we came to a grinding halt, air brakes hissing and brake drums squealing. Al turned to us and said, "Well, my friends, it's that time."

We swapped addresses and made all sorts of promises about staying in touch, then he turned the truck north and slowly disappeared into the distance, lost in the heat haze long before he reached the horizon. We watched him for a long time, sad to see him go but elated that we'd found him. A special time and a special man.

Decision time again. Night was falling, so we made the call to rent a hotel room in Denver once we got there and maybe hang out there for a couple of days while I made some money busking.

We didn't have to wait long. An old Dodge truck took us right into the heart of the city and dropped us at a street of cheap hotels. They all looked pretty much the same, and cost pretty much the same as well, so we picked one at random and booked the cheapest room they had.

Briony was completely exhausted and I wasn't far behind, but I took a short walk to try and find the heart and soul of Denver. Maybe I walked in the wrong direction, but it didn't seem to have any. I could have been on any street in any American town, all McDonald's and Burger King and glass-fronted car yards. After fifteen minutes I gave up and went back to the hotel to get some sleep. I couldn't see any way I'd be able to busk here. We might as well keep moving on.

I stared into the darkness that night with Briony sleeping beside me and tried to take stock. Briony's face had been steadily healing, but was now a mask of peeling road rash scabs. She didn't talk about it, but it must have hurt. Maybe this was why she had so much less energy than normal. After two days crawling ant-like across the vast central plains, we were both in a strange headspace. I realised I was probably going to make my trans-USA dream come true. We were over halfway now, and apart from the minor obstacles of the Rocky Mountains and about a thousand miles of desert, we were getting close – a week away at the most. It was difficult to work out how Briony really felt about all this. Most of her enthusiasm seemed to reflect me getting what I'd dreamed about; I'd given up trying to work out what she wanted to get out of the experience. It felt like we should have been feeling closer, but it wasn't happening. We were drawing apart, bickering our way across the country when we should have been together on the crest of a wave. As usual, analysing the situation with Briony didn't get me anywhere, and I put my energy back into the road.

It was time to head west. We were waving the enormous 'California' sign I'd made the night before when two young guys pulled over. They were fascinated by us being English, not just because of our accents but because they were mad keen fans of The Exploited, a seriously punk skinhead band. After they dropped us off, we got another short lift from a crazy bastard who went screaming past us, stopped, then reversed back full tilt to pick us up. We weren't sorry to get out.

We were now twenty miles west of Denver and all the traffic would be going a decent distance, so we focused on looking interesting enough to pick up. I wanted a lift at least through the mountains, to avoid any chance of getting stranded somewhere cold and miserable. I would have preferred to get across the desert as well, but this would have meant a two-day drive. We turned down a couple of lifts that were just going up into the mountains, but after an hour or so hit exactly what we wanted. Tony was going all the way to

Salt Lake City, about five hundred miles west. He was driving an old Capri fastback and had a fair amount of gear, so we had to cram to get us and the gear in. Twice he thought it was too hard, but we kept pushing and got it all in. Briony was jammed in the back and I had the big tube bag stuffed down by my legs, but we grinned and told him it was all fine, and he shrugged his shoulders and started driving.

Going up into the mountains was wonderful after two or three days on the plains. Even the names of the tiny settlements along the highway were more interesting: Parachute, Antlers and the unbeatable No Name.

Tony was a Mormon and on his way to meet up with his wife in the Mormon state of Utah after graduating from law college after nine years' study. He pushed me into one of my pet hate conversations in America, the subject of Ireland. Plenty of people who picked us up had strong views, but all seemed dazzlingly ignorant of how difficult and complex the whole situation was: the 'Brits Out' call was common from people who didn't know the difference between the Falls Road and the Shankhill, and had never heard of Ian Paisley. I made the atmosphere in the car quite tense by implying that Tony didn't know what he was talking about, and had to force myself to shut up and look out of the window for a while. Getting chucked out of a whole day's ride would have been a really bad idea.

We wound our way down the west side of the Rockies to another endless stretch of wide-open plains, but it was barren and desolate – no cornfields here. As we drove along we spied a freight train to our north, inching its way ahead of us, with the mountains as a glorious back drop. The train was over a mile long and we could see it end to end. It took a hypnotic amount of time to pull ahead of us, and

# 10 HEJIRA

I found myself deliberately looking away for as long as I could bear just so I could see some progress.

As we drove down a long, sweeping hill I spotted a hitcher standing in the middle of nowhere. He was wearing an army camouflage uniform, complete with forage cap. Seeing that our vehicle was crammed to bursting he withdrew his thumb and threw us a perfect salute. I worked out as we passed him that he was standing on a bridge that had a little stream under it, so at least he had water. God knows how he got there, he was fifty miles from anything, including the nearest junction. He must have had a falling out with his driver to get dropped somewhere so remote.

Through Grand Junction and into Utah, the Mormon state. Salt Lake City was a couple of hundred miles northwest, but we wanted to go due west. Tony kept trying to make us go with him to Salt Lake City but this would have added over 200 miles to our journey and we weren't interested. We got to the fork in the road and Tony decided if we wouldn't go to Salt Lake, he'd take us in the direction we wanted then cut back north.

An hour or so later we spied a raft of flashing lights in the distance: a police roadblock. Tony got flustered as the rego on his car had expired. We felt bad; he would never have been on this road if it hadn't been for us. As we crawled to the top of the queue, Tony told us to say we were with him if asked. The cop gazed down at us, taking in Briony crammed into the back seat.

"Where you guys goin'?" Tony told him Salt Lake City.

"You've picked a strange route, sir, you should have turned right about an hour and a half ago". Tony grinned weakly and said we were going via Nephi 'to pick up some stuff'. Eyeing the car packed to the gills, the cop helpfully suggested that we didn't pick up too much stuff or the car would be unsafe. He wasn't interested in the car rego. Tony asked why everyone was getting stopped.

"Well, partly to check on traffic going to LA for the opening of the Olympics ..." We didn't even know it was on, and the opening ceremony was tomorrow night. No wonder there was so much traffic.

"The other reason is that a couple of hitchhikers got murdered out on the road today, and we're just checking if anyone knows anything. Did you see anything suspicious?"

Briony and I were too shocked to talk, but Tony managed to mumble something about the soldier out in the middle of the desert. The cop thanked us and we drove off, no-one saying anything for a good ten minutes. Tony looked me in the eye.

"I'm dropping you at a motel in Nephi and you're going to book in, and we are not going to talk this back and forth anymore. OK?"

In the circumstances I couldn't think of anything to say, and so agreed.

Murdered. On the same road we were hitching on. Two hitchhikers. Fucking hell.

It was a fifty-mile detour north to Nephi. As we rolled into town it was dark, and Tony dropped us in front of a comfortable but ubiquitous, boring-looking motel, the facade covered in fizzing bug lamps. We pulled all the gear out and wished him luck, waving him goodbye as he pulled out of the front lot of the motel.

I suspected what was in my mind was in Briony's also. It was an awesome desert night, with giant stars hanging over our heads, and I had no desire to book into a tacky air-conditioned box when we could sleep under a sky like that. I raised my eyebrows at Briony and she nodded excitedly, and so, after Tony going two hours out of his way to get us to a place he considered safe, we walked back out into the desert to find a good place to swag out. We found a dirt track off the highway and followed it a couple of hundred yards back, found the flattest piece of dirt we could, then tried to make ourselves comfortable.

I lay in my sleeping bag gazing up at the stars, so big and real I felt like I could just reach out and pluck a handful from the velvet of the sky. It was magical. I slept very little but loved every minute. An unforgettable night.

We woke with the dawn, stiff, sore and cold. Overnight the desert ground sucked all the heat out of your body, and by morning we were cold to the marrow. We decided to walk back into town to warm up and eat a proper meal. There were a few turned heads and muttered conversations when we walked into a roadhouse. They would have seen us walking up the highway for a good ten minutes before we came through the door, so they knew we had come in off the desert after sleeping rough. The waitress had hostile eyes and a tight-lipped manner so I gave her my best plummy English accent to throw her. It worked a treat, and we became the darlings of the diner.

We finished up our breakfast feeling like film stars, with people peering at us, the mad strangers who walked out of the desert. It was a beautiful clear morning and as we left the diner I felt on top of the world. We were more than two-thirds of the way across the USA now, with only Las Vegas between us and California. I knew we would make it, it was just a question of when. We could go anywhere we felt like, we had no deadlines, no-one to go home to. The mountains were behind us and the desert was in front of us. I don't think I ever felt freer in my life than on that day. In hindsight, you'd think it might have crossed my mind that two hitchers had been murdered the day before on the road we'd just travelled, and that the murderer might just pick us up the next day. But it didn't.

We strolled up onto the highway and started walking out of town. Nephi was pretty much a one-street town and you could see one end from the other. We turned to face the traffic, and stuck out our thumbs. It turned out to be the day of the Mormons. First was Whitney, who took us an hour south to Fillmore. Fillmore was a tiny settlement scraped onto the desert, where we waited an hour, with hardly a car on the road. We soon got picked up by Jeff, a very laidback Mormon who chewed tobacco. I tried some. It was foul, like sucking used cigarette butts. Jeff had spent an adventurous night on a trampoline under the stars with his girlfriend and was completely exhausted, and after an hour or so asked if I wouldn't mind driving as he felt himself nodding off. This was fine by me, and it felt great easing the big car up to a slow cruise of fifty-five miles an hour across the rolling desert. We stayed with Jeff a couple of hours. He dropped us off in St George, an unremarkable town nestled between the red desert hills, right on the border between Utah and Nevada. Las Vegas was only 150 miles away.

We then scored our most bizarre lift yet. It was an oily old truck with a cab crammed with young men and women in party mode. They looked fun but we couldn't see how they could possibly fit us in. The driver hopped down with a huge grin, saying, "It's your lucky day guys, you're gonna travel into Vegas in style." He pulled down the tailgate of the truck and there were two sun lounges set up in the empty tray. It was ludicrous, hilarious, and perfect. The sides of the truck were too high to see over easily, but we'd haul ourselves up to get a look at the changing desert, the wind knocking the breath out of us. Then we would stretch out on the sun lounges and laugh and laugh. It was just so ridiculous. There was a distinct change in the weather as we started to come down off the desert plateau, and even in the open truck it was humid as hell. We stopped for a stretch break at a filling station with a pet camel, and once we stopped moving, the humidity got even worse. Our chauffeurs grinned into the back of the truck, asking if we were OK. We made it clear we were on top of the world. They told us it looked like rain, but we just laughed and told them to drive on.

The rain started, and at first we jigged around in the huge warm drops, still laughing away. Then, incredibly, it turned to snow, big sloppy wet flakes that melted as they fell in the humidity and slid down our skin like melting butter. The rain then *really* started to come down and it stopped being funny. There was zero shelter in the back of the truck and we huddled in opposite corners hugging our knees as the rain pounded our heads and dripped off our noses and chins. They pulled over and asked if we wanted to get out. It would have been physically impossible for us to fit inside the cab, but I knew we would have zero chance of getting another lift when we were this wet. It was best to sit and take it, so we said to drive on again, though slightly less exuberantly this time.

We rumbled down off the plateau and into the city. Our grand entrance into the Las Vegas strip was made dripping wet, peering over the back of an open truck in a torrential rain storm. The clouds were so heavy that it was almost like night, and the famously excessive neon lights reflected vividly in the torrents of water pouring across the road and down the flooded gutters. We drove past The Golden Nugget and Caesars Palace and a hundred drive-in chapels and then to a cluster of casinos – Circus Circus, Stardust, Sands, the Silver Slipper … all pulsing light and crazy reflections in the water. Finally, our crazy ride was over. We thanked them and stood shivering under the eaves of a motel, watching the rain hammer down and the roads flood higher. Briony checked the price of a room at Circus Circus and it was fifty-five bucks for the night. We couldn't bring ourselves to pay this much and stood shivering, watching the chaos of the traffic as cars and trucks snaked through the floods, trying to avoid the deepest parts. One car tried to take it too fast and disappeared in a cloud of steam as the up-splash boiled off the engine. What the hell would we do? I noticed something on the pavement, and instinctively ran out into the torrent to pick it up. It was a twenty dollar bill. We took this as a good omen. Suddenly the price of a room looked affordable. We booked into the Stardust Casino, putting the receptionist into no end of a flutter as we staggered in dripping water from everything and everywhere, all rucksacks and banging guitar case and bedraggled hair.

It had been a crazy day.

Exhausted as we were, we were still euphoric after our journey, and once we were revived by a hot shower and dry clothes, we decided we should hit the casinos. We promised each other that we wouldn't be hypnotised by all the hype and start throwing money into the machines. Easy to say. Las Vegas casinos are famous for snaring in hapless punters to perfection. They offered free food and champagne and gave you a booklet of vouchers which entitled you to a prize every hour as long as you stayed there. If you were prepared to sit it out for five hours you could get twenty dollars' worth of gaming chips, but the prizes for the first three hours were pretty lightweight. We headed outside to wander the strip; the clouds had finally run out of rain. As we walked, some of the old familiar tension reappeared. Briony pulled her usual trick of working out where to go by following the vibes again and confidently strode off in the direction of the desert. I had a minor strop and herded her back in the right direction. Circus Circus was remarkable: suspended above the gambling floor were three circus rings going at the same time with trapezes and clowns and unicyclists doing their thing while the punters sweated away at the tables below.

But beneath the glitz and glamour, it was clear to see some pretty sad stories: the shifty men in crumpled fraying clothes who would edge to the faucets of champagne and free food, stuffing their pockets before they were moved on by the burly porters in their ridiculous purple and gold regalia, who had a pin-on smile for the punters and an ice-cold stare for the people who actually needed the food. We watched one couple drive into a filling station that had been converted into a chapel with the tackiest neon and stucco grotto effect imaginable, and drive out married ten minutes later.

We decided that Dunes was the place to go, the food seemed better, the glitz and glamour positively excelled in tackiness and, the deciding factor, the booklet appeared the most tempting. But it soon became apparent how hard it was to get through that book. It took ten whole seconds to fail to win the zillion dollar jackpot, then you had to wait for fifty-nine minutes before you got your next free gift. We survived the first hour, went on some spinning wheel gambling thing, and lost again. All around us there was money falling out of machines, and rows and rows of people hypnotised by rolling numbers and flashing symbols. The serious punters sat at green baize tables and called for cards with gestures that we could hardly see. It was all set up to be irresistible and Briony cracked first, feeding a few dollars into a machine and watching the dials spin and stop, with no result. Then I had a go and the same thing happened. While I was distracted Briony slipped away and cashed one of the sacred travellers cheques – fifty bucks – and by the time I found her most of it was inside a machine. I blew my stack, able only to think of how we'd been prepared to shiver outside in a rainstorm for the sake of fifty bucks, and in ten minutes she'd fed the same amount to an insatiable money monster.

Briony blew right back at me, pointing out that she'd lived in a squat for four months with no power and a leaking roof so she could have those travellers cheques, and how she spent them was her own fucking business.

It was on then. I told her she could keep her precious travellers cheques, and I'd keep my busking money. She reasoned, loudly, that she'd earned a piece of whatever I could earn because she'd carried the guitar virtually right across America, and her legs had the bruises to prove it. And in any case, the guitar had only seen the light of day twice since leaving New York, once playing in a truck rolling across Nebraska and once when I was pretending to be a rock star in a shitty Denver hotel room. With the cacophony and sensory overload of the casino all around us, it would have been quite hard to get anybody's attention, but we were slowly getting a crowd. I decided I'd had enough; her last point had gone deep. I walked off, noticing when I glanced back that she was following me. I weaved my way around the casino till I lost her, then wandered the strip from casino to casino, drinking it all in and occasionally putting a couple of dollars in a machine. All up, I spent nearly thirty bucks.

After about three hours I realised that I had the only key to the room, it was booked in my name, and, knowing Briony, she wouldn't be able to remember the room number – or the name of the hotel, for that matter. But when I got back she was sitting outside the room, huddled up in a ball, crying. I was overwhelmed by guilt and squatted down beside her to give her a hug, gushing apologies. She leaned against me, dissolving into open sobs, saying, "Don't apologise, you were right, those fucking machines." The hairs on the back of my neck stood up. I drew back and looked at her. "How much?" She shook her head. "Don't ask – too much". It was time for honesty, and I owned up to how much I'd fed to the machines. I'd never asked exactly how much she had in the magic wad of travellers cheques in her top pocket, and I never found out how much she spent. But it did seem as though our one safety net had pretty much disappeared.

We went into the room and quietly talked things through. Unless we found somewhere very different to anywhere we'd been yet, I had to admit that the busking was pretty much a no-hoper. I hadn't seen anywhere I'd have been happy to play: New York and Las Vegas would have been suicide, Ottawa and Denver were car cities with shopping malls where buskers would get moved out in ten minutes. It was impossible to say what it would be like in the small towns along the highways, but it probably wouldn't be profitable. Our money situation was likely to get quite desperate. And we'd just blown large amounts of it in those hypnotic shiny machines, getting hooked in completely by all the dazzle.

Viva Las Vegas, indeed.

I woke up in the morning with a foul hangover from guzzling too much cheap champagne after a huge day. I was dog tired, but knew we had to get moving early if we were to have any chance of getting through LA and on to San Diego, where we'd planned to visit Kastle. It was miles back to the interstate from our hotel, but it was Sunday and we figured that a lot of people would be heading out of town after a weekend stay. We might even come across someone at the breakfast buffet who was going right in our direction. We split up, keeping our ears open. Standing behind a mellow elderly couple, I heard the guy say to his wife he hoped the traffic wouldn't be too bad on the way back to LA because of the Olympics. I glued myself to them and found some excuse to start talking to the lady, signalling to Briony with my eyes that I thought we had a chance. They were really nice people and fascinated by what we were doing. I avoided asking upfront about a lift, and as we chomped our way through a huge mound of fried breakfast it seemed I'd made a good choice in terms of nice people, but they weren't going to make the connection and offer us a lift. I was resigning myself to slogging out to the freeway when the man looked me in the eye and said, "You guys mind travelling in the back of a camper truck?" I said we would absolutely love to travel in the back of a camper truck, if it was going in the direction of Los Angeles. And it was that easy.

They wanted to get moving quickly before the heat got into the desert, and so we rushed back and threw all the stuff into the bags, and got picked up at the door. Then we sat in the back of their camper truck and watched Las Vegas disappear behind us. I felt I should be sociable, so I stuck my head through the little door into the cab. I asked if we were going to hit Route 66, as I'd been reading *The Grapes of Wrath* and would really like to travel along it into California. The old guy smiled and with a strange look in his eye, glanced across at his wife, who turned to me and said, "You know, that book is so true."

And they'd done it. In the thirties, they'd come west from the dustbowl of Oklahoma to the promised land, with hardship and trouble on the way and a desperate clawing to stay alive once they got there. I listened in awe as they talked about some of the extraordinary things that happened to them. Of all people that could have picked us up and taken us into California, that we would get a lift like this. But it was more what they didn't say that made an impact, there was clearly so much sitting there behind those eyes. They were so nice, and wise, and amazing.

As we rolled across the desert I was confused to see it green and lush. The rains had come big that year and the desert was making the most of it. Apparently we were really lucky to see it like this. I didn't feel lucky; I wanted it to be like in the book, with the heat boiling off the desert and having to drive at night to stop the car from blowing up. But being with them made up for it.

While we talked, Briony was sprawled out on the lounge of the camper van, taking little notice of what was going on, still nursing an aching head and probably nightmare visions of dollar coins disappearing into machines. It did us good to have some time apart, to let the tension go for a while.

The guy was a house painter, and he fished around on the dash and gave me a business card: *John Arnold, Painting – Interior and Exterior*. "If you guys need any help while you're in the west, you just call. You know these days Jill and I own our own house and we have a real good life, but we never forget where we came from and the hard times. Everyone deserves a chance in life, and I believe everyone is a good person if you just give them the right opportunity." They were wonderful. The journey seemed to go almost too quickly and soon we were coming into LA. John had his eyes fixed on the road as he said, "It seems to me you folks have just fulfilled a dream. If you had your wish, what would you like to do the most of all when you reach the west coast?"

I didn't even have to think. "I want to dive into the Pacific Ocean." John laughed. "Then we would be most honoured to have the privilege of driving you to Long Beach, California to make your dream come true, young feller." And that's just what he did. We stopped on a long wide boulevard and the two of us tumbled over each other and saw the giant curving horizon of the Pacific Ocean for the first time in our lives. We raced down onto the sand and just charged into the water, me almost in tears and Briony whooping and yelling. I ducked my head under and as the water closed over my head I felt all the wild things that had happened over the year wash over me. I suddenly felt weightless. All that restlessness and longing, with the idea sitting in my mind for so long, yet never letting it get too real in case I got disappointed. And here we were. I surfaced and looked back up the beach, and John and his wife were waving gleefully at us from the promenade at the top of the beach. I spread my arms high and let myself fall backwards into the water again, hamming it up something rotten and thinking, "Well fair enough. It's not often your dreams come true." I finally calmed down and Briony looked into my eyes and said, "Well done, and thank you," and for those few moments we were truly close. We finally staggered back out of the ocean and back up to the car, holding on to each other, giggling and laughing, water dripping off our clothes and our hair. Jill was in tears of joy, and John wasn't far behind, and as we got back to the car she gave us the hugest hug then stood back, wet and laughing. "Gee you guys are having fun, aren't you!"

Finally it was time for us to leave them. They dropped us at a healthily busy junction, wished us luck one more time, then swung around and back into the traffic, Jill waving at us until they were out of sight. What a way to get to the west coast.

Standing by the highway in salty drying clothes waiting for another lift was a strange anticlimax after the euphoria of our ocean dip, but it didn't take long to settle back into our well-worn routine. 'San Diego' sign across the chest, Union Jack bag hanging off the wrist of the thumbing arm, luggage placed side on to make it look smaller, ten minutes each, look into the eyes of the driver coming at you and dare them not to stop. Look desperate – but not too desperate. Smile, if it looked like it might work. In fact, do just about anything if it felt like it might work. It wasn't too long before a guy in a beat-up old car pulled over. We were in deepest Los Angeles and not expecting any huge lifts from this point, but he was going all the way to Mexico, right through San Diego. Unbelievable luck. We asked his name and he announced grandly that his name was Gilberto Juan Miguel Balboa, then laughed fit to bust at our goggle-eyed expressions.

We passed through endless perfectly sterile suburbs of palm trees and lawn sprinklers all the way to San Diego. We were committed to going straight to Kastle's, but the idea of going to Mexico somehow drifted into the conversation. I could see Briony was keen, but I kept thinking how far we'd pushed our luck getting this far, and to keep pushing it into Mexico with a guy we only just met and wasn't coming back would be pushing our luck right off the end. Plus, we would be leaving America, and I didn't know if we would be guaranteed entry back in again. Getting stuck in Mexico with our flight home out of New York would be a total nightmare. I didn't explain any of this to Briony, not wishing to hurt Gilberto's feelings, and she went into a sulk. I mentally shrugged my shoulders – it was my job to make sure we stayed alive, and I'd managed it this far.

We drew into San Diego and Gilberto proclaimed that for the end of such an incredible journey we should finish in style, and he would take us right to Kastle's front door. I looked up the address, found Evergreen Street on the map and showed Gilberto. He raised his eyebrows and said, "I hope they let me drive in there, my friend – that's the rich end of town." He was right. As we got closer the houses got bigger, the lawns got wider and the cars parked outside got more numerous and more shiny. We found Evergreen Street, which ran along the top of the ridge overlooking San Diego harbour. The views were stunning, and Kastle's house was vast.

We suddenly felt very ragged and smelly, invaders in a foreign land. Gilberto kept the engine running as I got out, in case we were in the wrong place and they got narky. I walked up the huge half-moon drive to an enormously large and ridiculous over-the-top double-fronted white door with a Romanesque entry porch, and pushed the big gold doorbell. An intercom crackled and spluttered. "Yes, what is it?" I asked if Kastle was home. "No, she's working right now, would you like to call again later?" This didn't sound too good. I explained who we were, that we'd rung Kastle from the UK and again from Vegas and she'd said we would be welcome to stay. There was a long silence at the other end of the intercom, and I thought the person had hung up before it crackled into life again. "Give me a second, I'll be right down." Briony was making questioning gestures from the car, and I shrugged my shoulders, feeling like this wasn't going to be what we'd expected. The door opened and a lady who I presumed was Kastle's mother floated into view, draped in dazzling fabric and big hair and looking for all the world like she was dressed to appear in an episode of Dallas. I felt even more ragged then, standing in my salty clothes on her porch with the beat-up old Datsun smoking away behind me.

She did a poor job of trying to conceal how aghast she was at the sight of me and the car, and introduced herself as Mrs Demerazzo, Kastle's mother. She asked me to go through the story again, and I thought about telling her to forget it, realising that Kastle hadn't said a word about us coming, but I took a breath and ran it through again. She was smoking, and while I explained, smoke crawled lazily out of her nostrils and into the big hair. She reminded me of Cruella de Vil in Disney's *101 Dalmatians*. She took a deep breath. "Well, Kastle hasn't said a word to us about all this, which makes it all a bit difficult, but I can see you've come a long way and were expecting to stay, so, welcome to San Diego." She smiled and tried to sound warm and almost achieved it. I walked back to the car and Briony and I pulled our gear out, bidding a fond farewell to Gilberto Juan Miguel Balboa.

We staggered with all our gear into the enormous hall. Our embarrassment must have been obvious. Clearly wondering what to do next, Mrs Demerazzo asked if we would like a glass of lemonade. I asked if it would be possible to ring Kastle. Mrs Demerazzo thought that was a fine idea, and went into the next room to make the call. After the sound of an abrupt, one-sided conversation, she tersely handed me the phone. "Kastle would just love to talk to you." Kastle was squealing her head off. "Gee, it's just so fucking wild you guys are here. I've fixed it with Ma and it'll be cool, don't you worry. Fucking wild!!"

This relaxed us a bit, but the atmosphere remained tense. The home was huge, and the views out of the lounge windows was like a movie – the whole of San Diego harbour rolled out beneath us. I'd guessed from our time in Paris that Kastle was a poor little rich girl, but not quite this rich. Kastle had a much younger brother and a sister, and we spent an uncomfortable evening playing video games with them, with the sister making dark threats to the effect that if we didn't let her win, she'd get her daddy to throw us out of the house. Mr Demerazzo made a brief appearance later in the evening, dressed in a very sharp suit. He expressed his surprise at our presence then disappeared to some other part of the house.

I was allocated the couch in the picture window room, where I fell into an exhausted slumber only to be woken in the middle of the night by an ecstatic Kastle jumping all over me, giving me huge hugs and kisses and proclaiming how bored she'd been living at home and how great it was all going to be now. This felt a lot more welcoming, and we whispered for a few minutes while I described our amazing journey across America. Then, with a final squeeze of my arm, she disappeared.

And I lay there in a state of disbelief. We'd done it. We'd actually done it.

## 11 PRISONER OF THE WHITE LINES

*I tried to run away myself*
*To run away and wrestle with my ego*
*With this, this flame*
*You put here in this Eskimo*
*In this hitcher*
*In this prisoner*
*Of the fine white lines*
*Of the white lines on the free, freeway*
Coyote. Joni Mitchell, 1976

Many times over the next few days I kicked myself for not taking up Gilberto's offer to go to Mexico, or even staying with John and Jill in Los Angeles. I had to admit that if we'd followed Briony's vibes, life would have been a whole lot more interesting. After spending two days recuperating from our epic journey – me devouring the rest of *The Grapes of Wrath* and Briony writing letters and catching up on sleep – we realised we were effectively stranded. Kastle was working all day, the house was in the middle of big-money suburbia, and the only buses each day were to ferry the Mexican cleaners in and out. We were in Mrs Demerazzo's way, and she wanted as little as possible to do with us. Things were getting increasingly tense in the mansion on the hill.

The evenings were a bit better but not much. Kastle's enthusiasm for having us stay was mostly so she had someone to talk to other than her family. In Paris, she had never been very big on doing anything except sitting around smoking and talking, and she was no different at home in San Diego. Her mother suggested we go to a few places in the evening and dropped us off, which was a nice gesture, but they were weird evenings. We spent one night at some new marina development designed to appeal to tourists – all quaint little bridges and fancy lighting and little food stalls. We cringed about for a couple of hours before Mrs Demerazzo picked us up again, and we tried our best to sound grateful while Kastle simmered in the back. She was very much the child of a first marriage and more than a little in the way; we were just an extension of this. Another night we went to some local disco with some of Kastle's friends. You had to be twenty-one in California to drink alcohol. This was an underage disco and all they sold over the bar was soft drinks and amyl nitrate. Every kid in the place had a bottle of the amyl. The coolest trick was to take such a huge sniff of the stuff that the adrenaline and huge blood pressure wave made you momentarily pass out. This seemed infinitely more likely to cause brain damage than a couple of beers.

A highlight was going to Mexico for the day. Tijuana is less than an hour south from San Diego and nothing like 'real' Mexico, but it was a lot more interesting than sitting in the Demerazzo mansion. We wandered the streets, looking for the cheapest duty-free tequila we could find. Briony bought a very stylish felt hat that wasn't quite a Stetson but very cowgirl, and which I was forced to admit looked very cool. Crossing the border was hilarious; the American side had a huge shiny concrete and glass building about the size of an airport terminal, while the Mexicans had a tin hut with one guard asleep with his hat over his eyes. In the middle of town was a large store with 'Woolworths de

## 11 PRISONER OF THE WHITE LINES

Mexico' proudly splashed across the glass-fronted windows in giant gold letters. Parked outside was a big old Dodge truck with a goat tethered to the fender. It was glorious. We came back across the border with a litre and a half of tequila each, and of course got pulled up because Briony was under twenty-one. I asked the customs official what our options were, and he was very relaxed about it. "You can either leave it with me, go back down the road and drink it, or see if you can find someone to carry it over for you." After taking a swig of the stuff and nearly retching it straight back, we chose the last option.

We got back to the house very late that night, only to find that Mrs Demerazzo had chosen that evening to cook us a special Mexican meal. Five different dishes were sitting forlornly in the kitchen; she had obviously gone to a lot of effort. Kastle rang us from work the next morning to let us know we had to be out of the house before the end of the week.

What to do next. Our guidebook mentioned 'driveaway firms' as a good cheap way of getting across the country, by delivering cars long-distance. It involved a lot of paperwork and deposits, and there were major penalties if you damaged the car, took too long or exceeded the direct line mileage by more than an agreed amount. But it seemed reliable, and the only cost was the fuel. I rang the firm and left my details first thing in the morning, saying we would be interested in going as far east as possible, as soon as possible. My English accent went down well again with the woman on the phone, and I made the most of it, thinking it might make the difference between a car to Phoenix or New York.

She rang back all excited that afternoon. "I think it's your lucky day. We just got a drop off at short notice, a red

Mustang that needs delivering to New Orleans. You'll need to get over here as soon as possible to sort out the paperwork, and I need this in a hurry. If anyone else rings I may have to let it go." The place was miles away, and it would be fifty bucks or more in a taxi. I used up the last dregs of goodwill from Mrs Demerazzo in almost demanding she give us a lift. She drifted around the house in a vague imitation of hurry for two hours, and I did a very bad job of hiding my frustration, sitting in the car quivering with rage and dreading getting there to find the car was already gone. Looking back on it, I'm amazed she didn't just tell me to get out and walk at that point, I was being such a prick.

We got to the office and the woman heaved a sigh of relief. There were a couple of other people on the way to sign up, but she'd really wanted to give the car to us because of our great 'Monty Python' accents. It turned out we needed a reference from someone local, so Mrs Demerazzo had to write out a letter on the spot. I was scared stiff at what she might say about us: "Arrived uninvited in stolen car driven by drug runner, freeloaded for a number of days, bullied me into driving them across town, will be very glad to see the back of them." But she managed to come up with something suitably complimentary, I imagine because it would mean she got us out of her house. We got all the paperwork sorted out, signing all sorts of scary things which committed us to big bucks if anything went wrong. Then we got to see the car. It was fire engine red, a V8 Mustang. And I was driving it all the way to New Orleans. Wow.

By the time we finished all the paperwork it was rush hour and the whole city was pulsing with moving vehicles. The first few minutes of left-hand side driving were tense to say the least. I kept putting my hand into the map

## 11 PRISONER OF THE WHITE LINES

pocket on the door to try and change gear, even though the car was an automatic. I was acutely aware that I really wasn't in control of the situation, so decided to treat it all as a video game. Suddenly it was all much easier; I could concentrate more on the driving and less worrying about it. I briefly entrusted Briony with the map reading but we ended up heading in the wrong direction within five minutes, misdirected by those vibes again. I pulled over to work out where we needed to go, and as I was tracing my way across the freeways of San Diego my eyes strayed to all the beaches along the west side of the city that we hadn't seen. There was nothing calling us back to Kastle's in a hurry, so we made a diversion. We were finally in charge of our destiny again, and it felt good. We'd been climbing the walls at Kastle's since we arrived. We decided to leave that night, partly to get some miles under our belt, but principally to be free again. Al's words about it being the journey and not the destination that was important drifted through my head.

Kastle was highly unimpressed that we were deserting her, but ironically she was going out somewhere we weren't invited and left before we did. Long ago in Paris I'd come to realise that the only way to keep Kastle happy all the time was to follow her around nodding, so I didn't worry about it too much. I doubted we would see or hear from her again. Packing the car was made more interesting when we found an enormous framed print sitting in the boot of the car that took up a huge amount of room. We ended up with most of the gear in the back seat. It didn't take us long to get everything in, by now we were very used to organising ourselves and getting our gear into cars in the space of a minute. And then it was time to say goodbye.

The kids stopped playing video games for a couple of minutes to come and listen to the growl of the Mustang, and Mrs Demerazzo did her best to appear sorry but, quite reasonably, was obviously very happy to see the back of us. I gunned the car a couple of times to get the kids excited – impressing myself a bit as well – then pulled out of the enormous driveway, Mrs Demerazzo waving half-heartedly for a full two seconds before herding the kids back inside. Staying at Kastle's had been a mistake, and a dissatisfying experience for all involved. Under the circumstances, Mrs Demerazzo had made a very brave effort.

The plan was to travel due east before branching off north, as we wanted to see the Grand Canyon on our way to New Orleans. After twenty minutes, the temperature gauge had climbed to just below the red line and the handbrake was too hot to touch. We pulled over at several garages along the way to ask if we should be worried, and each time got a curious look and a "Where are you guys FROM?" This was initially useful, but after a solid month of it, it was getting on my nerves. We were starting to feel like some carnival side show. A couple of people told us that Mustangs just ran hot, and we would be OK. We kept driving and the car didn't explode. I needed to be sure of this – we had 150 miles of nothing but sandhills and desert ahead of us. If we boiled out there, it would be serious. The turnoff was at El Centro, just over one hundred miles east of San Diego. I took a breath and pointed the car north. Soon we were in the middle of nowhere in the dark, with giant desert stars hanging above us. I started to enjoy myself, feeling the big engine thundering gently in front of us as we drove through wide savanna country, heading out into the desert, free again. The moon set in the west, the

## 11 PRISONER OF THE WHITE LINES

night came down inky black, and everything beyond the white glow of the headlights was nothingness. We, and the car, relaxed into the easy fifty-five-mile an hour pace. The country was dead flat and the road was arrow straight. The urge to see what this car could do was irresistible, and I pushed it a couple of times, getting up to eighty and ninety without the car even trying, then coasting slowly down.

A white speck in the distance turned into an amateurish hand-painted sign of an upside down 'L'. As we passed it, I wondered what it meant. It meant a sharp right-angle turn to the left, and I hit it at full speed, flying off the edge of the road and into the dirt. I hauled the wheel around, desperately trying to get back to the road, feeling the wheels cut into sand. If we stopped, we'd be up to the axles and stranded. As the car fish-tailed crazily, a huge wall loomed above us out of the dark. It was the biggest haystack I'd ever seen, and if I hadn't hauled us around, we would have hit it head on. I kept pushing the gas to keep us moving and, still fishtailing, hit the highway and shot right across the tarmac to the other side with a howl of rubber. I over-corrected back and forth a couple of times, with the smell of burning rubber seeping through the floor. Finally, we were back on the road and heading straight in the right direction. It had only been seconds, but Briony had been braced back in her seat for the whole saga, paralysed with terror. Once it was over, we glanced across at each other and dissolved into hysterical, relieved laughter.

The country started to change, with the road undulating snake-like through ghostly looking sandhills glowing stark white in the headlight beam. As we crested each rise, our headlights picked up the cats-eyes stretching for miles ahead, staring back at us from the inky black. We really were out in the middle of nowhere now, and I could feel the heat of the desert seeping into the car. My eyes strayed to the temperature gauge every few seconds watching for any movement, but it stayed just below the red line.

I imagined I saw bobbing lights ahead, and finally worked out they belonged to three off-road dune buggies coasting on the dunes just ahead of us. The buggies had huge spotlights on the front and a light on a long plastic pole at the back that whirled crazy patterns in the desert star sky as they rolled over the dunes. As we drew alongside and watched them rise and fall over the dunes, it gave the impression of being at sea. They were clad in full boiler suits, goggles and masks, looking for all the world like Mad Max extras. They raised a hand in a long salute as we coasted past them. Most surreal.

The plan was to sleep in the car at Blythe, but it was so hot and the car was so cramped I decided to keep driving all night, crossing into Arizona as the sun rose, dazzling and hot in our faces. We avoided the big interstate to go through Riviera, then picked up Route 66 at Kingman after getting directions from a man with skin of old brown leather who called the road 'Ol' 66'. We were now travelling the same road the Joads travelled in Steinbeck's novel. I was dog tired and cramped and irritable, but still felt some strange pull to know we were driving on the road that had harboured the dreams of so many people all those years ago. A rusting old hulk of a 30s car sat in a sun-scorched cornfield to remind us of the legacy, and we coasted past it as the sun crawled higher, lost in our thoughts. We joined the interstate for a while until we reached Williams to head north for the canyon. I was so tired now it was getting dangerous, but the canyon was less than fifty miles ahead,

## 11 PRISONER OF THE WHITE LINES

and the temperature got more bearable as we climbed slowly up onto the Coconino plateau.

We drove into an overcrowded carpark around mid-morning. The Grand Canyon. I'd driven nearly six hundred miles in the twelve hours since we left San Diego and hadn't slept a wink. My body was crying out for sleep, but I wanted to see what all the fuss was about. From the viewing platform, I gazed down and down and down into the biggest hole in the ground on the planet, layer upon layer of red and yellow and gold forming impossible sculptures and castles and towers. As I squinted in sleep-deprived disbelief at the river snaking through the vast landscape far below us, a trick of the wind suddenly pounced on us from out of the canyon and we were caught in a screaming updraught for ten seconds. Then all was serene again. It was all too much, and I staggered back to the car and collapsed, sleeping like a dead man for four hours or more.

We spent the next day driving along the southern rim of the canyon, stopping every five minutes to get another look. There was an ancient serenity about the place that was wonderful, of a thousand years passing like a second as the rock was sculpted by the wind and the rain and the heat and the cold. Briony was lost in thought for a couple of hours then, in a small voice, declared that this was the place to liberate 'The Rock'. This was still her security talisman and a big thing for her. In a surprisingly moving ceremony, she stood alone on the edge for ten or so minutes, talking secret words to the little sculpted stone that had travelled so far with us, then let it fall gently from her hands to bound down into the endless depths below. We imagined some geologist finding it and sending himself mad trying to piece together how a piece of French limestone ended up in the Grand Canyon.

A crowd had gathered at Desert View to watch the sun go down. As the sun sank, the giant eastern ramparts turned blood-red and there was an awed hush at the majesty of it all, and applause when the wondrous show was over and the sun disappeared. Despite the signs saying camping wasn't allowed, we figured we'd hide somewhere out of sight. We found a little ledge to lie on, on the edge of the giant hole, feeling the air breathe gently in and out of the canyon and the heat seep out of the rocks. But a ranger found us, so we said goodbye to the canyon and found an informal campsite just outside the park boundary. We slept out under the stars listening to small groups of people talking quietly under the stars. Again, I felt very close to the Joads.

The next day we drove all day across Arizona and New Mexico. Wide, open skies, empty arrow-straight roads, and Joni Mitchell's Hejira – the only cassette we brought with us – locked on an endless play loop. Briony and I had done all the talking we had to do, and so for hours we would just gaze at the land passing by us and under us, content to coast in the rhythm of the music and the tyres humming along the road.

We slept at night on picnic tables to escape the scorpions and spiders and the terrible heat of the desert ground. I loved sleeping in the crystal-clear desert night air – the only problem was that I was so fascinated with watching the night sky unfold from the east and sink in the west, with the satellites spinning overhead, that I struggled to get enough sleep.

The next day we rolled across New Mexico, through Albuquerque, over the Rio Grande and into Fort Sumner – the stamping ground of Billy the Kid. It was the only thing that made Fort Sumner different from a thousand other mid-western towns, but it was refreshingly free of the hype and froth that seemed to permeate just about anything in America worth seeing. Billy the Kid was buried in a desolate piece of red dirt on the edge of a decaying boardwalk town called Hells Half Acre. His was one of the very few marked graves, a bizarre oblong chunk of rock surrounded by a padlocked cage. Apparently someone had decided to souvenir the headstone once, and it had taken the city fathers some strenuous effort to get it back. There were lots of faded noticeboards in glass cases around the town telling the story of Billy's final showdown with Pat Garrett, when he was shot in the back at the age of twenty-one. There was a ramshackle dusty collection of curios and artefacts on display in seven termite-ridden old sheds – optimistically called a museum. Ploughs and horseshoes and strange old farm implements without a name or obvious purpose, and the prize exhibit – an eight-legged stillborn calf mounted in a dusty glass case on a gorgeous antique table complete with sepia lace cloth. It was like walking through an album of Tom Waits songs, and I loved it.

For two days straight we crawled ant-like across New Mexico and Texas, through a hundred tiny mid-west towns, stopping only to grab something to eat in yet another nameless diner, drinking too much coffee, leaving grime and sweat on the shiny black leather seats of the Mustang as we could never find a shower, legs and backs cramped and tired from sitting in the car for twelve to fourteen hours a day. The air conditioner died, the cassette player died and, as the miles ground on beneath our wheels, the urge to keep moving finally, slowly, almost imperceptibly, started to die as well. It was the hypnotic sameness of everything – the never-ending road stretching before us across the aching, empty flatness of the desert, the soporific pace of fifty-five miles an hour, the vast open skies that never held rain, the endless diners with the same smell of over-brewed coffee and donuts, bored waitresses with tired pinned-on smiles that masked a quiet longing and waiting for something to happen that never ever would. I knew as I drove and drove that those restless demons that had been pushing me on all year were slowly trickling out of me – like sand from an hourglass, under the bright red Mustang, scattering behind me in the wake of the car across the hot dry desert. It was a strange feeling.

As we moved across Texas we passed long rows of nodding donkey oil rigs, sucking the black crude out of the ground, primitive flaring stacks tacked on to some wells, the gyrating flare scorching the stunted desert trees surrounding it, another Mad Max vista in the desert landscape. Texas was big on hats, and in one diner we walked through the door to see five fat-arsed Texans all wearing white Stetsons and white pants sat in a line on bar stools, turning to stare at us in perfect choreography as we walked in. It was like a scene from a Cohen brothers movie, ten years before they started making movies.

Towards the end of the fourth day we arrived in Fort Worth, on the outskirts of Dallas. We'd broken the back of the trip and were now just one day's long drive – just over 500 miles – away from New Orleans.

The car had been guzzling gas and our money was disappearing at a scary rate, even though we were eating almost nothing. The drive across America finally put a year's worth of wandering demons to rest. I knew on that last day in the Mustang that I finally didn't need to keep moving anymore. I was tired of the road, and the flaming desire to travel was all but burned out, even though there was still a good fifteen hundred miles of highway before we would be back in New York.

But amidst this strange, complex feeling of completion and resolution, there was a much simpler feeling of frustration. Since New York, America had in general been a very dissatisfying experience. The high points had been Al the trucker, and our two lifts into and out of Los Angeles. Niagara, Denver, Las Vegas and San Diego had all been spectacular duds. The Grand Canyon was awesome, but could have been anywhere on earth, it just happened to be in America. Nearly everything and everyone seemed vacuous and shallow. It seemed all the clichés about America were true, but were even bigger in real life. How could a nation take such national pride in serving the same crap food under a franchise sign from one side of the country to the other? This was what these people called their culture. It felt way more alien than Paris ... the language barrier there was nothing compared to meeting endless legions of people who weren't even sure where England was, just that it consisted of London, green hills, a bunch of faceless oppressors of the Irish, Buckingham Palace and a queen who everyone knew personally. I was sick of being treated like some carnival sideshow freak because of the way my voice sounded: "Gee, say some stuff out of Monty Python (accent on the 'thon') or Bennie Hill." *Bennie Hill??* The only satisfaction had lain in the miles unfolding beneath us, tracking our ant-like progress across the vast country day after day, and in certain small and unexpected wonders like Fort Sumner.

As we headed east, I prayed that New Orleans would produce something new. I didn't know much about New

Orleans except that it was the home of jazz, and there was some French Cajun influence there. I dreaded getting there to find another chocolate-box Walt Disney packaged place. Briony and I were hardly speaking; being in each other's company 24/7 had finished what little spark we had felt for each other, and we both knew we would rather be with other people. It felt strange to be feeling so down about everything. Here I was driving a wild red Mustang through Louisiana to meet the great Mississippi River and travel into New Orleans. But that's just how I felt that day.

The weather got hotter and more humid. The air was heavy with pressure, and we knew a storm must break soon. It did so, big time, in Baton Rouge, about an hour and a half out of New Orleans. The wind howled, spinning torrential rain in mad curves across the sky. The roads ran like rivers, the power went out and cars snaked along at ten miles an hour, occasionally aquaplaning down the camber of the road and bouncing off parked cars. I drove at snail's pace, praying. A hundred metres ahead of us, a traffic light suspended on wires overhead shook free in the crazy wind and smashed into the road. But there was nothing to do but keep driving. For the last hour we drove through a steaming mangrove jungle, on what seemed like a long bridge through a swamp. Steam rose either side of us, the cloud was low and heavy, darkening the sky. It felt like we were driving into Conrad's Heart of Darkness.

Finally, thankfully, we were in New Orleans. We spent the night in the car, in a suburban street, but the heat and mosquitoes and cramped seats meant once again I got no sleep.

We got completely lost delivering the car back to the owner's brother. We'd pushed our luck too far in trying to hand over with the minimum fuel and ran out of gas on a level crossing. We dragged the car to a place of reasonable safety and I sprinted back to a garage and hired a gas can and a litre of fuel. Meanwhile Briony was trying to sort out six days of crap so we could be ready to hand the car over. She'd stacked it on the roof to sort out, and as she slid it off, a big scratch appeared in the dazzling red paintwork. Great. I topped up the fuel and looked under the car and there was water pouring out of something in the engine. Great again. We went back to the garage to hand back the gas can, and the pump attendant reckoned the water was only the bleed from the air conditioner. I hoped he was right.

The concern about handing over the car was misfounded. The owner's brother showed up in a black Trans-am and was very amiable about everything. He had to sign papers to say the car was in good condition; we had most of our remaining money riding on this, and so were in tense agony while he did so. But he was happy and signed off. It was a bit of a shock then when we realised we had no car and would need a lift to get anywhere! He offered us a lift somewhere, and we told him we were after the cheapest part of town. He suggested the French Quarter. Sounded good to us.

He drove us right to the heart of New Orleans. My heart sank at the concrete and glass, until we turned a corner and were suddenly a hundred years back in time. Tiny streets were lined with terraced balconied houses crammed in together, and the streets were alive with people. It was wonderful. He let us off, bade us farewell and we watched the car – our constant companion and home for the past week – drive away until it disappeared, turning heads as it rumbled through the tiny streets. Then we turned around to face the bubbling energy of Bourbon Street.

Busking with Tim on Bourbon Street, New Orleans.

## 12 A HOUSE IN NEW ORLEANS

*There is a house in New Orleans
They call the Rising Sun
And it's been the ruin of many a poor boy
And God, I know, I'm one.*
House of the Rising Sun. American folk song, origins unclear.

The place was pumping with life, and we loved it instantly. There was music coming from virtually every shopfront – modern jazz and Trad jazz and blues and singing – with people crammed onto the streets like nothing we'd seen since New York. I beamed at Briony. "Now here I *can* make a buck, guaranteed!" We went into a hotel and found the rooms were 140 bucks a night. The receptionist looked taken aback at our amazement. "Anyone would think you didn't know the World Fair is on right now," she said. She was right, we didn't.

The tourists flurrying in and out of the hotel lobby looked far too rich for our budget. More than this, I knew that if we stayed in a place like this, we would have a room that could be anywhere on earth, with a colour TV and a shiny bathroom and perfectly folded white towels and a room service menu that said something like 'fresh garden salad lovingly drizzled in the cook's own secret balsamic vinaigrette dressing.' It wasn't what we were looking for and we got out of there, away from the stare of the receptionist who just wanted us to disappear and stop tarnishing the image of her shiny-floored, concealed-lighting, pot-planted entrance lobby.

Every other hotel on Bourbon Street was in the same price range. Things didn't look good. With our current funds we could last about three days in New Orleans at these rates, and we had about three weeks still to last in America.

We knew we had to find the New Orleans equivalent of the Nesle, but if we didn't track something down by nightfall, the only option would be to keep moving. I was loath to do this. I knew I could make money in New Orleans, but the money had to more than match the rent. We headed by instinct a few streets north, where the houses were less showy but still with the same vibe. It was as if nothing had been built or changed in a hundred years or more; we stopped at a little corner store that smelled of strange secret spices and had dried chillies and other strange looking things hanging in bundles from the ceiling. A tiny old black woman stood behind a counter wearing an apron and bright red headscarf. We asked her where the cheap places to stay were. She flashed a careful smile of huge perfect teeth and said all the hotels were back on Bourbon Street and we were heading in the wrong direction. I looked her in the eye and told her we just didn't have the money and we were desperate. She looked at us long and hard, nodded, and came back to us this time without the theatrical smile and accent reserved for tourists.

"OK, I hear ya young feller. There's other places. I ain't sayin' they're safe and I ain't saying their real nice, but they might just be what you can afford right now. There's one two blocks north from here up on North Rampart Street. If that ain't in your price range, then the only other place

## 12 A HOUSE IN NEW ORLEANS

you'll be sleeping is the park. But remember – you asked for this, and you take care, OK, there's some pretty crazy people hang around up there."

This sounded much more promising. We thanked her profusely and headed up to North Rampart Street. Protruding from a second-storey balcony on an old house was a sign in amateurish wobbly letters of faded white paint proclaiming rooms for rent. The whole place had an air of damp and crumbling decay. It felt perfect. There were two guys sitting on the front porch who looked like residents, and we asked who we should see about a room. The larger of the two guys answered us in a huge booming Texan accent. "Why you should see me, that's who, but I ain't sure your lookin' in the right place young man, you might want to look back on Bourbon Street." He was a huge guy with a solid angular face, a craggy beard with a hint of grey, and flashing eyes that he fixed on me with an arch of his eyebrows as he spoke. He looked macho, but in a theatrical way that made me sense he was gay. We gave our honest but small budget speech again, and the gay theory was confirmed as the other guy spoke. He was tiny and wispy and camp as they came, and as he spoke, he patted the big Texan's bronzed leg in excitement.

"Charles, darling, where are your *manners*. If these lovely people want to grace our little place with their presence, then we should be *inviting them in* not sending them down the road. And they have the most *gorgeous* way of talking that I just know I want to hear more of. Of *course* they should stay with us." 'Charles' gave a big theatrical snort, but I could see we were in. "Well, if you *insist* Johnny, but I have to say they are *not* what I would consider to be our *usual* clientele." The piercing eyes switched back to me. "You are *very* lucky, we are in general a *residential* establishment, but this very morning one of our long-term friends has vacated a *beautiful* little room on the ground floor. If it's what you're looking for, we would be *proud* to have you as one of our *illustrious* guests." He was so much larger than life it was hard to believe, with every word backed by wonderful theatrical gyrations of his arms, twirls and tugs of his beard and a constant interplay of jutting chins and arching eyebrows. He reminded me of the guys you saw in old western films who travelled around in a horse and cart wearing a battered top hat and tails, selling some magical elixir in a glass bottle that would cure all the ills of the world for just fifteen cents a bottle.

He stood and led us through the open front door to a room just down the hall. It had a huge slumping double bed, a dressing table with a cracked old mirror, peeling damp wallpaper, a giant whirling fan in the roof and the special luxury feature of a small bar fridge. Charles made a highlight of this in his magnificent oration of all the features of the room, finishing up with, "we don't charge extra for the cockroaches, and they put on a mighty fine show, though I say it myself. They will dance La Cucaracha every night for you my friend, first performance shortly after sundown." His chin jutted forward as he finished, daring us to say anything against his beloved cockroaches. It was twenty dollars a night and it was perfect, and we said yes immediately. Charles and 'Little Johnny' fluttered around us for ten minutes or so getting details in books and a day's rent in advance, then retired back to the front porch, saying we would be welcome to join them once we had unpacked. When they had gone, we stretched out on the bed in hysterical ecstasy – the last time we'd slept in a

## 12 A HOUSE IN NEW ORLEANS

bed was San Diego, half a continent away. We sensed that this place could be as wild, or possibly even wilder, than the Nesle. Finally, we had found somewhere in America other than New York that went beyond endless shopping malls and fast-food franchises. This was going to be fun!

The French Quarter of New Orleans was a unique bubble in the plastic sameness of America, and we took to it like ducks to water. Within a day I had busked on Jackson Square, down past Bourbon Street near the giant Mississippi River, and found that I could make just enough to pay the rent and feed us with about three hours playing. This wasn't brilliant, but at least we were even and not going backwards. We could hole up in New Orleans and leave ourselves a few days to hitch back to New York. The busking was strangely simple in this place; it had a European feel, designed for people not cars, and had music running through its core. But despite busking being a part of the landscape, it often didn't seem to occur to people that you were there to make money.

One time I had a crowd of about ten people around me, all clapping and smiling before they all drifted off happily without one putting a cent in the hat, oblivious to me seething behind them. There were plenty of other buskers around, almost all black, and we spent a few hours watching them do their stuff to pick up the local tips. Two brothers playing trumpets were great; the younger wasn't more than twelve years old. They made a big show between songs of, "You like the music, people, we like you for that, but the rent man don't care, he wants your MONEY, so, for the rent man, not for us mind you, if you like the music, put some money in the hat, our landlord will looooovvve you." This would result in a flurry of money from the audience. It worked well if you were a twelve-year-old black trumpet player with a larger-than-life southern accent and a big brother to back you up, but I doubted I could pull it off on my own. I tried a couple of times without much success, trying to ham up my best English accent. If I'd known lots of Noel Coward songs or something else frightfully British, I think it would have worked better, but as most of my repertoire included Bob Dylan and Neil Young, the English accent didn't fit the image too well. I knew there had to be a better way, but I doubted I would find it in the time we had available. No matter – we could stay alive, and in the most fun place we'd come across in the whole country.

We learned quickly that the place ran the same way as Saint-Michel, with Bourbon Street being the equivalent of Boulevard Saint-Michel in Paris. If you were a tourist with buckets of money and wanted to say you'd had a drink on Bourbon Street, you paid for it the same as if you wanted to eat your lunch with a view of Notre-Dame cathedral. For the likes of us, Bourbon Street was for looking and absorbing the vibes, not for buying, and Jackson Square and the area around the World Fair site weren't far behind. The vibes were well worth absorbing, but the beer was a whole lot cheaper in bars two streets back.

New Orleans was a mecca for every kind of jazz. Old guys in white shirts and bow ties deftly worked the silver keys of their clarinets, sweating in a hundred degrees, faces wrinkled and lined with fifty years of playing. Enormous black guys cradled trombones like babies, bursting out of their shirts, eyes and cheeks bulging as they whipped the glittering brass slides back and forth, using their bowler hats as mutes on the trombones. Weedy little banjo players hid up the back, chugging away on the beat with drummers who played almost without moving, all economy of movement, tickling away on the hi-hat and the snare and occasionally snapping in a rifle shot against the beat to show their real skill. Sharp young dudes with bootlace ties and wide-legged stances pushed out sensuous tones from tenor and alto saxophones, and above it all, the sound of trumpets arcing and flying in soprano mastery, played by blacks and whites, young and old, men of a hundred different shapes and sizes.

Most bands played Trad but there was more than a smattering of progressive jazz stuff that changed form so quick I could never keep up with it. And then there was the Cajun and Zydeco stuff, music I'd never heard before, dirtier and darker, the beat pushed along at a chugging two-time beat by anything from giant chrome-trimmed accordions to weird little squeezeboxes, with a clipped strum of guitar behind it – which looked easy but seemed to hit every beat the opposite way round to how I would normally accent it. Weird French American lyrics wailed above the driving beat, and it all combined to produce a music that had an animal, feral, voodoo feel on the surface, and something dark and dirty underneath, all swamps and alligators, mangrove jungles and dark, mosquito-ridden nights on front porches in the middle of nowhere. The bars were all open-fronted, and we would lean on the doorpost and take in the music till the bouncers asked if we were coming in, and then move on to the next and the next. It was a never-ending musical kaleidoscope. New Orleans was the only city in America where drinking on the street was legal, so we got a six-pack and took our drinks with us down the pavement, and when we finished that we went and got another, drinking in the music and the feel of the place along with the ice-cold beer.

We drank too much and wove our way back to the hotel to find Charles and Johnny and a couple of other gays on the balcony cat-calling the cutest men as they walked past, often getting an appreciative call back; New Orleans was packed to the seams with gays. Charles was effusive in his welcome now that he knew I was an *artist*. "I *insist* that you sit here on the porch with us with that lovely instrument of yours and play away this shitty afternoon heat". I agreed to keep playing as long as the cold beer kept coming, and Charles and Johnny disappeared inside at regular intervals to keep the deal, coming back with something to nibble on as well as a beer every time my can was empty.

It was a wonderful afternoon and by the end of it Briony and I were both completely hammered and were firmly part of the tapestry of the hotel, with Charles and Johnny being friends not just landlords. A tired-looking black woman, who was probably only a couple of years older than us, came in towards the end of the afternoon. She sat on the stairs of the porch, leaning against the banisters with a quiet smile and world-weary eyes. After listening for a little while, she asked if we'd had any Cajun food and when we answered no, she said, "Well, you're in New Orleans, children, and you surely must try some right now." She disappeared into her room and came out half an hour later with an enormous plate of fried fish dusted with wicked spices, and as the dusk came down, she insisted we eat the lot – with much encouragement from Charles and Johnny. I asked how she made her money, and that tired smile came back. "I don't do nothin' honey, 'cept put other people's washin' and dryin' in and out of machines for 'bout twelve hours a day. You do what you can." She probably earned as much in her twelve hours sweating away in the laundry as I had in strumming away for three hours on the street and yet she'd produced this feast for us. I tried to give some money back to her and welled up inside when she said "Honey, you playin' your music there has made my day special, and this is my way of sayin' thank you for that, so don't you go tryin' to stop me from sayin' thank you, you hear?" with a mock firm tone and those beautiful smiling eyes. I played my heart out for her, thanking our fickle guardian angel for guiding us to this wonderful, wonderful place.

The only darkness in that wonderful afternoon was watching Johnny occasionally dissolve into fits of coughing that seemed to drain his whole body of any energy, and realising that, like Jonathon in New York, he was a very sick man. The flickers of haunted concern in Charles' eyes when Johnny thought he wasn't looking spoke volumes. It seemed we were witnessing the brutal reality of AIDS in New Orleans as well as New York.

I was with Briony setting up to busk in Jackson Square when we spotted a guy tuning up a banjo and wandered over for a look. He was wearing thick corduroy trousers and huge steel-capped boots, and his pale complexion contrasted starkly with his jet-black hair and clipped moustache. He looked as though he'd stepped out of an English winter and into the humid sweat of New Orleans in August. His banjo was a four-string, with a shorter neck than the five-strings everyone seemed to play in America. He started playing Irish jigs and reels, of all things. The American love of all things Irish meant he had plenty of people stopping, but he wasn't talking to them, or getting much money out of them. I knew if we played together, we could break through that barrier. And that's how we met up with Timothy from Ennis, Ireland. He was Irish to his boots, which was hugely refreshing after all the pretend Irishmen we'd endured in our hitching. He'd arrived from Athens, east of Atlanta, Georgia, escaping from woman troubles. We got chatting and hit it off immediately over a couple of beers in a pub, so we dragged him back to our place up on North Rampart Street for a jam.

An appreciative audience gathered in the doorway within five minutes of starting up – Charles, Johnny, Lewis the jivey black guy from the room in front of us, his wise-cracking big mama of a wife, and a couple of other gay guys from down the hall. Tim had been struggling to get enough money playing to get by, so was keen to give the duo thing a try. The music was simple enough to play along with, all three-chord trick stuff, and Tim made it even easier by showing me a wild open tuning that included putting the G-string all the way down to a D. This gave the guitar a huge fat sound like a bouzouki, and you could play any chord just by stopping the two strings together and letting everything else drone away at the back of it, almost like bagpipes.

After our practice warmup we went big straight away, going to the main show pitch down by the river, near where the paddleboat steamers came in on their way to the World Fair site. Briony came along to take round the hat. We had to wait for the break-dancers to finish their spot and then started up. We'd discussed giving the punters some 'Irish larrikin' talk between songs to tap into that American Irish thing, and also agreed a set of signals for Tim to flick me when he was going to change tune or key. This of course fell apart as soon as he got ripping; in typical Irish fashion he completely forgot, but I hung on and didn't cock it up too much. The chugging guitar behind the tight-stringed tenor banjo pushed out the tricky melodies with triplets and doublings all over the place. It sounded bloody wonderful.

## 12 A HOUSE IN NEW ORLEANS

After the first set of tunes we had a crowd of twenty people round us, after the second that had doubled. Briony tipped my trusted Paris trilby off my head and weaved her way through the throng, hat out in front just like she used to do on the Metro. We tried not to stare too hard as she made her way, but we would see there was plenty of coins going in and even the odd note or two, though this might only be a dollar. She came back looking flushed, and we knew we'd done well. We played for an hour, Briony doing the rounds every ten or fifteen minutes. We counted the takings on the benches that overlooked the river and the paddleboat steamers. Even after we split it down the middle, the money was more than triple what I'd earned the previous day. Suddenly busking in New Orleans was something we could do to get ahead, rather than just scraping by. The only embarrassment was that, though Tim was the real thing when it came to playing, he wasn't really a showman between tunes. I found myself chipping in with one liners and crowd teasers in a mock Irish accent to liven things up a bit. It worked – the punters would laugh away at the quips and banter – but occasionally it had Tim writhing and spluttering when I came out with some blarney expression that I'd made up, which was total crap to anyone who actually knew Ireland for real. But the money was so good he was happy to put up with it.

We watched the paddleboats and big commercial vessels passing by until Tim had to go. We agreed to meet the next morning on Jackson Square to do it all again. Briony and I were like kids in a sweet shop; for the first time in America, we had a little more money than we needed just to avoid starving. We went into an old seafood gumbo bar near the harbour and ate the biggest shrimps I'd ever seen, washed down with cold beer, and I bought a big shiny sticker for my guitar case saying 'New Orleans'.

We wandered back to the hotel to find Charles and Johnny still lounging on the porch. They were unbelievable tarts and would say the most outlandish things to any guy passing who they thought looked good. "You have the cutest little ass this side of the Texas state line honey, why don't you come up on my porch and sit on my knee and let me squeeze it for you?" Now that they knew us better, I started getting similar treatment, which freaked me out a bit. Charles proclaimed loudly it was such a waste that I was a 'breeder' and off limits. It was becoming a bit of a hassle for me to go out alone in New Orleans, as there were so many gay guys around on the pick-up that I couldn't walk ten feet without getting propositioned or cat called. At least when Briony was with me I only got suggestive looks.

For the first time in my life, I stood in front of the mirror to analyse whether I might actually be wearing something that might be too suggestive, and decided the tight cut-off jeans I'd acquired from the New York apartment were a bad idea on the New Orleans streets. I experienced a bizarre close call in a laundry near our hotel, when I was brazenly chatted up by a guy who brushed up against my leg. It made me feel like a schoolgirl getting perved at by a dirty old man. I was in a corner, literally, proclaiming my straightness, the guy simpering and wheedling and saying why not just try it once sweetheart, I just *know* you'll like it, when Briony walked in. Boy was I glad to see her! The guy eventually slunk off, but Briony was highly unsympathetic "At last you know what it's like for us girls, every day of our fucking lives we get guys trying to chat us up."

## 12 A HOUSE IN NEW ORLEANS

I resolved to try and look as unlovely as possible for the duration of our stay in New Orleans, except when I was busking, when I would attempt to appeal to the tourist bracket and not the gay end of town.

Life slipped into a marvellous routine of busking and getting in the money with Tim, floating around the French Quarter drinking in the scene – and just plain drinking – and playing our part in the day-to-day dramas of the hotel.

One slightly alarming characteristic of the hotel was the largely gay population leaving their bedroom doors open when they were getting up to some boy-meets-boy gymnastics and wanted to make the party bigger, so to speak. They would often call out for me to join their fun. I soon learned to walk very quickly past an opened door, particularly at night. Charles was a great help in situations like this, giving guys who were latching on to me a stern lecture on how it was a real shame, but I was definitely straight and he would not have his guests being made to feel uncomfortable by tarty behaviour focused in the wrong direction, and they could tart at *him* instead because he just *loved* it.

Lewis, the black dude from the front room, found a room across town, and when he and his wife moved out the fridge also disappeared. Charles spun into a rage, proclaiming all sorts of dire consequences and declarations of penalties, with Johnny twittering along behind him trying to calm him down. The fridge reappeared with an apparently truly apologetic Lewis, who reckoned his friend had loaded the fridge onto the truck when his back was turned, and the first he knew of it was when Charles appeared on his doorstep threatening to kill him.

After Lewis moved out, all sorts of wild characters suddenly started appearing at our door asking if we were selling, or if we knew anyone who was. Turns out Lewis had been pedalling a wide range of drugs to make ends meet. I was sitting strumming on the edge of my bed with the door open one night when two black guys appeared in the doorway and walked into the room. One was young and appeared friendly, but the other, much older one, immediately went on the prowl around the room looking for things to steal. Spotting Briony's hat from Mexico, he placed it on his head and flicked a New Orleans baseball cap across the room at me saying, "Here buddy, let's swap," in a less than friendly tone. He had the most amazing teeth I'd ever seen. A sliver of gold framed each tooth, giving him a bizarre smile like the grille of a 50s American car. He caught me staring and paused in his roaming long enough to say, "I used to own my own goldmine, boy, but this is the only gold I got left now," gritting his teeth with a cat-like leer and tapping on the metalwork as he did so.

My radar was well into alarm mode now, but the young one stayed friendly and chatty, and even asked if we wanted to tag along and find a party with them. I noticed the older guy had my watch curled into his hand. I asked him to put it down and give back the hat, and that if he did, we'd play a couple of songs for them on the balcony. The watch came back, but the hat didn't.

Briony flashed me a look that said, 'go with them and get that hat back'. I dithered until she came up behind me and pushed me towards the door, saying in no uncertain terms that I was going and that I wasn't coming back without her hat. For some stupid reason I obeyed and chased after the two men out into the New Orleans night. I looked back to see Briony on the balcony watching as we disappeared up the road past Louis Armstrong Park and then north away from Bourbon Street, where I had never set foot before.

I decided to stick with it as long as the younger one stayed friendly. He suggested we get a bottle to share, and I really couldn't say no. We got a half-bottle of Thunderbird liquor from a tiny bottle shop where the guy behind the counter tried not to look too curious at this white boy in the wrong company and heading for the wrong end of town. We found a party a few streets further north and sat on the porch to drink the Thunderbird. I got talking to a huge black guy sprawled on the boardwalk steps with a girl on his arm. Turned out he was in the navy and having a couple of weeks of R and R. He'd been to England and other European ports, and actually knew real things about places rather than the American TV version. He was fascinated to find a white kid in this part of town – I was the only white face at the party. He dwarfed the gold-tooth man, and I felt I'd be OK if I stayed close to him.

This was about as good a time as I would get to try and get the hat back, so I lifted if off Golden Teeth's head as he drank, laughing that it was time to swap hats back now. He turned and grabbed it back onto his head, and the young guy gave a barely perceptible shake of his head at me, looking just a shade scared. The bottle of Thunderbird was going around, and when it came to me I took a couple of swigs and tried to hand it back to Golden Teeth. He turned his back on me and told me I might as well kill it as I'd left so little anyway.

There was about a third of a bottle left. I shrugged and handed it to the young guy, who took one gulp and then passed it back to Golden Teeth, who took it without comment. Then he said he wanted to find somewhere else to hang out as he didn't like the company. He stood up and started walking away. The young guy followed him, and everything I knew told me I should stay on the porch, but I decided to try one more time for the hat. I caught up with the young guy. "Just get the hat off him," I said, "and I'll give him back his baseball cap, and disappear." Golden Teeth was starting to talk at the walls about how there was a bad smell around here, then picked up a couple of bricks that were lying on the pavement. He started banging them together in time to his bad mouthing of me. The young guy just turned to me and said "Man, I'm sorry, but it's time for you to run."

I knew he was right. I started jogging ahead of them to get a comfortable distance, then went into a full sprint as a brick came sailing over my shoulder and smashed into pieces on the sidewalk. I ran as fast as I could through the pitch-black streets heading south. I knew if I could cross Louis Armstrong Park I would be back on North Rampart Street, close to friends and under streetlights. There were huge iron gates to the park and just as I was getting up to them, a security guard closed them, snapping on an enormous padlock. I yelled that I needed to get through NOW, but he shook his head, nodded to the next gate round the corner, another hundred metre dash to my right. There was no time to debate, so I charged round the corner of the park, barely noticing that the guard was deliberately walking slowly to give me time to get through before he got there. I had no idea whether Golden Teeth was behind me and didn't want to risk looking behind and falling over. I reached the second set of gates and made it into the park, still running full tilt. Once I was inside the guard quickened his pace and ten seconds after I was in, he locked the enormous gate behind me. In the shadowy street away from the lights of the park I thought I saw the silhouette of Briony's hat prowling back and forth, but I'll never be sure. I lay on the grass under a palm tree hyperventilating to get my breath back as the security guard walked slowly over to me. He waited till I was breathing a bit more normally, then said he would let me out of the park on the south side, with a firm look that said, 'stay on your own side of town from now on, you idiot'.

Briony was sitting in our room when I got back. One look at my face and she dissolved into huge apologies for pushing me into going after the hat. But it was no good. As I'd walked back from the park, thinking how I'd nearly got myself beaten senseless or maybe even killed for someone else's twenty-dollar hat, something inside me seemed to snap, finally and forever. Briony and I were completely over.

We may have been completely over, but I knew I couldn't abandon her fifteen hundred miles from New York. We had to stay together until the flight out. Despite having the closest shave yet in America with potential disaster, and all the unwanted attention from the gay component of the population, for the first time since leaving Paris I wasn't in a hurry to leave somewhere. It wasn't just that I could make money in New Orleans. The French Quarter, away from Bourbon Street, was thoroughly comfortable with being what it was, and wasn't trying to dress itself up as something else. Maybe the final snap with Briony made me less restless as well: I'd finally faced up to the inevitable and made a decision.

Days slipped by, all different but all the same. Tim and I got to know some of the other buskers, though I noticed that it was only the guitar-strumming troubadours who were sociable – the jazz musicians spurned us as being beneath notice. The main two we met were Colin, a wild-looking guy who looked like Cat Stevens, and a beautiful willowy woman who not only looked like Joni Mitchell but could also do a reasonable job of playing her as well – just about the hardest acoustic artist there is to do well. It turned out they were a semi-ex couple; he had come all the way from San Francisco to get away from the relationship, only to have her turn up on the streets of New Orleans a few days later. It was like Bob Dylan's *Tangled Up in Blue*, and I got the sense the two of them were playing it for the theatrical romance of it; whatever, they were both great street singers and good company.

The tequila we'd bought in Mexico was still sitting in our room, but it was so foul we knew we would never drink the stuff. We had to get rid of it before we left – three kilos of spirits we didn't want was the last thing you needed in a backpack by a highway. I offered it to Colin. His eyes brightened as he proclaimed that he would teach us how to love tequila, and why Mexico was the only place in the world where the hangover was an inherited characteristic. Our instructions were to purchase a large bag of ice, two large bottles of soda water, a packet of coasters, and to make sure we had some solid chunky glasses. This sounded like fun, and we got the required goods set up in our room.

In typical Irish fashion, Tim showed up when he showed up, and Colin introduced us to the tequila slammer. More a piece of theatre than a drink, it suited Colin's dramatic approach to life. The stage directions were as follows: mix equal proportions of tequila and soda water in a thick-bottomed glass loaded up with ice. Place a coaster over the top of the glass, slam it down on the table and when the soda was fully fizzing, knock it back in one. Then wait for the belt this gave your stomach, closely followed by your head, from the alcohol hitting you so quickly. Then pass to the next person.

After slamming two each in the first twenty minutes we were giggling hysterically. The evening then turned into something quite legendary. Colin talked of his roaming around the US, I talked about mine in England and living in Paris, and Tim of blasting away in bands in Ireland and playing in Athens, Georgia – the town where the B52s, of Rock Lobster fame, came from. We got the instruments out and played songs and jammed together between rounds of slammers, and Briony got her trusty diary out and tried to do her stream-of-consciousness recording bit for the night – though as the slammers kept coming round it deteriorated into more of a stream of unconsciousness. We played songs of the road and songs of the streets and there was nowhere else on earth we wanted to be that night than with each other, playing the songs that were our life. We weren't play-acting, we were as real as it got. We'd been all the way round the world, boys, and we were trying to get to heaven before they closed the door. Looking back, that was the night I achieved perfection – the nirvana of the dream I had carried in my head for so long. I was the real thing. The songs kept coming in rounds, just like the slammers; *Tangled Up in Blue* and *Piano Man* and *Simple Twist of Fate* and *Mr Bojangles* and *Southern Cross*. We made up songs that started off sounding good but got fuzzier and fuzzier as the night wore on until we reached a shambolic state. It was a long, long night and – quite scarily – at the end of it we'd drunk three litres of tequila between the four of us: a standard bottle each of spirits. About two in the morning Colin announced blearily that he would be on his way and weaved out the door. Tim was unconscious in the corner of the room, and Briony and I retired to bed, where, for the first time since New York or even since we got to America, we got tangled up with each other. Maybe she was trying to say sorry for the hat debacle, maybe I was using some weird kind of reverse logic on us being finished, or probably just because of the wild romance of the night, I don't know. Tim never stirred from his place on the floor during our antics.

The next morning we were in a dreadful state. A bottle of Mexico's cheapest tequila was, in retrospect, probably actually poisonous if drunk in those quantities, and I certainly felt like I'd been poisoned. We spent the day wincing, wishing the sun wasn't so bright. Charles and Johnny invited us to go with them to a fire sale where a guy was selling anything he had to get the money together to go somewhere. It was like another Tom Waits song – the whole of a man's life laid out on the French Quarter sidewalk for anyone who had a couple of bucks to buy the faded memories and old shoes and musty books. Charles was in fine form, rummaging through the treasure and finding trinkets to display to Johnny, who twittered and clucked like a hen over where they would put all this stuff. A tequila hangover and a fire sale with a couple of gays on the streets of New Orleans – it could have made a great song, but I never got round to writing it.

Tim had offered us the use of his room in Athens for as long as we wanted it. It was pretty much a perfect fit, about a third of the way back to New York and only about eighty miles out of our way. But if we were going to meet up with all the people Tim had lined up for us in Athens, and get to New York in time for our flight out, we'd only have time for a couple more days in New Orleans. I didn't want to leave, but I knew it was time. It felt good to be feeling sad to be leaving somewhere at last.

At the same time, we needed to make the very most out of the last couple of days, both in terms of making money, and by squeezing every last drop of life we could out of the streets. And so I started busking at night on my own, as well as during the day with Tim. This wasn't work, it was the best fun I could think of having in New Orleans. Playing *House of the Rising Sun* at midnight on Jackson Square and having a guy who just oozed French Quarter listen to the whole song then come over at the end of it to shake my hand, almost in tears, and say it was the best he'd ever heard it sung, was a perfect moment. I befriended a hot dog seller on Jackson Square, who would stroll over every half hour or so for a quick chat between songs. He was a Bob Dylan nut and would bribe me with hot dogs to play his favourites. *Tangled Up in Blue* and *Tambourine Man* got me fed three nights straight, and he would tell every person who bought a hot dog off him that they should stick around and listen to the show and give me a couple of bucks. A surprisingly large number did and this, together with the excellent money Tim and I were making, meant we should have enough money to survive to the end of our time in America.

Playing with Tim was brilliant fun and dead easy, and we got gutsier and gutsier over where we were prepared to play until we were busking on Bourbon Street itself, using the crash barriers that blocked off the street as our stage backing. The police came to talk to us a couple of times, but when the Irish accents came out, they forgot about rules and we were allowed to carry on. The only thing we had to be careful about was Briony threading her way through the crowd actively asking for money, as panhandling was one of the few street laws they took seriously in New Orleans. We could generate a crowd of fifteen or twenty people when we got cranking, and learned that the best way to make money was build them up to a crescendo, send Briony round with the hat, then sit down for ten minutes to let them disperse, and then do it all again. In between playing we kept exploring the Quarter and loving every square inch of it. We looked at the idea of going into the World Fair but didn't look for long when we saw the prices. I only ventured into the modern business district of New Orleans once – I endured the faceless, glass-towered city for a whole twenty minutes before rushing back to the womb of the Quarter.

In between all this I investigated getting to Atlanta and found there was a bus that left from just across the street that would get us up to the interstate. The only golden rule in hitching in the south was to cross the state of Alabama in one lift, and not get dropped off anywhere in the state. When I asked why, I was just told that Alabama was different, that's why, don't worry about it – but just don't get dropped off there. This was easier said than done, because it would be a good five-hour lift to get clear across Alabama.

We didn't announce to Charles and Johnny when exactly we would be leaving, because the original deal was that you paid the rent by the week and Charles had let us slip a bit on this and we didn't want to get hit for a week's rent just for the one extra night. I'll never know, but I think Charles had worked out we were going to skip out owing a day's rent. He announced he was taking us all out to dinner to thank us for all the wonderful music I'd been playing on the porch and in our room and pretty much everywhere around the Quarter. It was to be a dress-up night, and Johnny lent me his razor so I could have a shave for the first time since I got to America. I was out of practice and cut myself a couple of times. My face felt raw as we all set off, but we were an exotic-looking band.

Briony and I were feeling guilty for not telling him we were going to leave and tried to insist we pay for our own meals, but Charles would have none of it. This was partly because we wanted to buy a takeaway burger to save money and, as Charles loudly proclaimed, "I am *not*, repeat *not* eating my dinner in the middle of the fucking *road* darlings, I have *standards* to uphold". So, we went to the restaurant of Charles' choice and he sat at the head of the table and proclaimed toasts to everything and everyone he could think of all night long and was magnificent. We crawled home late yet again, knowing that we were going to get up at the crack of dawn the next morning to hitch out of town. We packed quickly as usual, both very sad and very nervy about getting back on the road. I had this overwhelming feeling that we'd used up all our good luck and it was only so long now before something terrible must happen. That night, crazily, we made love again, and it felt something like the condemned man's last hearty meal before the hanging.

Chicago
Gary
s Moines
ILLINOIS
OHIO
Peoria
INDIANA
Springfield
Dayton
ssouri
Indianapolis
Cincinna
Ohio
Jefferson City
St. Louis
Frankfort
Evansville
Lexingto
MISSOURI
KENTUCKY
Springfield
Nashville
Knoxvill
TENNESSEE
Tennessee
Memphis
Chattanooga
APPA
ock
Huntsville
ANSAS
Atlanta
Athe
Birmingham
GEORG
MISSISSIPPI
ALABAMA
Macc
eveport
Colambus
Jackson
Montgomery
Mississippi
Baton Rouge
Mobile
Lafayette
Tallaha
LOUISIANA
New Orleans
FLOR

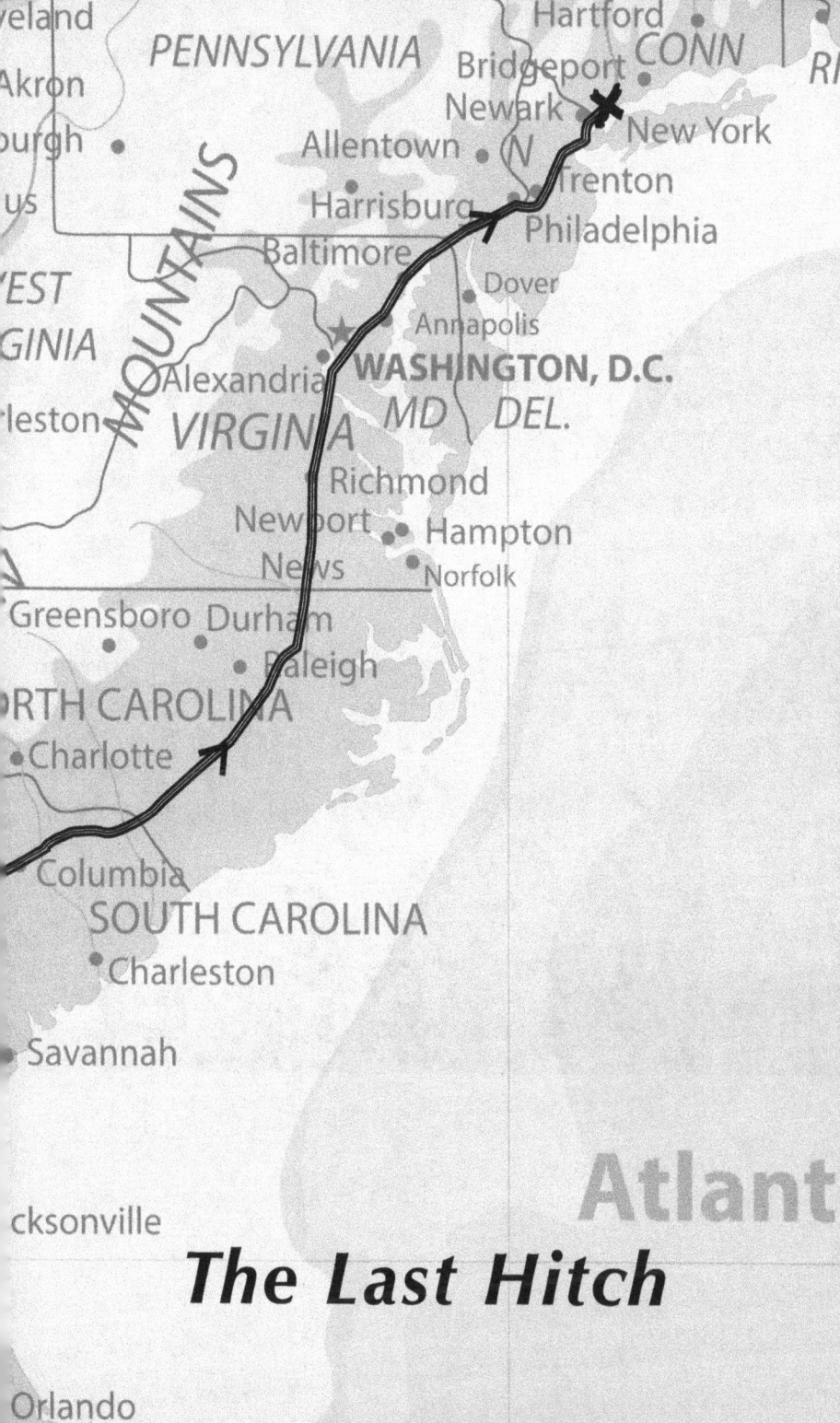

# The Last Hitch

## 13 NOTHING LEFT TO LOSE

*Freedom's just another word
For nothing left to lose
And nothin' ain't worth nothin' but it's free
Me and Bobby McGee.* Kris Kristoffersen, 1969

I'm not sure why, but I was spooked hitching out of New Orleans. We'd hitched so far already without worrying about it. Maybe it was my scare trying to retrieve Briony's hat, but I think it was more that the burning need to keep moving had finally been extinguished by the epic drive in the Mustang and the brilliant time we'd had in New Orleans. Moving was now something I had to do, rather than wanted to do.

On our final day, we tip-toed around the room getting things ready. I left a 'thanks for everything note' for Charles and Johnny, which probably wouldn't make them as happy as a cheque for the day's rent we owed. I also left Johnny's razor and shaving cream on the dresser, having washed the razor to get all traces of blood off it from my inept shaving attempt. (I have a vivid memory of a time two years later, watching someone on TV talking about how AIDS was transmitted by blood products, and realised how easily I could have picked it up, simply from the offer from a dying man who was just trying to be friendly. It was another two years before I got the courage to have the test and find out I was OK.)

We left the hotel and humped our gear across to the bus stop. Athens was well over five hundred miles away, and I thought we'd be lucky to make it in a day, but it didn't really matter. We would either hole up by the highway or, if the mosquitoes were impossible, use some of our hard-earned cash from busking to get a motel room, if we could find one.

The traffic was different in the south; there were far fewer trucks and those who picked us up were only going fifty miles on, not five hundred. We got a series of short lifts out of New Orleans and crawled over the state line into Mississippi.

The rule about Alabama went out the window when we got offered a lift that would take us to just past Montgomery. It was our first decent lift, but would drop us off bang in the middle of the state. I couldn't bring myself to knock it back, so we took it and took our chances in the heart of Alabama. It did feel different; there seemed to be a dusty, corn-cob primitive feel to the place, a vague smell of Klu Klux Klan and midnight lynchings. There was also very little traffic, and we waited almost an hour before a big beat-up Dodge pulled over, all dusty and road worn. It was being driven by a weathered-looking black guy, with a huge black mama sitting beside him on the front bench seat. He didn't say a word to us, he merely nodded when I asked if he was going up the highway. When I asked how far, he muttered something I couldn't pick up. It didn't feel good. I would have knocked back the lift, but we'd been there for over an hour and I didn't think anything dangerous would happen with the big black mama in the car.

We loaded ourselves in and as he set off I noticed all the dials on the dashboard were out of their housings and

## 13 NOTHING LEFT TO LOSE

hanging from wires. Both the tacho and the speedo were disconnected. There were beer cans all over the floor of the back seat and crushed cans on the dash. This didn't feel too good either. About three miles in, he turned off the highway. I declared loudly that we would get out here, thank you very much. He kept driving, and my heart sank through the floor. I glanced sideways at Briony, who was obviously terrified. I could see she was rummaging through our daypack to find our pathetic little penknife. We were still travelling parallel to the highway, and I said loudly again that we wanted to get out right here please, as we weren't interested in lifts that took us away from the main highway. The guy waved his hand in some non-committal way and kept driving. There was nothing we could really do, and I clung to the hope that as long as we could still see the highway, he might just be taking some kind of detour, though I didn't really believe it. What felt like an hour later but was probably about ten minutes, we drew up at a filling station and he stopped.

The highway was still in view, but there was no exit ramp at the intersection, so you would get no custom for the gas station from the interstate. It was where they lived, and he parked up on the apron of the gas station and waved us in the general direction of the shiny new black tarmac interstate. I realised that highway must have torn their lives apart, turning a halfway viable way of keeping yourself alive into a worthless millstone. Every day he would sit and listen to the cars whistle by on the new road, knowing they couldn't stop to get gas from him anymore. After he'd pointed at the interstate he turned and went into a dusty tired-looking workshop without saying a word, and without looking back. The big mama followed him; she had never even acknowledged our existence. An emaciated dog hobbled around in the dustbowl at the front of the filling station, crickets chirruped dry and hollow, and an exhausted dust devil grew out of the dust and waltzed across the forecourt of the gas station. Everything and everyone seemed to be rusting to pieces waiting for something to happen, knowing nothing would. It felt like we were in the most desolate, desperate spot on earth. We picked up our gear and sweated our way down through the landscaped cut of the interstate. Looking back from the highway, you could only see the filling station if you knew where to look. One man and his family's dream destroyed. I think it was the saddest lift I ever hitched.

It was only ten minutes until we got our next lift and left them behind forever. The rest of the day continued with a series of short unmemorable hops, except that the whiff of desolation stayed with us right through Alabama, and I knew the advice from New Orleans was right. As evening approached we were dropped off right on the state line between Alabama and Georgia. We would need some serious luck to make it to Athens that night, even though it was only a bit over a hundred miles. We'd have to get right across Atlanta and pick up the right exit to get us to Athens. We were tantalisingly close to our destination, but not quite there yet.

As the sun dipped nearer the horizon, we got a lift from a guy going all the way to Atlanta, but not through it. Odds were, we would end up in a motel somewhere on the ring road, but I held back on telling him this straight away. If we could sell ourselves well enough, he might take us right through the city to our exit. He was very proud of the way Atlanta had 'come on' in the last few years, and obviously regarded it as the most happening

## 13 NOTHING LEFT TO LOSE

place in America (and therefore, obviously, the world). Development was going on everywhere and there were exciting new office blocks springing up on all sides. I did my best to reflect his enthusiasm, while Briony curled up in the back and got some sleep. She'd lugged the guitar and the second bag down the highway too many times in one day, and her legs were a mass of small bruises. The guy lived on the wrong side of the city for us, and I knew we would not get round the city without a major detour on his part. When I asked that he just drop us at a motel on the highway, he was desolate that we wouldn't get to see all the great things about Atlanta. After some thought he offered to give us a quick drive round the centre before dropping us off. I said fine, on condition that he drop us at the right spot afterwards to hitch out. He was happy to do this, and I reflected on my deceit, playing the game to get what I wanted. He would never know he'd been taken for a ride while taking us for a ride, so to speak.

Sadly, Atlanta was almost exactly what I'd expected, except the shiny office buildings were less tall and a bit further apart than I would have predicted. He drove us around new freeways and pointed out new concrete edifices and it could all have been any western city in the world. I was generally a sucker for anyone who was truly passionate about what they were into, but it was hard to reflect his ardour for a few concrete and smoked-glass buildings and some big new roads. The grand tour took an hour, during which Briony woke up and gazed in confusion at the scene through the window. We were right out of hitching country, weaving our way through the city tollway systems – a hitcher's nightmare. I radared her a confident *it's all OK* look. More glazed boredom as he waxed on about one more sexy concrete building, then finally it was dark. He honoured the agreement and drove us to the Athens exit. As he dropped us off, he wished us luck and expressed genuine satisfaction that even if we couldn't stay in Atlanta, he could sleep easy knowing he'd shown us how great a place it was. It was all a bit lost on us.

It was pitch black now. The route to Athens was more of a country road, and this was the first time we'd hitched off the highways. It was less than fifty miles, but anyone's guess as to how long it would take. Our first lift was from a cowboy in a big flatbed truck going to see his girl ten miles down the road. Within a minute of us getting in he asked if we smoked, pulled a bag of grass from the map pocket in the door and tossed it to Briony, who rolled a serious number that we just had time to finish before he dropped us off at a tiny junction in the middle of nowhere. We stood by the road in a dope haze, thinking this had to be the end of the line, but the first set of headlights that came through five minutes later stopped. It was an even bigger trayback truck, and this time we travelled in the back, sprawled out with our gear, mesmerised by the giant stars overhead. Five minutes after we started, the sliding window of the cab opened and a hand appeared offering another huge glowing joint, with a "You make sure you enjoy yourselves back there, you hear." Once again, we just had time to smoke the thing before they dropped us off. I had no idea how far we were from Athens.

By this time I was unable to string two words together, and I had to prop myself up just to stand by the road with my thumb out. Eventually someone stopped and we got our final lift into Athens – with yet another offer of a smoke – after hitching for about sixteen hours straight.

## 13 NOTHING LEFT TO LOSE

It was the most extreme day of hitching we had the whole time we were in America.

Tim had told us to go to the Old 40 Watt Club in Athens, which he reckoned everyone in town knew, to ask directions for the Print Shop, where he lived.

We floated into the club in an extreme dope haze and asked someone behind the bar for directions. I vaguely took them in while watching a mirror ball twirl and dance in the lights, thinking someone else should really be in charge of getting us to where we were going, as I was clearly not capable. We wandered outside and set off in what I thought was the right direction. The streets were deserted. It was about a mile walk the girl reckoned, and we were to look for an old stone building set back from the road on a corner. I was almost certain we had the right road, and a big stone building on a curve in the road looked promising, though I thought she'd said it would be at the bottom of the hill. We'd been told the place was never locked and to go on in, so I prowled around trying doors, and found them all locked. There was also no sign saying it was a Print Shop, or any indication it was one. I decided we must have the wrong place; if anyone had been home, I'm not sure how we would have explained it.

We continued slogging down the road and I was starting to have serious doubts as to whether we were going in the right direction when, finally, a place that looked right appeared. And it was. We humped the gear inside and, following Tim's instructions, headed up a tight little staircase to a deserted flat. It must have been close to midnight by this time, and we were completely exhausted. We crashed out on what we presumed was Tim's bed. I slept like a dead man for I don't know how long until I was woken as if by an electric shock by someone shouting at us in the room. It was so intense that both Briony and I inadvertently screamed. A woman was in the room, screeching like a wall of pissed-off sound. It took a minute or so for us to get our heads together to explain who we were. She wasn't impressed, and I thought we were going to be out on the street, though Tim had assured us that the room was his and it would all be cool. I stressed this to the woman, but it didn't seem to cut much ice. She disappeared from view but continued her loud angry diatribe on other subjects. She seemed to be talking to someone but after I'd pulled some clothes on and followed her, I realised she was talking to herself. She was one wired-up lady.

I found out that her name was Sonny and that she didn't actually live there but was a friend of the landlord. She sure treated the place like hers, though. She kept coming in and out of the room telling us all sorts of rules about the place, number one being that the fridge must have no meat in it as 'meat was murder' and she wouldn't have the place polluted by such things.

She was also going on about some local band that were about to go on a tour that included New York, and this was the next step in their blossoming career on the way to mega stardom. I had heard this so many times that year from just about every busker I'd met that I tuned out completely. She was extraordinarily hard work and never shut up so after ten minutes or so I decided to go back to bed. She was committed to being pissed off with our presence, and her abrasive manner was really getting on my nerves.

Eventually she drifted away in a haze of noise and sandpaper irritation, and we could explore our new resting place in peace and quiet. It was a quirky spot, with the

## 13 NOTHING LEFT TO LOSE

kitchen being reached from the top of the stairs via the toilet, which was basically a corridor – each side of the loo being a door. The door on the stairs side was missing so when you went to the loo anyone coming up the stairs got a full view. The back lounge was shelved floor-to-ceiling with a treasure trove of a thousand books, mostly pick-ups from second-hand stores. I was elated to find a dog-eared history of Billy the Kid that I devoured avidly, recalling our dry parched day back in Fort Sumner.

The kitchen was a nightmare, with every surface covered with stuff, clean and dirty. A grateful colony of cockroaches feasted off the food remains. Inside the scariest fridge I'd ever opened was a mass of unidentifiable items (admittedly, not meat) that had been there a long, long time. The freezer had iced over so often that the weight of the ice had pulled away the metal frame of the ice box, so food, ice and fridge parts formed one decaying iceberg mass that dripped onto the rest of the fridge contents, making everything damp, soggy and mostly rotten. It was quite repulsive.

The view to the back looked over a grove of tall trees and a garden that could have been idyllic if it hadn't been used as a rubbish tip: cans, bottles and builders' rubble fought with choking weeds in a bewildered chaos. The Print Shop downstairs didn't look as though it had done any serious business for a long time. A tricolour with 'IRA' painted in red hung from the antlers of a moose's head on the wall. I knew from chatting with Tim on the subject that it would not be his flag; this was the work of naive Americans. Tim's room was at the front of the flat and looked out onto the road we'd weaved along last night. It was a short walk back into town past a mechanic's spot that specialised in fixing VWs called the Bug Shop.

As had become our habit after a marathon hitch, we took it easy that day, watching the clapped-out TV, finding a small supermarket down the road to get in some rations, and me strumming away on my guitar. Briony and I had little left to say to each other. We both knew that when we got back to New York, the relationship would be over. For the first couple of days in Athens, Briony seemed to make an effort into putting some spark back into our relationship, and seduced me quite convincingly a couple of times, but it was no good. I was burned out with the travelling, with the constant need to be looking over the next hill to work out how to get over it safely, and with the endless conversations with her that never seemed to go anywhere or sort anything out. We got on better if we didn't talk at all, or kept things to simple and mundane practicalities.

I was quite comfortable with this, but at one point in that first day I came across her quietly weeping in a corner. She had thought I was out in the garden and tried to hide her tear-stained face. I couldn't think of anything to say and left her to it.

A variety of people wandered in and out of the flat at will. After our run-in with Sonny, we remained cautious, cool and uncommunicative. Most of them seemed to be either members of, or hangers-on, of the band that was going up to New York. It was all they seemed to talk about. Sonny came back a couple of times and sputtered around the place like an egg in hot fat.

Occasionally the place was empty, perfect for the head space I was in. I would settle down to read *Billy the Kid* while Briony scribbled away in her trusty diary. We spent the time in almost total silence without having to think about anything at all, which was complete bliss as far as I

## 13 NOTHING LEFT TO LOSE

was concerned. I'd reached the end of my rope as far as the big adventure was concerned, and just wanted to hole up somewhere and look at the view for a while.

Tim arrived back from New Orleans. He'd left only a few hours after we did, but it took him twice as long, and his hitching tale was even more epic than ours. It was not easy listening. He'd had a gun pulled on him, been picked up by a gay guy looking for action, had his wallet stolen and been picked up by the police. All in Alabama. I thought back on our scare in Alabama and contemplated what we would have done if the guy had REALLY been bad. Not much that would have been helpful, I suspected. Tim also filled us in about the Print Shop. Apparently it had traditionally been a musician's open house; it was owned by Andreas, and was somehow linked with Athens' legendary 40 Watt Club, where the B52s got started.

We met Andreas at the Bug Shop up the road. He was very laidback and good company. He suggested we check out a few local bands that night in one of the many venues round town. We took him up on the suggestion, and it was a great night. We saw three bands and they were all solid, in fact they were dauntingly good for what were essentially uni campus bands. Various acquaintances of Tim's were there, and we met up with a woman who was involved with the local uni radio station. When she found out what we'd been up to, she insisted we go on her show for an interview and play a few songs.

The show was a weird experience. Our enthusiastic DJ interviewer made a big deal out of our adventures in the US, UK and France, which, when I talked them through, did sound pretty impressive! Playing was tricky though, as Tim and I had only ever winged it on the street and had never played live in front of a microphone. She also asked me to do some solo stuff, and I played on the English thing and pulled out a couple of Jam songs, John Otway's *Geneva* and, of all things, *Streets of London*. Briony sat in the corner of the tiny studio the whole night staring at the floor, hardly saying a word.

Tim and I wandered round the streets of Athens afterwards looking for a place to busk, but it was so tame after New Orleans that we just couldn't summon up the enthusiasm.

One morning I was walking past the toilet with no door and found Briony vomiting carefully and quietly into the pan. When she saw me, she shrugged, wiped her mouth and tried to smile. I wanted to be sympathetic, but just couldn't bring it off. Months later I woke in the middle of the night with the sudden realisation that she might have been pregnant, but at the time it didn't even occur to me. Briony and I continued to operate in a kind of vacuum, not really speaking or touching other than the occasional lapse into a bout of passion. It was a strange time.

In what seemed like no time at all, we'd been there a week and it was time to start moving again. Maybe I should have felt frustrated that we didn't do more with our last chunk of serious time in America, but I was by then tired of everything and everyone. Maybe if I hadn't been, I would have taken the time to get to know the band that kept wandering in and out of the Print Shop, or maybe even gone to hear them before they set off on their quest for fame. It was years later that I was listening to a radio and heard a singer with a voice that hypnotised me, with lots of gorgeous jangly guitars going on in the background. The program was on how the band got started. They were from Athens, Georgia, and their base was the Old 40 Watt

Club and the Print Shop. The name of the band was REM, and the singer was Michael Stipe. The only time I ever recall saying anything to him was to ask him to get out of the way of the TV. Funny how life turns out sometimes.

Tim had promised us that he'd organise a lift for us to the highway, even though the only car available had no registration and pretty much no brakes. Each time I raised this, he declared in typical Irish fashion that he would get us to the highway if it was the last thing he ever did, while failing to do anything at all about actually doing it. I'd pretty much written it off as an option, but it soured what should have been a much fonder farewell, more because Tim felt bad, rather than us feeling let down. It was one of the toughest starts to a hitch I'd ever had, with not a prayer of getting a lift from anywhere near the Print Shop, and no clear direction to walk to get started. We just started walking north, as this was the way to the interstate. Briony was waving her thumb vaguely in the direction of the road, and, remarkably, a guy pulled over. He could drop us on the edge of town heading towards the interstate, and apologised profusely that he couldn't do more for us, though his offer was copy-book perfect for getting us started.

It was about twenty miles to the interstate, and then another eight hundred or so back to New York City, where we'd set out what seemed like a lifetime ago. Our flight left in a little under three days, so we had to do reasonably well. If it all went disastrously wrong I was relying on being able to get a Greyhound bus, or even a flight – but of course that meant we would need to be near somewhere we could actually catch a bus or a plane.

We got our second lift very quickly, up to Interstate 85. From there it was interstates all the way to New York, but with some tricky cities to get round on the way, in particular Washington DC, the sprawl of Baltimore and then New Jersey to the north of it. I was praying for good long lifts, and on what would have to be easily the luckiest hitching day in my whole life, within fifteen minutes of putting up our New York sign, we got a lift that was going to take us the whole way. Seven states. Eight hundred miles. I doubt if anyone ever hitched from Athens to New York in fewer lifts.

Our wonderful chauffeur was named Guy. He was in the American forces and was on his way to New York to be posted to Hawaii for four years. Because of this, he declared almost as soon as we got in that speeding tickets were not a concern, as they wouldn't be chasing him all the way to Hawaii to pay his fines. As a result he consistently drove at twenty miles over the speed limit, and we gobbled up the miles. We got stopped a couple of times in the first few hours by traffic cops who, when they found out where he was going and why, generally shrugged and smiled, handing out the ticket but joking with him about not getting it paid.

We made our way north then east – South Carolina, North Carolina, Virginia, endless highways and fast-food joints, Taco Bells and MacDonald's and KFCs, everywhere looking the same as everywhere else. Suddenly my biggest worry was that we were going to get to New York too quickly and would have nowhere to stay – unless we could call on Jerry again, which I doubted. At least after our good fortune busking in New Orleans, I knew we could pay for a night's accommodation.

Clearly we weren't going to make eight hundred miles without Guy getting some sleep, and as the end of the first day closed in, we talked through what to do for the night. I said we would find a bridge to sleep under and meet up with him the next morning, but he insisted on paying for a double room so we could sleep safe, and also fed us. A really nice guy. Briony and I were in terminal orbit around each other, and lying next to her in the bed in the motel room with our driver snoring contentedly in the next bed was a strange feeling; a feeling that was magnified because I knew it would be her birthday the next day. I'd done nothing about getting her a present, and there'd be nothing to buy on the road except a Big Mac and maybe a road map. I knew I should have got something organised in Athens, but I justified to myself that getting her back to New York alive on her birthday was a pretty good present. I knew I should have done more, but I also knew I didn't care. We were very much at the end of our story.

When we woke in the morning I muttered a 'Happy Birthday'. She seemed startled I'd remembered at all. Guy was horrified that I had no presents or cards and went out and bought her some chocolates, which of course made me feel even more of a heel.

We soon moved from the wide-open country of the south into more densely populated areas. Washington DC was a blur of wide boulevards and enormous government buildings; we even caught a flashing glimpse of the White House. The area surrounding the hub of American politics was surprisingly rundown and ghetto-like, and Guy told us it was one of the highest crime rate areas in the country. This made about as much sense as most other things in America, and I just filed it away with all the other extraordinary things I'd learned crawling over the vast sprawl of the US.

North of Washington, the speeding tickets started to come in like clockwork, and we got stopped and booked at least four times on the second day. Guy joked that it would probably be quicker not breaking the limit because we wouldn't lose so much time filling out paperwork by the side of the highway. Not one of the traffic cops ever gave him a hard time when they found out he didn't care about their little piece of paper. It all seemed a bit pointless and made me realise that I could have done the same thing in the Mustang and just thrown the tickets out the window.

Finally, as night was coming down on the second day, we got to the edge of the enormous New Jersey sprawl and started to crawl our way back into New York City. We would be entering the city on the Verrazzano-Narrows Bridge, an enormous and graceful suspension bridge that Briony and I dubbed 'The Last Bridge'. As we approached, I insisted we pull over so we could get a photograph of something so momentous. As we stood looking across the harbour, it finally felt as though I was giving Briony a present.

"Happy Birthday Briony, here is my present to you – New York City!" She cheered up a bit, and in fact we rekindled some last embers of feeling as we got back in the car and crossed the bridge. We'd travelled through twenty-six states and over seven thousand miles in a bit under two months and had done and seen some wild things together. The flame that had burned inside me to keep moving and looking round the next bend had finally guttered out somewhere on the endless stretches of highway we had travelled. Finally I wanted to have somewhere to call home, and not be constantly on the move – at least for now. It was a very strange feeling, and as we hit Manhattan I felt a huge weight finally lift from my shoulders: the weight of needing to worry about an eighteen-

## 13 NOTHING LEFT TO LOSE

year-old girl who was one step away from the fairies at the bottom of the garden and had travelled clear across America and back at an age when most kids haven't even left home. So, in some ways, maybe it was a pretty good birthday present.

Guy dropped us at our second home, the bus terminal on 42nd Street. We rang Jerry, who was less than overjoyed to hear from us, as his new flatmate didn't see the exciting side of having strangers sleeping on his floor, but when he found out it was our last night in the US and how far we'd travelled, he said we were welcome to stay.

It was dark by the time we got there, and Jerry was out living the typically frantic New York lifestyle. He'd left instructions with the bellhop to let us in, and we found a congratulatory note, a couple of sleeping bags and the gear we'd lifted from the dead opera singer's flat, including the shiny chrome microphone. Somewhere in the back of my mind there'd been a plan to go out and get Briony a present now that our journey was finally over, but I knew I'd left it all too late and there was nothing appropriate I could think of that I'd be able to buy at this time of night in New York anyway. Well, that's what I told myself. So we crashed out, and I tried to pretend I was asleep as Briony cried and sobbed quietly to herself on the couch on the other side of the room. It seemed a desolate end to such a huge experience, but I just couldn't bring myself to walk across that room and deal with it.

The next morning Jerry poked his head in for two minutes before he left for work, shook our hands, congratulated us on seeing more of America than he probably ever would, bid us goodbye and left.

We had almost all day to kill before our flight, but the idea of trying to do something touristy was just too much, and besides, if we left Jerry's we wouldn't be able to get back in, and we had all the gear with us. I had the idea of going up to the roof of the apartment building and it was perfect. We could look out over the crammed labyrinth of the city, the smart facades of buildings betrayed by the chaos of aerials, air conditioners and other junk on the roofs, the 'over belly' of the city. There was a water tower on the roof of the building, and we climbed up and took some last photos of ourselves, Briony looking tense and distant, but suddenly livening up with the idea of taking photos of me playing my guitar on the roof. They turned out well, and were a fitting close to our great American journey.

When it came time to leave, we stuck our New York hitching sign on a spike on the top of the building, a bit like leaving a flag on Everest, and made our way to the airport.

Bizarrely, English Colin was there, having completed his studies in Ithaca. He'd managed to miss his flight and so was waiting on standby at the airport till he could get a seat. He'd been there two days and wasn't allowed out of the place because his visa was now expired. I was glad to see him, as it gave Briony and I someone to talk to other than each other.

As we flew out of New York, I knew a whole lot of things were finishing in my life: Briony and I, my busking life, all the travelling and all the uncertainty. It felt good that this was the way things were going to end. At last I was free of that cold dread of the day-to-day survival stuff.

Briony had bought a bottle of vodka at the airport and got in with a group of Contiki airheads and drank most of it in the first few hours of the flight – a delayed birthday celebration, I imagine. I fell asleep, only waking when Briony finally crept back to her seat after several hours,

## 13 NOTHING LEFT TO LOSE

with a rosy-red face and the sickly-sweet smell of vodka coming off her skin.

My mind was churning. It was trying to deal with the fact that we'd made it, and yet I couldn't summon up any joy or elation. Now, all this time later, I can look back with some perspective and remember the pure joy of the moment when we plunged into the Pacific Ocean at the end of our epic western hitch, and at the euphoria of how I felt pretty much the whole time we were in New Orleans, playing on the streets at night, and the crazy night drinking and playing with Tim and Colin as being the absolute pinnacle of what I had been looking for. But sitting on that plane, with Briony unconscious beside me, I just felt empty, drained and desolate.

As we made our way through customs at Heathrow, I tried to think about what we would do on the other side, but being that organised was a struggle so soon after already mentally 'signing off'. Fortunately, I was spared the need to do anything. Mum and Dad were there to pick us up. I couldn't even remember having given them my flight details. It was a truly surreal experience to walk into Mum's well-meaning fuddle so unexpectedly. Much more telling was the long look Dad gave me, with the single nod that said so much. It was funny how I could communicate so much with Dad without saying a single word, and yet Mum and I could talk all day long without us ever seeming to say very much to each other.

Dad headed for a train station to drop Briony off for her trip back home to Cornwall. We were halfway there when she suddenly seemed to shake herself out of a daze. "No… no. I can't finish this with a train ride, I have to hitch. I just have to, that's all." Dad looked at me in the mirror and I

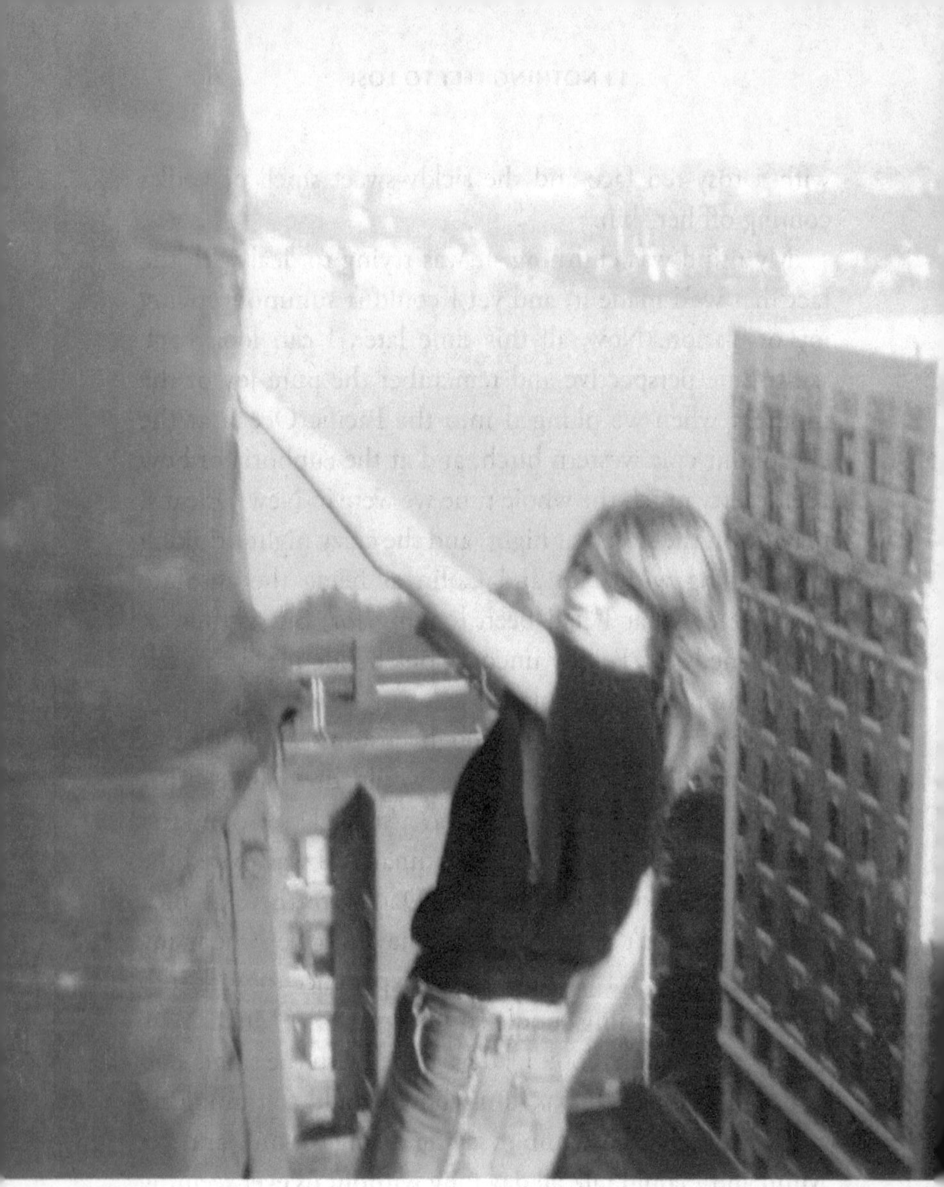

## 13 NOTHING LEFT TO LOSE

shrugged. He wanted to drive her to a good starting point, but she was adamant that she wanted to do it 'properly'. We pulled over on a road that led to the motorway. As she dragged her bag out of the car, I gave her a wave and an attempt at a smile, which she returned with about the same amount of enthusiasm before walking off purposely to finish her journey in the way it should be finished – as it started. Two minutes after she disappeared from view, as we were driving back to Bedford, I realised she'd been walking in the wrong direction.

I never saw her again.

# EPILOGUE

Well, that's not quite true. I saw her once briefly in Nottingham about six months later, when I was helping Chris the DJ out at a show, and she turned up. We managed to stumble through a minute or so of inane safe talk. Then, fifteen years after that, when I had the idea to write this memoir, I tracked her down to do some remembering with her. She was remarkably generous and even lent me the famous stream-of-consciousness diary, which recorded some of the deep, dark depression she went through towards the end of our American saga. But, as she said, it was all a long time ago. She was a mum, with a beautiful spacy little daughter and a confused husband, who had done the honourable thing after Briony had found she was pregnant after a lightning romance. She openly said that she thought things weren't working out, and they split a few months later. She was using their house as an informal animal sanctuary; there were cats, dogs, budgies, tortoises and rats secreted all over the place, with more arriving each day. She was as loopy as ever, but had grown into being comfortable and relaxed with her loopiness. It was good to finally put some skeletons to rest with her.

After that, our contact waxed and waned, until eventually she disappeared herself from all forms of social media and, sadly, we lost touch altogether. But I will never forget her.

I saw Simon a couple of times back in Nottingham, but not long after I got back he went down to London to get famous and make his fortune and we lost touch. (He didn't get famous enough for me to hear about him again!).

I met Garry the ex-legionnaire one day right on the spot where I'd first busked in Nottingham, and he immediately asked if I wanted to buy his 'truss' – a portable Vox amp – and a microphone taped onto a harmonica stand. When I asked why he was selling, he said bluntly there was no smack in Nottingham so he wanted some money to get to Paris so he could score. He was very matter-of-fact about it. I said I didn't want to give him money to do something so daft, but he shrugged and said he would sell it anyway, and at least if I had it, he'd know it had gone to a good home. Somehow I allowed myself to be persuaded by this and bought the thing. I still have the Vox amp on a shelf in my shed. I look at it occasionally and feel guilty. I never saw him again after that.

I kept in touch with the Nottingham buskers for a while, but the crew slowly turned over and I didn't play often enough to be known by the new set. Busking in Nottingham pretty much died out over the next two years. I think I was lucky I hit the city at the time I did.

Years later I caught up with Irish Tim in a pub in Ennis when I was travelling across Ireland. He'd sold his banjo to help set up his own business, and, though it was good to see him, it was one of those nights when you sat there trying to think of something to say. About the strongest theme was, "Fuck me, REM stole our food from out the fridge!!"

Martin from Bedford got chronic fatigue syndrome, gained a permanent limp, married a sixteen-year-old and sold his guitar to buy a carpet. The marriage lasted less than a year. I think all that dope and acid took its toll.

Al the trucker and I wrote to each other for five years or so, and I loved getting the feel of his reflective, gentle voice from the spidery scrawl of his handwriting. He just kept driving and driving and driving, but hardly referring to it in his writing, concentrating more on the quality time in between. Eventually we ran out of things to say, and the letters dried up.

I am still close friends with Rob, Helen and Sarah. Rob is my son Callum's godfather, and Helen is his godmother.

I never saw or heard from anyone from Paris again, not even another card from Andrea. I still look at the photograph of Nathalie looking through the broken window with that haunted look in her eyes and wonder what happened to her. I hope her story had a happy ending, but I doubt it did. Every few years I'd go back to Paris, and one time when I stuck my head in at the Nesle, Renée pretended to remember me. The hotel had been through huge renovations and the rooms were triple the price. There wouldn't have been any artists or actresses living there at those prices, and in fact over the years the entire Latin Quarter smartened up and became a chic address. The artists had to move east and north to places where they could still afford the rent. The clochards disappeared altogether.

I went back to university, feeling like a creature from another planet. I never really fit back in, but somehow earned a degree. The guitar stayed a big part of my life and I carried on busking, mainly in Bedford, partly to top up my bank balance and partly because I still loved that feeling of total freedom.

I started up a band at uni. The money was never more than enough to pay for beer and petrol, but it was great fun and put me in touch with a whole culture of people trying to make a buck out of the precarious music industry: sound engineers and recording engineers and stage hire people. That was about the only thing that kept me sane while I was plodding through the tedium and toil of getting my degree.

My restlessness to move eventually returned and stayed with me for fifteen or more years. I backpacked across the world and sailed across oceans as a ship's musician on a square-rigger sailing ship, the guitar as my only constant travelling companion. It was great while it lasted. But the fire in my belly that wanted to keep moving finally faded. I have ended up in Western Australia, which has more space and big sky than just about anywhere else on earth. I love it. My life here in Fremantle is filled with wonderful music and musical projects; the place is a musician's paradise. Over the years I've finally learned how to play well with other musicians and even write some reasonable songs of my own. I count myself lucky.

I started writing this memoir a year or so after my son Callum was born in 1998, for him to read when he turned twenty-one. Even back then, I didn't think you could do what we did in 1984, and I'm damn certain as I write this Epilogue in 2022 that you absolutely couldn't; the world is a tougher and more selfish place in many ways. Apart from anything else, people don't pick up hitchhikers, and

# EPILOGUE

a cashless society has largely destroyed the easy busking way of life. COVID also changed the way we think about our place in the world, and how we travel through it. It's made what we managed to do all those years ago seem all the more unbelievable. And the fact that Briony agreed to go with me to America seems all the more extraordinary now; I would never have got to America, travelled all those highways and crossed paths with all those wonderful crazy people if it hadn't been for her.

Watching Callum grow beyond the age I was when I took those extraordinary chances has made me think about my own dad. Only as I reach the age Dad was when I first dropped out of uni and left home can I appreciate how hard it would have been for him to believe in me and support me to do all the crazy things I did, and become the person I am. That's the reason I wanted to share this memoir – to pay homage to my dad.

So this book is for Briony, for Callum, and for my dad.

And even now, some days I lie in bed and listen to the crows and remember the smell of hot tarmac and dry grass as we stood beside all those highways across the vast bulge of America. I recall the sound and lights of the Metro carriages barrelling into Montparnasse station, and me shouldering my guitar for the twentieth time that day to get those extra few francs so I could sit at a table to eat for a change … the countless shopfronts and subways and street corners and tunnels where I walked up, set my case down, and went through the carefully choreographed start-up routine. Never in a hurry, never worried. No matter how broke you were, look easy boy, look easy. And I smile. Because I did it. I made my dreams come true.

## ACKNOWLEDGEMENTS

This book wouldn't have happened without the assistance of some and the considerable tolerance of others.

Thanks to Fran for giving me the space to download all those memories night after night many years ago while she was feeding Cal and trying to get him back to sleep. Huge thanks to Ingrid Waltham for firstly giving me an honest appraisal as to whether this memoir was something that others may want to read, and then doing a magnificent job of decluttering and honing it into something hopefully entertaining and readable while still sounding like ME. To Cath Viol for rigorous proofreading and in particular transforming my school-boy phonetically remembered French place names and expressions into actual French! To Lindy for great photos of me now, and patience in getting them right. To Rob Hatley for finding time to take photos of the London Underground, I was too busy busking! And to Anna Maley-Fadgyas for giving this book such a wonderful feel and look.

To all the singer songwriters whose wonderful songs kept me alive busking and gave me the inspiration for the chapter titles of this book: Bob Dylan, Paul Weller, Jacques Brel, Edith Piaf, Joni Mitchell, Neil Young and so many others. You are my heroes.

And most of all to the crazy wonderful people I came across in my travels, without whom there would not have been a story to tell!

Me with my busking guitar, present day.

## About the Author

Nick Turner was born and raised in the UK, spending his early years moving around England, gaining and losing different accents as his dad changed jobs around the country as a museum curator. He received a scholarship to the poshest private school in Bedford while living in social housing, providing him with a varied view of life at a young age. He got his first guitar when he was ten years old and taught himself to play.

Nick left the UK at the age of 26 and roamed the world for several years. He worked as a water engineer in New Zealand, Sydney, Perth and the northwest of Western Australia; sailed from Uruguay to Portugal on the square rigger *Soren Larsen*; and hitchhiked back to the UK through Portugal, Spain and France, busking on the way. He has managed to juggle a successful career in the water industry with crewing on square riggers across oceans, all the while enjoying a wide range of musical adventures: busking across Europe and the USA, backpacking through the Himalayas with a mandolin, and performing in multiple bands, venues and music festivals over decades. Nick has recorded several albums of both his own material and covers.

Nick is now happily settled in the port city of Fremantle in Western Australia, the perfect place for a sailor musician to live. He remains a keen songwriter and sailor, performing regularly at local Freo venues, and sailing on his yacht *Farruca* to Rottnest Island and other wonderful spots with partner Lindy.

www.ingramcontent.com/pod-product-compliance
Lightning Source LLC
Chambersburg PA
CBHW010706020526
44107CB00081B/2663